China's Past, China's Future

China has a population of 1.3 billion people, which puts strain on her natural resources. This volume, by one of the leading scholars on the earth's biosphere, is the result of a lifetime of study on China, and provides the fullest account yet of the environmental challenges that China faces.

The author examines China's energy resources, their uses, impacts and prospects, from the 1970s oil crisis to the present day, before analyzing the key question of how China can best produce enough food to feed its enormous population. In answering this question the entire food chain – the environmental setting, post-harvest losses, food processing, access to food and actual nutritional requirements – is examined, as well as the most effective methods of agricultural management. The final chapters focus upon the dramatic cost to the country's environment caused by China's rapid industrialization. The widespread environmental problems discussed include:

- water and air pollution
- water shortage
- soil erosion
- deforestation
- desertification
- loss of biodiversity

In conclusion, Smil argues that the decline of the Chinese ecosystem and environmental pollution has cost China about 10 per cent of her annual GDP.

This book provides the best available synthesis on the environmental consequences of China's economic reform program, and will prove essential reading to scholars with an interest in China and the environment.

Vaclav Smil is Distinguished Professor in the Faculty of Environment, University of Manitoba, Canada. He is widely recognized as one of the world's leading authorities on the biosphere and China's environment. He is the author of many books, including *The Earth's Biosphere*, *Enriching the Earth*, *Feeding the World* and *China's Environment*.

Asia's transformations
Edited by Mark Selden
Binghamton University and Cornell University, USA

The books in this series explore the political, social, economic and cultural consequences of Asia's transformations in the twentieth and twenty-first centuries. The series emphasizes the tumultuous interplay of local, national, regional and global forces as Asia bids to become the hub of the world economy. While focusing on the contemporary, it also looks back to analyse the antecedents of Asia's contested rise.

This series comprises several strands:

Asia's transformations aims to address the needs of students and teachers, and the titles will be published in hardback and paperback. Titles include

Asia's great cities: Each volume aims to capture the heartbeat of the contemporary city from multiple perspectives emblematic of the author's own deep familiarity with the distinctive faces of the city, its history, society, culture, politics and economics, and its evolving position in national, regional and global frameworks. While most volumes emphasize urban developments since the Second World War, some pay close attention to the legacy of the *longue durée* in shaping the contemporary. Thematic and comparative volumes address such themes as urbanization, economic and financial linkages, architecture and space, wealth and power, gendered relationships, planning and anarchy, and ethnographies in national and regional perspective. Titles include

Hong Kong
Global City
Stephen Chiu and Tai-Lok Lui

Beijing in the Modern World
David Strand and Madeline Yue Dong

Bangkok
Place, Practice and Representation
Marc Askew

Shanghai
Global City
Jeff Wasserstrom

Singapore
Carl Trocki

Asia.com is a series which focuses on the ways in which new information and communication technologies are influencing politics, society and culture in Asia. Titles include

Asia.com
Asia Encounters the Internet
Edited by K. C. Ho, Randolph Kluver and Kenneth C. C. Yang

Japanese Cybercultures
Edited by Mark McLelland and Nanette Gottlieb

RoutledgeCurzon studies in Asia's transformations is a forum for innovative new research intended for a high-level specialist readership, and the titles will be available in hardback only. Titles include

Chinese Media, Global Contexts
Edited by Chin-Chuan Lee

Imperialism in South East Asia
"A Fleeting, Passing Phase"

Internationalizing the Pacific
The United States, Japan and the
Institute of Pacific Relations in War
and Peace, 1919–1945
Tomoko Akami

**The American Occupation of
Japan and Okinawa ***
Literature and Memory
Michael Molasky

Koreans in Japan
Critical Voices from the Margin
Edited by Sonia Ryang

* now available in paperback

Critical Asian scholarship is a series intended to showcase the most important individual contributions to scholarship in Asian Studies. Each of the volumes
presents a leading Asian scholar addressing themes that are central to his or her
most significant and lasting contribution to Asian studies. The series is
committed to the rich variety of research and writing on Asia, and is not
restricted to any particular discipline, theoretical approach or geographical
expertise.

China's Past, China's Future
Energy, Food, Environment
Vaclav Smil

**Women and the Family in
Chinese History**
Patricia Buckley Ebrey

China Unbound
Evolving Perspectives on the
Chinese Past
Paul A. Cohen

Southeast Asia
A Testament
George McT. Kahin

China's Past, China's Future

Energy, food, environment

Vaclav Smil

RoutledgeCurzon
Taylor & Francis Group

NEW YORK AND LONDON

First published 2004
by RoutledgeCurzon
29 West 35th Street, New York, NY 10001

Simultaneously published in the UK
by RoutledgeCurzon
11 New Fetter Lane, London EC4P 4EE

RoutledgeCurzon is an imprint of the Taylor & Francis Group

© 2004 Vaclav Smil

Typeset in Baskerville by Taylor & Francis Books Ltd
Printed and bound in Great Britain by TJ International Ltd,
Padstow, Cornwall

British Library Cataloguing in Publication Data
A catalogue record for this book is available from the British Library

Library of Congress Cataloging in Publication Data
Smil, Vaclav.
China's past, China's future: energy, food, environment/Vaclav Smil.
p. cm.
Includes bibliographical references and index.
1. China–Environmental conditions. 2. Power resources–China. 3. Food
supply–China. I. Title.
GE160.C6C63 2003
304.2'8'0951–dc21

                                          2003006064

ISBN 0–415–31498–4 (hbk)
ISBN 0–415–31499–2 (pbk)

For is and is-not come together;
Hard and easy are complementary;
Long and short are relative;
High and low are comparative;
Pitch and sound make harmony;
Before and after are a sequence.
Laozi, Dao de jing

Contents

Illustrations

Tables

Figures

Preface

All but two of my books have had the same randomly methodical genesis. Months or years after coming up with the initial idea (as far as I can recall the shortest period was less than half a year, the longest one nearly a decade) I eventually put together a brief proposal for a publisher, and then got down to intensive writing, with the book's title being usually the last thing. The first exception was *The Bad Earth*, the first book on China's environment: after reading my paper on that topic in *Asian Survey*, Doug Merwin of M.E. Sharpe suggested that I write the book, and he also chose its title. This book is the second, and even more notable, exception.

I would have eventually done a broad survey of China's environment even without Doug's prompting – but I am not so self-indulgent to come up with the idea of a retrospective volume of my China writings. In fact, if Craig Fowlie and Mark Selden had asked me merely for that I would have hesitated, and likely said no. But their idea of the *Critical Asian Scholarship* series as the combination of rethinking and commenting on previously published work together with new, or unpublished, material was immediately appealing – and I began working on the book in July 2002, within weeks of finishing *Energy at the Crossroads*. Mark also suggested, upfront, what I think is a very apposite title.

My thanks go also to Doug Fast, who reproduced all old illustrations and who created a number of new ones, and to journal and book publishers who gave permissions to reprint selections from about twenty-five different publications. These reprints take almost three fifths of the book. The remainder is made up of unpublished (and updated) pieces, and of new essays on China's rural fuel use, energy intensity of the country's economy, the 1959–1961 famine, dietary transition, nitrogen in China's agriculture, and on worrisome and desirable megaprojects.

Thanks to Zoe Botterill for guiding the typescript through the publication process.

Finally, a few technical details. For the sake of consistency, all Chinese names are transcribed in *pinyin*. The metric system is used for all measurements, and because so many units, scientific prefixes and acronyms are used in the book I have provided detailed explanations of these. The Harvard system of referencing is not used only in a few instances where the reprints of complete, or slightly abridged, articles retain their original referencing or a numbered combination of references and notes.

Acknowledgments

The author and publishers would like to thank the following for granting permission to reproduce material in this work:

The American Geographical Society for reprinting parts of "Controlling the Yellow River", *The Geographical Review* 69: 253–272, 1979.

The *Asian Wall Street Journal* for reprinting "China's megaprojects for the new millennium", 22 April 1999, p. 8; "China's unstable past and future", 30 September 1999, p. 8; and " 'Water, water everywhere…' ", 22 August 2000, p. 12.

The *British Medical Journal* for reprinting "China's great famine: 40 years later", 7225: 1619–1621, 1999.

The China Quarterly for reprinting "China's energy and resource uses: continuity and change", 156: 935–951, 1998.

Current History for reprinting selections from "Food in China", 75(439): 69–72, 82–84, 1978; "Eating better: farming reforms and food in China", 84(503): 248–251, 273–274, 1985; "Feeding China", 94(593): 280–284, 1995.

Food Policy for reprinting selections from "China's food", 6(2): 67–77, 1981.

Helen Dwight Reid Educational Foundation for reprinting Vaclav Smil, "China shoulders the cost of environmental change", *Environment* 39(6): 6–9, 33–37, 1997. Reprinted with permission of the Helen Dwight Reid Educational Foundation. Published by Heldref Publications, 1319 18th St, NW, Washington DC 20036–1802. www.heldref.org/html/env.html. Copyright © 1997.

Institute of International Relations in Taipei for reprinting selections from "Communist China's oil exports: a critical evaluation", *Issues and Studies* 11(3): 71–78, 1975; "Communist China's oil exports revisited", *Issues and Studies* 12(9): 68–73, 1976; and "Food availability in Communist China: 1957–1974", *Issues and Studies* 13(5): 13–57, 1977.

Johns Hopkins University Press for reprinting "China's environment and security: simple myths and complex realities", *SAIS Review* 17: 107–126, 1997.

Kluwer Academic/Plenum Publishers for reprinting Vaclav Smil, "Energy flows in rural China", *Human Ecology* 7(2): 119–133, 1979.

MIT Press for reprinting the final chapter from *Feeding the World: A Challenge for the Twenty-first Century*, Cambridge MA: MIT Press, 2000, pp. 291–315.

Praeger Publishers for reprinting selections from *China's Energy: Achievements, Problems, Prospects*, New York: Praeger Publishers, 1976, pp. 11–23, 31–41, 74–84, 93.

M.E. Sharpe for reprinting selections from Vaclav Smil, *The Bad Earth: Environmental Degradation in China*, Armonk: M.E. Sharpe, 1984, pp. 68, 78, 79, 198–200, copyright © 1988 by M.E. Sharpe, Inc.; Vaclav Smil, *Energy in China's Modernization: Advances and Limitations*, Armonk: M.E. Sharpe, 1988, pp. 46–54, 60–68, 71, 91–94, 162–171, copyright © 1993 by M.E. Sharpe, Inc.; Vaclav Smil, *China's Environmental Crisis: An Inquiry into the Limits of National Development*, Armonk: M.E. Sharpe, 1993, pp. 38–51, 101–104. Reprinted with permission.

The New York Review of Books for reprinting selections from "Is there enough Chinese food?", 43(2): 32–34, 1996. Reprinted with permission from *The New York Review of Books*. Copyright © 1996 NYREV, Inc.

Oxford University Press for reprinting a short selection from Vaclav Smil, *Energy, Food, Environment: Realities, Myths, Options*, Oxford: Clarendon Press, 1987, pp. 86–87.

Population and Development Review for reprinting selections from "Food production and quality of diet in China", 12: 25–45, 1986, pp. 27, 29, 31, 38–39.

Routledge for reprinting the complete text of Smil, V., "Three Gorges Project", in *International Encyclopedia of Environmental Politics*, eds J. Barry and E.G. Frankland, London: Routledge, 2002, pp. 449–451.

Every effort has been made to contact copyright holders for their permission to reprint material in this book. The publishers would be grateful to hear from any copyright holder who is not here acknowledged, and will undertake to rectify any errors or omissions in future editions of this book.

Abbreviations

BBC	British Broadcasting Corporation
BP	British Petroleum
CIA	Central Intelligence Agency
CNPC	China National Petroleum Corporation
EI	energy intensity
EIA	Energy Information Administration
EU	European Union
FAO	Food and Agriculture Organization
FYP	five-year plan
GDP	gross domestic product
ICOLD	International Committee on Large Dams
IDRC	International Development Research Center
IEA	International Energy Agency
LNG	liquefied natural gas
NBS	National Bureau of Statistics (Beijing)
NCNA	New China News Agency
OECD	Organization for Economic Cooperation and Development
OPEC	Organization of Petroleum-Exporting Countries
PPP	purchasing power parity
PRC	People's Republic of China
ROC	Republic of China
RWEDP	Regional Wood Energy Development Program
SB	Statistics Bureau (Tokyo)
SSB	State Statistical Bureau (Beijing)
TPES	total primary energy supply
UNDP	United Nations Development Program
UNO	United Nations Organization
USDA	United States Department of Agriculture
WHO	World Health Organization
WTO	World Trade Organization

1 Introduction

China's biophysical foundations

Western writings on China have always been dominated by social perspectives as anthropologists, economists, ethnographers, historians, journalists, linguists and students of military and political affairs provided a wealth of interpretations ranging from overzealous ephemera produced by instant experts to balanced and well-argued exposés authored by long-time observers with deep and nuanced understanding of the country. As a natural scientist with a keen interest in history and politics I enjoyed reading many surveys, appraisals and forecasts that were reevaluating China's achievements and prospects during the early 1970s. But every society is created by a complex interplay of natural and human factors – and I felt that some fundamental perspectives concerning China's biophysical foundations were covered only marginally or that they were entirely absent.

In 1973 I decided to start filling some of these gaps. Energy was the first obvious choice, as its conversions are required for every natural and human activity; and as any nation's fortunes, be they economic or political, are closely tied to the modes, rates and efficiencies of its use. This focus was especially apposite at the time when OPEC's quintupling of crude oil prices in 1973–1974 finally led the Western world to pay more attention to energy resources and uses. Converting my resolution into reality was not a matter of weeks, or months. My interest in energy studies predated by a decade the sudden burst of interest in fuels and electricity brought about by OPEC's actions, and so by 1973 I knew a great deal about Europe's, Russia's and America's energy. But information on China's energy accessible in the West, or even inside China, was at that time extremely limited, and the few available publications were authored by Sinologists whose impeccable knowledge of the language was not matched by the understanding of scientific and engineering realities that is needed to evaluate energy systems.

My Chinese experiences

For two years I immersed myself in what Alexander Eckstein labeled, so memorably, "economic archaeology" as I looked for shards of energy-related information and studied many ancillary aspects of China's energy situation. Only then did I write my first short China energy papers, which came out in 1975. The first major survey piece appeared in *The China Quarterly* in May 1976; and just before the end of that year I published *China's Energy*, the first comprehensive analysis of the country's energy resources, uses, impacts and prospects.

During the following ten years, my work on China's energy both broadened and deepened as I considered nearly all of its major aspects, ranging from the use of traditional biomass fuels to the prospects of offshore oil and gas exploration, and from the performance of coal-fired electricity generation to the fate of (at that time rather fashionable) small rural biogas digesters. I did not plan to write another book about China's energy, but after I finished a lengthy report on the topic that was commissioned by the International Development Research Center, I still had so much new material that the expanded and revised report appeared as *Energy in China's Modernization* in 1988. Unlike my first China energy book, this new book dealt with the complications and implications of rapidly growing and no less rapidly innovating energy industries. I returned once more to the topic in a more systematic manner to prepare a long-term retrospective that appeared in *The China Quarterly* in 1998, twenty-five years after I began my studies of China's energy.

As a long-time practitioner of the systems approach, I found my interest in China's food to be an inevitable outgrowth of a broader interest in the country's energy supply. After all, no energy is more vital than that contained in nutrients we produce largely through cropping, and a systems approach to human nutrition dictates that this inquiry should not stop with the production of food, but that the whole food chain – including the environmental setting, post-harvest losses, food processing, access to food and actual nutritional requirements – be examined.

This is why my earliest studies of China's food situation attempted to quantify national food balance sheets, and why in my work published during the 1990s I argued that China's prospects for feeding itself would be greatly enhanced by managing better not just the production, but the composition of the demand by promoting the most efficient production of animal foods (carp and chicken vs. pork and beef). Given the critical influence that China's highly variable climate, recurrent water deficits or excesses and much-degraded soils have on the country's agriculture, my work on China's food has also always stressed the necessity of appropriate environmental management.

At the same time, I have had always little use for naive exaltations of China's traditional farming based entirely on renewable resources, and I have shown how these – albeit in many ways admirable – practices clearly limited the country's food output. Only a radical shift to intensive agriculture – unlike in the West this transformation was not primarily one of massive mechanization of field tasks but rather one of rapidly increasing reliance on nitrogenous fertilizers – made it possible to support today's 1.3 billion people. This dependence has made China the world's largest producer of ammonia, as well as the country with the highest existential dependence on synthetic fertilizers.

And, again, as a student of complex systems it was an obvious step to move from energy in general and food energy in particular to the study of China's environment. Extraction and conversion of energies and the production of food are the two most important reasons for the anthropogenic degradation of the biosphere. By the time I was ready to take a deeper look at China's environment, I was helped by a long-overdue, but still unexpected, shift in the country's affairs. Just before Deng Xiaoping rose yet again to power, some Chinese publications began to print astonishing revelations about the parlous state of China's land, air and waters, and by the early 1980s there was a veritable flood of this previously absent information.

I used these publications to write my first papers dealing solely with China's environment (for *Asian Survey* and *Current History*, both in 1980), then in the first fairly comprehensive briefing on the topic commissioned by the World Bank. A year later I completed the first, Western or Chinese, book on China's environment: *The Bad Earth*, an interdisciplinary survey of China's ecosystemic degradation and environmental pollution. The book not only spurred a great deal of interest (more than forty favorable reviews in publications on five continents), but also some disbelief rooted in the persistence of a naive Western image of China as a civilization living in harmony with its environment and in the residual infatuation of some Western intellectuals with Maoism.

During the following years I continued to publish papers on different aspects of China's environment and, exactly ten years after the publication of *The Bad Earth*, *China's Environmental Crisis* came out in 1993. This was a deeper inquiry into the biophysical constraints of China's development. Soon after completing the book, an invitation to spend some time at the East–West Center gave me the opportunity to complete a detailed evaluation of the economic costs of China's ecosystemic decline and environmental pollution. I was able to demonstrate that this burden is equal annually to at least 10 per cent of the country's GDP.

An extensive summary of this study deserves particular attention, as these accounts question what is perhaps the country's most touted post-1980 achievement, its high rates of economic growth. In addition, environmental selections in this book will survey not only such key concerns as water supply and chronic Northern water shortages, water and air pollution, soil erosion, deforestation, desertification and loss of biodiversity, but also such notable failures of environmental management as the Three Gorges dam and mass afforestation campaigns; and such current concerns as the Three Gorges reservoir and the South–North transfer of water.

From the mid-1990s my attention focused on the studies of global energy, agriculture and environmental change. *Global Ecology* was followed by *Energy in World History*, then came *Cycles of Life* for the Scientific American Library and *Energies, Feeding the World, Enriching the Earth, The Earth's Biosphere* and *Energy at the Crossroads*. None of these books deals explicitly with China, but all of them drew on my China work, and some of them contain lengthy discussions devoted to China. This is particularly the case with *Feeding the World*, whose entire closing chapter, reproduced almost completely in the third chapter of this book, appraises China's food production constraints and potential.

Another recent return to China-centered research arose from my interest in the global nitrogen cycle and in the history and impacts of nitrogenous fertilizers.

China is now their largest producer and user, and hence it is a perfect choice for examining several key features of the dependence that makes the difference between adequate diets and malnutrition, hunger and famine. That is why this book's food chapter (Chapter 3) includes a new contribution that looks at the history and consequences of China's uses of agricultural nitrogen. Similarly, my recent appraisal of global energy prospects led me back to some key issues of China's energy use, particularly to the impressive decline in energy intensity of the country's economy. Most of this new work is included in this book's energy chapter (Chapter 2).

Finally, a paragraph on access to my publications on China. Between 1975 and 2002 I have published four books, just over 100 papers in nearly fifty different periodicals, and about forty book chapters dealing with the three big topics featured in this book, as well as with China's population, economic development and future. Roughly a third of these publications are listed in references, and all papers and books published since 1990, including those that do not deal with China, can be found on my regularly updated website (http://home.cc.umanitoba.ca/~vsmil).

Challenges of understanding

There are several important commonalties in studying China's energy, food and environment, some universal and others country-specific. Perhaps the most important universal factor is that the understanding of complex, and inherently interrelated, matters of energy, food and the environment benefits from interdisciplinary perspectives – but such insights cannot be gained either from brief visits to a studied country or from cursory reviews of published materials. Only a long-term commitment, and the combination of deeper specific inquiries and a broad familiarity with relevant foreign circumstances and international comparisons, will do.

Unfortunately, during the 1970s and 1980s too much information on China came out as a result of brief visits by herded groups of experts. Until the early 1980s these trips were almost entirely choreographed well in advance, and included such compulsory highlights as inspection of Potemkin's communes of Sino-Albanian Friendship or model kindergartens with flag-waving toddlers. Eventually, the access improved – both in geographical and in personal terms – and some collaborative studies were able to come up with unique and valuable information. The two rounds of extensive health and nutritional surveys by the Cornell–Oxford–China Project (Chen *et al.* 1990; CTSU 2002) come to mind as an excellent example of the latter category. As for the uncritical reliance on published Chinese materials, I could spend many paragraphs on some embarrassing quotations taken not just from the writings of overt Maoist sympathizers, but also from the work of some Western academics who were convinced, among other things, that the world's greatest famine never took place, that China is a model of environmental management, and that the best guidance for national modernization can be found in Mao's little red book.

Another important universal imperative is not to succumb to the fashionable conclusions and biased stresses with which the studies of energy, food and the environment abound. Even readers not particularly well versed in these fields will recall that the two successive energy "crises" (1973–1974 and 1979–1980) persuaded many energy experts that the era of readily available and inexpensive energy is over. Yet just a few years after the Western media overflowed with dire forecasts of the lights going out on Western civilization, the price of oil collapsed and it is still a lot cheaper than that of the fake mineral water that has since flooded the North American continent. A quarter-century ago acid rain was seen as the most important cross-border environmental problem (just try to find news references to global warming in 1977), and during the mid-1990s Lester Brown's sensationalist catastrophism convinced many people that China would not be able to feed itself. I have been repeatedly involved in combating some of these unjustified yet annoyingly persistent misconceptions, and a number of selections in this book address some of their notable China-related examples.

By far the most important China-specific challenges to the understanding of complex matters of the country's energy, food and the environment are the country's immense natural and socio-economic diversity, and the quality of Chinese statistics.

Natural and socio-economic disparities

Dealing with averages of any kind, and also with modes, is a perilous business, particularly when they apply to natural conditions and socio-economic achievements of large nations. They both reveal and obscure, they are very meaningful and rather meaningless at the same time. When measured on a human time-scale, the environmental averages shift exceedingly slowly, governed as they are by processes that take 10^2 (rapid regional climatic change) to 10^6 (major surficial remodeling caused by plate tectonics) years to unfold. In contrast, human activities can move a long array of national socio-economic averages quite significantly in just one or two generations. East Asia offers many excellent examples of this rapid progression as the economies of Japan, South Korea, Taiwan, and now also China, have traversed the road from subsistence and shared poverty to incipient or, in Japan's case, undeniably widespread, affluence.

Rapid economic development is able to erase some traditionally embedded regional inequities: Guangdong became just in a matter of a few years China's richest province, and Shenzhen, an insignificant town in 1980, was rapidly converted into a quasi-Hong Kong. But laggard regions can be found even in the most rapidly modernizing major economies, including the relatively highly homogeneous Japan, where the outlying areas of the archipelago continue to be noticeably poorer than the traditional heartland of the Kanto Plain. Consequently, what is more notable than China's persisting regional disparities is the post-1980 widening of the gap that has been documented by many publications (World Bank 1996, 1997; Khan and Riskin 2000; UNDP 2001; Gustafsson and Shi 2001; and Wei and Kim 2002 are only a small part of this output).

This literature draws our attention to multiple widening gaps: one is urban/rural; another is class-based; a third is the difference between coastal and interior provinces; a fourth is related to ethnicity; a fifth, more complex, is gender-related. Deng's radical economic reforms have been a powerful tide that has, indeed, lifted all boats – but, unfortunately, some much more than others. And so while the nationwide averages of just about every important economic indicator as well as most of the quality-of-life measures are (whatever the desirable direction is) either up (income, savings, access to schooling, ownership of appliances) or down (malnutrition, illiteracy, sulfur dioxide levels in large cities), provincial and regional disparities have actually increased considerably, and they remain far greater than in Japan.

Energy consumption may actually be a more accurate measure of these disparities, as China's average income totals ignore rural subsistence production of food and local barter. During the late 1990s China's annual national consumption mean was about 30GJ/capita, or about 1.5 tonnes of coal equivalent (all units and their abbreviations are listed in the Appendix), but the rates in coal-rich Shanxi (which also wastes a great deal of the fuel because of its easy availability) and in Shanghai, the country's richest city of some 15 million people, were nearly three times as high, and the total primary energy supply of the capital's 13 million people averaged about 2.5 times the national mean (Fridley 2001). In contrast, the mean for more than 60 million people in Anhui province, Shanghai's northern neighbor, was only about 20GJ/capita and for more than 45 million people in land-locked and impoverished Guangxi it was as low as 16GJ/capita.

And the difference was even wider for per capita electricity consumption, with the annual national mean of about 0.9MWh/capita, and the respective extremes 3.4 times higher in the country's most dynamic megacity (Shanghai), and 50 per cent lower in its southernmost island province (Hainan). Household surveys also show that during the late 1990s urban families in China's four richest coastal provinces spent about 2.5 times as much on energy as did their counterparts in four interior provinces in the Northwest (NBS 2001). There is no need to belabor this point: what is important is to be always aware of it, even if the use of a particular average is not (as is the case in the vast majority of instances) prefaced by any caveat.

Chinese statistics and realities

Caution is advisable when dealing with any aggregate statistics, and particularly those of large and rapidly modernizing nations where corruption is widespread and where the black economy accounts for a large share of all transactions. Still, China is in a special category. This is how I assessed the challenge in a recent essay (Smil 2001a).

In this age of ubiquitous statistics, China is now an uncommonly zealous contributor to the incessant flow of figures. This bounty was preceded by a no-less-uncommon absence of any regularly published statistical volumes. Between

1958, the year when Mao's delusions launched the disastrous Great Leap Forward, and 1978, the year of Deng Xiaoping's comeback, the world had to be thankful for a few figures sprinkled sparsely in official press releases. Reporting resumed first on a limited scale, but a generation later few countries can rival the amount of data issued by the National Bureau of Statistics. The hardbound copy of *China Statistical Yearbook* now weighs almost 2.5kg. With its nearly 900 pages of a large (21cm × 30cm) format, the yearbook is now more massive than the venerable *Statistical Abstract of the United States*, whose 120th edition contains 999 pages of smaller (15cm × 22cm) size.

The quality of this data flood is a different matter. Inaccurate reporting and questionable statistics are a universal problem. But the degree of misinformation that an average user may get by consulting official Chinese figures is exceptionally high. Moreover, China's dubious numbers are not only misleading about minor realities but about key indicators. For example, official statistics claim that between 1980 and 1999, GDP grew annually at an average of 9.8 per cent, with four consecutive years of double-digit expansion (as high as 14.2 per cent) between 1992 and 1995. But the numbers don't seem to add up.

Angus Maddison, a distinguished economic historian who has done the most extensive long-term comparisons of global economic growth, argues that the actual average expansion was more than two per cent lower, that is 7.6 per cent rather than 9.8 per cent (I will address this discrepancy in some detail when dealing with energy intensities in Chapter 2). Granted, GDP figures are often questionable, but it is difficult to explain the reasons for one of China's largest and most persistent statistical lies: the amount of the country's arable land. Few other factors are as critical in determining China's capacity to feed itself. During the late 1990s Chinese official statistics persistently claimed that the country's cultivated land is only about 95 million hectares, or a mere 0.08 hectare per person. The figure gave China less arable land per capita than Bangladesh, and it furnished one of the key arguments for the conclusions that China would be unable to feed itself.

But for years, thousands of people in the Beijing bureaucracy knew that, based on satellite studies and land-use surveys, the total was vastly undervalued. Finally, in the year 2000, China admitted that it has 130 million hectares of cultivated land. But is this 36 per cent boost enough? (in the third chapter of this book I will show that it is not: China's total of agricultural (and aqua-cultural) land is most likely at least 150Mha).

So the next time you pick up that heavy tome of China's statistics, or when you hear a mainland official claim a particular growth rate, stop and think what may hide beneath those, and thousands of other, figures, issued by a bureaucracy that has reported aggregate GDP growth that was 30 per cent too large for the preceding decade while overlooking half of the country's food-producing land.

Interdisciplinary perspectives

One of the most effective approaches to overcome these data weaknesses is to examine China's record from a number of different perspectives and compare it to the historical record of other countries at similar stages of economic development:

absence or excess of expected interdependencies and correlations, whose magnitudes and ranges are reliably known from the experience of other nations, will then more readily reveal some exaggerated or otherwise dubious claims. For example, the expected elasticity of energy/GDP growth in low-income countries during the last decade of the twentieth century was between 1.0 and 1.5 (that is, their primary energy requirements were growing at least as fast as, or faster than, their GDPs). In contrast, China's elasticity for the decade was not just marginally below 1.0, it averaged close to 0.5. Obviously, this is a claim that requires a close examination – and I will do so in the closing segment of this book's second chapter.

Keeping with the strategy of the multipronged approach to the understanding of China's reality, the energy chapter will span the post-1949 era and examine several different but interrelated topics, ranging from the largely failed reliance on small-scale energy techniques to the two topics that attracted a great deal of international attention during the 1990s: the emergence of China as a major crude oil importer, and the impressive improvements in the energy intensity of China's economy, developments with important consequences for the world's energy supply.

Similarly, the food chapter has its retrospective and forward-looking segments: I open it by recounting the genesis, the toll and the consequences of the world's largest, and overwhelmingly man-made, famine of 1959–1961, and close it by assessing China's prospects for feeding itself during the coming decades. And, after a brief review of China's environmental attitudes and constraints, in the book's last thematic chapter (Chapter 4) I take a closer look at the country's strained water resources, a possible security threat arising from nature's abuse, the economic cost of these degradations, and the impacts of some of China's controversial megaprojects. In Chapter 5, the book's closing chapter, I will look ahead by looking back. First, I will recount briefly some notable successes as well as some missed opportunities that I have been advocating for decades. But most of my attention will go to forecasting, now a ubiquitous and compelling activity, but one whose perils, as some choice examples will demonstrate, are particularly great in China's case. I will not add to these failed prophecies by submitting any date-bound quantitative predictions, but I will offer some broad probabilistic conclusions about the future trends of China's energy, food and the environment.

2   Energy

I open this chapter with brief surveys of China's energy contrasting the situation at the time of the Communist assumption of power in 1949, a quarter-century later at the end of Mao's era, and at the beginning of the twenty-first century. Those who are aware of major milestones along this journey will be reminded of the enormous progress, as well as of many remaining problems characterizing "Half a century of advances" of China's energetics. The second segment will take a different tack by paying attention to an undeservedly understudied topic. Beyond China's rich littoral there is still the vast interior where subsistence peasants continue to burn straw and grasses and wood. The overall importance of these inefficient and environmentally damaging practices will be covered in "Continuing importance of traditional energies".

The next section, "A failed strategy", will chart the history of what once seemed to be such a promising course to follow, as well as China's unique contribution to the expansion of the world's energy supply: development of small-scale energy projects and conversions including coal mining, hydroelectricity and biogas generation. A generation ago, exaggerated claims about China's potential crude oil resources led to speculation about the country becoming a major petroleum exporter; twenty years later China is on its way to becoming the world's second-largest oil importer. "From a new Saudi Arabia to concerns about oil security" will analyse this unexpected shift. An even more notable post-1980 development has been an impressive decline in the energy intensity of China's economy: this little noted process proceeded at a rate faster than in any other case in history. "A remarkable shift in energy intensities" will describe and explain this encouraging trend.

Half a century of advances: China's energy 1950–2000

When I began my work on China's energy in the early 1970s I had to reckon – as any other serious student of China's affairs – with the absence of official systematic statistics. China's pre-1960 statistics, although never abundant, were adequate for basic economic assessments, but their veracity became extremely suspect as Mao launched the Great Leap. Then all statistical publications ceased in 1960, and irregular and incomplete information became more frequent only after the Sino-US *rapprochement* in 1972. But some major uncertainties were not resolved until the late 1970s, when the resumption of official statistical reporting finally started to fill a generation-long gap, and some indeed not until the early 1980s when we learned about China's suppressed 1964 population census, got the first results of the country's properly conducted population count taken in 1982, and could study more data in gradually expanding editions of China's various statistical yearbooks.

This paucity of pre-1978 information was a challenge when writing my first book on China's energy (in 1975 and 1976). Diligent collection and critical evaluation of fragmentary information that appeared in numerous press releases, central and provincial broadcasts, interviews with leading officials and (after 1971) in accounts of foreign observers, made it possible to form a basic dualistic judgment about the progress of China's primary energy supply and its conversions during the quarter-century of the Communist rule: great quantitative advances coexisted with inferior quality in both energy-producing and energy-consuming sectors. Between 1950 and 1975 China's coal extraction increased from about 40Mt to nearly 500Mt a year, its crude oil production rose from a mere trickle (0.2Mt) to 74Mt, and its hydroelectric generation expanded from less than one to more than 200TWh (Fridley 2001) (see Figure 2.1).

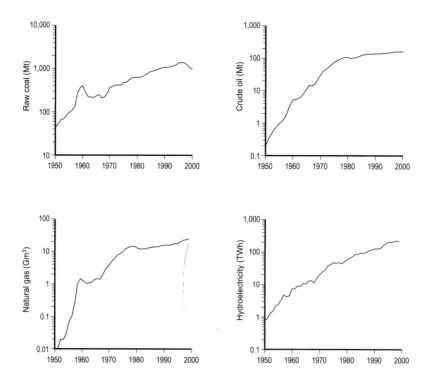

Figure 2.1 Growth of China's fossil fuel extraction and hydroelectricity generation, 1950–2000
Source: Plotted from data in Fridley (2001) and NBS (2001).

But, at the same time, this was an economy governed by the Stalinist–Maoist dogma of quantity, where overfulfilling the plan, rather than producing useful things, was the overriding goal. And so in the country which was the world's third-largest producer of coal more than 80 per cent of it was sold as raw, run-of-the-mine fuel, unwashed, unsorted, unsized, and burned mostly in boilers whose efficiencies were not much better than those of the steam equipment found in Europe and North America right after World War I. And sometimes worse: in 1982 I saw in Sichuan an English boiler built in the early 1880s! As the world admired the rise of China's hydrocarbon industry, the lack of refining capacity was forcing the Chinese to burn a great deal of raw crude oil in thermal power plants. In 1964 the country joined the small group of nuclear powers, but ten years later there were no kitchen refrigerators even in China's largest cities, and households were cooking, and throughout the northern provinces also heating their rooms, with primitive stoves that wasted 90 per cent of stoked coal, wood or straw. And the production and combustion of these low-quality fuels was generating inordinate amounts of air pollution, making China's cities the most polluted in the world. This is how I appraised the state of China's energy supply during the last years of Mao's regime (Smil 1976a).

Primary energy supply during the Maoist era

Coal mining was China's only readily and abundantly available source of commercial energy when the PRC was established in the fall of 1949. Between 1950 and 1952, seventy-seven large- and medium-sized mines were restored or reconstructed. The long-wall method – increasing the coal output and saving mine timber – was introduced to replace some of the traditional room-and-pillar extraction, and the labor productivity surpassed the best prewar levels. But essential difficulties mostly remained. The basic technical backwardness of the Chinese coal industry had hardly been altered; serious safety problems persisted, and the capacity of coal preparation plants was totally inadequate. A large-scale effort was clearly needed to expand and to modernize the production.

The achievements of the first five-year plan (FYP) contributed quite significantly to this goal. Between the years 1953 and 1957, construction commenced on 215 shafts and open mines with aggregate capacity of 63.81Mt. The total output of raw coal reached 130.7Mt in 1957, after growing by an average rate of 14.6 per cent since 1952. Yet this growth rate, as well as other industrial advances, seemed too slow to Mao's government. Another Soviet-style FYP, scheduled to start in 1958, was supplanted by the Great Leap Forward. Coal played a prominent role in this spectacle. Feverish construction of primitive small open-cast mines started all over the country. By the end of 1958 there were some 110,000 pits in operation, engaging an incredible number of 20 million Chinese peasants. Output of large mines was to be expanded at a similarly staggering pace, as more than 400 new mines were started in 1958. The total claimed 1958 raw coal output – 270.2Mt – surpassed that of 1957 by 106 per cent.

After the collapse of the Great Leap in 1960 the coal industry was thrown back almost to the 1957 level. The first half of the 1960s became a time of recovery and consolidation. Only twenty-eight new mines with the total capacity of 14.4Mt were opened between 1961 and 1965. Although a renewed expansion during the second half of the 1960s was temporarily halted by the turmoil of the Cultural Revolution, the addition of thirty-seven new mines brought the total 1970 capacity to 300Mt. While the Chinese official coal production statistics for the years 1949–1957 are generally considered genuine, the Great Leap figures, accepted uncritically in the late 1950s and the early 1960s by some researchers, were doubtlessly exaggerated. When the publication of all statistics ceased in 1960, the outside production estimates started to differ by scores of millions of tonnes.

By 1976 the PRC was the world's third-largest coal producer, with dozens of large, highly mechanized mines, an expanding coal-machinery industry, and abundant reserves to support future growth. At the same time, China's coal industry has been facing some rather intractable problems, and new difficulties will assume prominence in the not too distant future. Small coal pit extraction is not, even when approached in a planned and sensible manner, without many difficulties. Pit output is usually of a lower quality than in modern mine production, economies of scale cannot be attained in thousands of small and quite primitive enterprises, labor productivity is very low, and the actual cost of coal may be unexpectedly high.

Two main problems hurting the production of large modern mines have been the shortages of mine timber and extraction, loading, and transportation machinery. Another difficulty has been a very low capacity of coal-preparation plants. The key future problem and, inexorably, the ultimate limiting factor in the expansion of coal mining, is the magnitude of the task itself. If the 1950–1975 growth had continued for the rest of the century, total coal production would have reached at least 450Mt in 1980, 775Mt in 1990, and almost 1.34Gt in the year 2000 – more than a threefold increase in the already very high current production in just twenty-five years.

Perhaps nothing illustrates better the backwardness of the pre-1949 Chinese oil industry than the aggregate figures for forty-two years between 1907, when the first well in Yanchang started to produce, and 1948. During almost half a century there were only 123 exploratory wells that were sunk and forty-five wells that went into actual production, and the cumulative oil output reached 2.78Mt (that much is now extracted in about six days).The Great Leap techniques were also tried in the oil industry. Handmade equipment was used to drill many shallow wells, and hundreds of minuscule "distillation factories" were built near small shale oil deposits. Needless to say, the results were useless and ephemeral. Fortunately, the giant fields discovered during the latter part of the 1950s (Lenghu, Karamay, and Longnüsi) were coming into full operation at the same time. Daqing (China's first supergiant oilfield discovered in September 1959) went into full operation during 1963.

Very fast output increases since the end of the Cultural Revolution, initiation of crude oil exports to Japan, large-scale expansion of oilfields and refineries, and the promising offshore potential have made China's oil industry an object of widespread international attention. Insufficient pipeline transportation and tanker capacities have been major limiting factors in the expansion of China's oil and gas industry. Another serious difficulty has been the shortage of refining facilities. To eliminate some of the described difficulties, China might resort to large-scale, long-term cooperation with Japan or the United States. But whatever the future actions might be, one fact remains certain – the high growth rates prevailing in the country's oil industry could not be sustained over a long period. Had this post-1950 rate continued for the next two decades, China's oil output would have reached about 310Mt by the year 1980, and a patently ridiculous total of 3.2Gt in 1990. A decline of growth rates was absolutely inevitable.

Considering the admirable tradition of high waterwork skills, it is ironic – yet at the same time a fitting illustration of the economic weakness of the emerging Chinese republic – that the first large modern hydroprojects in the country (Supung on the Yalu between Liaoning and Korea, and Fengman on the Sungari near Jilin) were built by the Japanese during their occupation of Manchuria in the late 1930s and the early 1940s. Both plants were heavily affected by the Soviet removals of Japanese-built Manchurian industry after 1 September 1945. Reinstallation of Fengman units became the first large hydrogeneration project after the establishment of the PRC – a task conducted, ironically enough, with Soviet assistance. With a considerable Soviet and East-European (above all Czech and East German) help, the hydroelectric capacity at the end of the first FYP (1957) reached almost 1GW, that is 22 per cent of the country's total electricity-generating capacity.

By 1957 designs were finalized for a 1.1-GW station to be built at Sanmenxia on the Huanghe in Henan province (the fate of this megaproject will be described in detail in Chapter 4). The second-largest project was planned for Liujiaxia, 80km above Lanzhou. Grandiose as they were, the Huanghe projects constituted only a part of a strong shift in favor of hydro power, a move contemplated for some time and vigorously initiated in 1958. Thus the construction of a large number of hydroelectric power plants of all sizes became one of the most distinct features of the Great Leap years of 1958–1959. After the Leap's demise most of the projects had to be simply abandoned, and construction and installation was progressing, with great delays, on only a fraction of the original program.

In 1973 the PRC sent its first delegation to a congress of the International Commission on Large Dams, and its general paper provided the first useful summary of developments in the eventful period between 1949 and 1972. In those twenty-four years 12,517 dams higher than 15m were completed, of which smaller dams (15–30m high) constituted the overwhelming majority (12,321); there were 1,150 structures between 30 and 60m, and 46 dams were more than 60m. The largest hydroelectric station in the country, Liujiaxia, was finally completed just at the end of 1974, and it was only in 1973 that the PRC surpassed India in the installed hydro capacity. As with other Chinese energy techniques, the post-1949 growth rate of installed hydro capacities could not be sustained for the rest of that century.

A quarter-century later: continuity and change

Recent writings on China's achievements during the last quarter of the twentieth century stress, almost without exception, the enormity of change.[1] But, for both universal and particular reasons, this survey of the country's energy resources and uses (Smil 1998) will stress continuity as much as change. Taking the inertia of complex energy systems as the key universal given, the most important particular explanation lies in the peculiarities of China's resource endowment. Historical perspectives demonstrate that it takes a long time – usually half a century – for a new source of energy to capture the largest share of a market, and the capital spent on implementing the necessary extraction, processing, distribution and conversion infrastructure is a powerful reason for maintaining the existing arrangements.[2] The challenge of rising costs of extraction, transportation and conversion is mostly met through technical innovations, which not only keep most of the inflation-adjusted prices from rising but often lead to impressive secular price declines.[3]

The social consequences inherent in the rapid dismantling of labor-intensive industries (coal mining is the best example) or in depriving some regions of their major source of income (oil and gas extraction in otherwise industrially undeveloped locations) make it desirable to prolong the economic viability of such operations through technical innovation (or through costly government subsidies). These virtually universal considerations exert an expected influence on China's energy industries – but the country's peculiar resource endowment is an even stronger cause of the relative stability of its primary energy supply's composition.

China's energy resources: strengths and weaknesses

Given the size of China's territory (almost exactly as large as the US including Alaska), one would expect to find generous amounts of fossil fuel resources. The resource aggregate is, indeed, very large – but this is overwhelmingly because of China's huge coal deposits. China's global rank in what is, by definition, an only imprecisely known category, is – at worst – number three, behind Russia and the USA.[4] In any case, its coal resources could last for several hundreds of years at the mid-1990s rate of extraction. Moreover, most of China's coal has fairly high heating content, with inferior lignites accounting for only a small fraction of all resources.[5]

In terms of verified coal reserves China ranks third in the world, behind the USA and Russia, with roughly 115Gt, or one ninth of the world's total. This could support nearly a century of extraction at the current rate.[6] In contrast, at the end of 1996 the total of 3.3Gt of China's proved oil reserves amounted to just over 2 per cent of the global total (eleventh-largest in the world), enough for no more than two decades at the 1996 rate of extraction.[7] And the country's proved natural gas reserves are much smaller still, amounting to a mere 0.8 per cent of the global total, ranking only twenty-third worldwide.[8] China's poor natural gas endowment is conspicuously out of line with the proportions of the two fuels in other major oil- and gas-producing countries.[9] Both American and British natural gas reserves hold about as much energy as their respective crude oil reserves, and Russia has about six times as much energy in the already discovered gas as it has in commercially recoverable crude oil. In comparison, the energy content of Chinese gas reserves amounts to mere 30 per cent of the country's verified crude oil deposits.

This unusually low natural gas endowment disadvantages China in several important ways. Natural gas is both the most convenient and the cleanest fuel for a range of uses from residential and commercial heating to electricity generation during periods of peak demand. In addition, it is also the best fuel and feedstock for numerous chemical syntheses, including plastics and nitrogenous fertilizers.[10] A high share of natural gas consumption in a country's primary energy balance thus assures lower energy intensity (total amount of energy used per unit of GDP) while minimizing the emissions of CO_2, the world's most important greenhouse gas.[11] Because of its extensive coal deposits, China has large reserves of coal-bed methane, but this kind of natural gas is usually much more expensive and less convenient to recover than the resources in hydrocarbon fields.

Fortunately, China can claim global primacy in the other most desirable clean energy resource: it has the world's highest potential for generating electricity from flowing water.[12] This potential is never easy to develop for two major reasons: hydro generation has inherently higher capital costs than thermal power plants, and expensive long-distance transmission links – needed to connect remote dam sites with populated regions – add considerably to the overall cost of hydro power.[13] These fundamental realities mean that the dominance of coal in China's fossil fuel consumption is going to change only very slowly in decades ahead. In fact, coal's share has actually increased since the beginning of China's post-1979 modernization: the fuel provided about 72 per cent of China's primary energy consumption in 1980, and it supplied just over 76 per cent of the total in 1996. Consequently, it is most unlikely that its share will fall below 60 per cent by the year 2010.[14] This extraordinary dependence causes a number of problems whose impact has been aggravated by the generally low technical level of Chinese mining, inadequate coal processing, underdeveloped transportation and irrational pricing.

Chinese coal: straddling two realms

China surpassed Soviet production to become the world's largest coal producer in 1989. During the 1990s its coal production continued to grow strongly, but irregularly, by anywhere between 24 and 59Mt a year. Extraction surpassed 1Gt in 1989 and 1.3Gt in 1996.[15] But the last total does not represent 38 per cent of the global coal output, as a simple quotient of the two figures would indicate: Chinese totals do not refer to cleaned and sorted coal, but rather to raw fuel which contains large, and variable, shares of incombustible rocks and clay. A multiplier of roughly 0.7 has been used to convert this fuel to the standard coal equivalent – i.e. fuel with 29.3 megajoules per kilogram (MJ/kg). Typical raw

Chinese bituminous coal, representing the bulk of the country's solid fuel extraction, thus has an energy content just short of 21MJ/kg.

In reality, even this rate may be too high an average for the extraction of the late 1990s because of the rising share of raw coal with more than 30 per cent of incombustible waste. This qualitative decline arises from yet another long-standing Chinese peculiarity whose enormous effects go far beyond the coal industry: Chinese coal extraction originates from two very different kinds of enterprises, from large collieries owned by the state and administered from Beijing, and from a variety of local medium and small mines, most of which are run by counties, townships, collectives or individuals.

The first kind of enterprise, each producing annually more than half a million tonnes of coal, is now increasingly modernized and relatively highly productive.[16] This modern sector was considerably strengthened during the 1980s when mechanization became widespread in underground mines, and when China finally began to join the other great coal powers by increasing its share of efficient surface mining. In 1979, mechanized extraction accounted for slightly less than one third of the total output in state mines, but by 1990 the rate had reached 70 per cent. Before 1980 a handful of old small surface mines contributed less than 5 per cent of China's coal output. Then, with considerable foreign investment and technical cooperation, China decided to open several very large open-cast mines in Shanxi and in Inner Mongolia.[17] Even with these innovations, international comparisons reveal the continuing inferiority of China's large-scale coal mining. Typical coal recovery rates average no more than 50–60 per cent, compared to over 90 per cent in modern long-wall extraction. Even though per capita labor productivity had risen from just 0.9t/shift in 1980 to roughly 1.4t/shift in the mid-1990s, it still remains only 30–40 per cent of European, and less than 15 per cent of average US levels. The official target of 2t/manshift by the year 2000 may not be reached.

Large Chinese mines have a long way to go in order to achieve acceptable levels of coal dust and work safety. The current situation is truly shocking, as chronic bronchitis and pneumoconiosis incapacitate miners in their thirties, and fatal accidents are at least thirty times as frequent per million tonnes of extracted coal as in the USA.[18] Despite an increase of more than 50 per cent in the capacity of coal-processing plants during the 1980s, still little less than half of all coal produced by large mines is processed – i.e. crushed, washed in order to separate coal from incombustible waste and sorted by size according to the needs of different customers.[19] Nothing demonstrates the inadequacy of large-scale state-controlled coal mining in China better than the fact that it no longer produces the bulk of the country's coal. Its production share slipped from 56 per cent of the national output in 1979 to one half in 1984 and to 40 per cent by 1995. Since 1987, collectively or individually owned local mines have been responsible for virtually all output growth. This has gone a long way towards reducing China's long-standing coal supply shortages, as well as alleviating environmentally undesirable cutting of trees for fuelwood and the burning of crop residues in rural stoves.[20]

But, in line with a frequent phenomenon in China's development, this quantitative growth has not been accompanied by qualitative improvements. The race to open small mines, usually without any geological and technical evaluation, has led to an enormous waste of resources in an uncoordinated and often illegal quest for instant profits (at least at a third of some 80,000 small mines may have been opened illegally). The combination of primitive extraction methods and inexperienced operators results in very low recovery rates. Because of low productivity and insufficient profits, many small mines – in some counties a quarter or a third – have to close down within a few years, or even a few months, after their opening.

Coal extracted in local mines, including those owned by the state, is sold almost exclusively in raw state, without any cleaning or sizing. As a result (and in spite of increasing capacities of washing plants attached to large mines), the overall share of processed coal in China has remained basically unchanged during the past twenty years, fluctuating between 18 and 20 per cent. While the labor productivity of small mines is very low – typically just a few hundred kg of fuel per shift per worker – occupational risks are extraordinarily high, with fatalities two to five times higher than in large enterprises.[21] Mine-roof collapses and landslides are especially common in the absence of any operating regulations.

Given such a disregard for human safety, it is hardly surprising that the operators of small mines pay scant attention to the environmental consequences of coal extraction. Predictable results include extensive destruction of arable and grazing land, accelerated erosion of exposed topsoils, and increasing air and water pollution. A recent survey in coal-rich Shenmu county on the Loess Plateau illustrates these perils.[22] Streams filled with mine spoils and increased sediment aggravate local floods, and erosion caused by mining adds almost another 300Mt of silt to the Huang (Yellow) River already overburdened with eroded loess. Local air pollution has increased twenty-four times for sulfur dioxide (SO_2) and seventeen times for particulate matter. These are extraordinary increases caused by an unusually high concentration of inefficient coking plants and industrial boilers in one of China's most affected counties – but all of the country's industrial and urban regions have been experiencing unacceptably high air pollution levels, a state attributable to coal's dominance in China's energy supply, to inadequate coal cleaning capacities, and to inefficient combustion.

Most of the inferior fuel is burned either in the small boilers that fuel local industries, service establishments and housing estates, or in even less efficient household stoves (typically these are less than 30 per cent efficient). Only modern large coal-fired power plants and a growing number of newly installed industrial boilers are equipped with electrostatic precipitators which effectively remove particulate matter from hot flue gases. Consequently, Chinese emission factors per unit of delivered useful energy are extraordinarily high in comparison with rates prevailing in Western countries. No matter which yardstick is used – Chinese standards or the World Health Organization (WHO) levels – typical concentrations of particulate matter in Chinese cities are excessive. Indeed, frequently they are so high that their annual means surpass recommended daily maxima![23] And many cities fare much worse: Taiyuan and Linfeng in Shanxi, Lanzhou in Gansu, and Mudanjiang in Heilongjiang have recorded annual TSP means above $600\mu g/m^3$. Major southern cities are somewhat cleaner, with annual averages of around $300\mu g/m^3$ – but such values are still multiples of the WHO's guidelines (maxima of 60–$90\mu g/m^3$ as an annual average).

The average sulfur content of major Chinese coal deposits, about 1.2 per cent, is not high by international standards, and statistics for large state mines show that they produce coal with average sulfur content of just 1.04 per cent.[24] But some southern coals, most notably those from Sichuan and Yunnan, have unusually high sulfur content (up to 5 per cent). Official estimates put SO_2 emissions at 15Mt in 1990 and 19Mt in 1996 – but these totals do not contain a sizeable contribution from spontaneous combustion of coal seams. Mao and Li estimated that every year more than 100Mt of coal are lost to this difficult-to-control phenomenon, releasing at least 1.6Mt SO_2.[25] Given the anticipated increase of coal consumption, it will be extremely difficult to prevent a further substantial rise of SO_2 emissions.

Annual averages of SO_2 concentrations have been above the recommended WHO levels in every northern Chinese city and, because of high-S content of many southern coals, also in many centers south of the Yangzi. Beijing annual means have run between $80\mu g/m^3$ in the cleanest suburbs and twice that much in the most polluted locations. These are low levels compared to annual means (all in $\mu g/m^3$) over 400 in Taiyuan and Lanzhou. I have estimated that at least 200 million Chinese are exposed to annual TSP concentrations of above $300\mu g/m^3$, and at least 20 million are exposed to twice that level.[26] Clean coal techniques (both combustion and conversion to liquid and gaseous fuels) are seen as the best way of reconciling China's high reliance on coal with the need for environmental protection, but the short-term contributions of this approach are rather limited. Fluidized bed combustion is not commercially available at ratings now required for China's electricity generation (with annual capacity installations surpassing 15GW, in units of more than 300MW) and, as the costly and aborted US foray into coal conversion shows, imports of hydrocarbons are preferable.

In the future, flue gas desulfurization will be thus necessary not only in parts of southern China where highly acid rains (with pH commonly below 4.5) are already causing serious damage to forests, but also in the north. During the next generation that region will acquire the world's largest concentrations of coal-fired power plants, whose emissions will be carried eastward toward Korea and Japan. Current emissions are already causing concerns in both countries, but large-scale desulfurization is an expensive proposition.[27]

Yet another lasting challenge arising from China's high dependence on coal is the heavy burden which the shipment of the fuel places on the country's railroads and, increasingly, on its wholly inadequate road network. New electrified lines were built from Shanxi, the largest coal-producing province, to the coast to facilitate growing coal exports (rising from just 6Mt in 1980 to over 30Mt by 1996), but the main north–south lines of domestic coal transfers are chronically strained by coal shipments amounting to slightly over 40 per cent of all transported freight.

The most desirable solution of this problem – burning most of the fuel in large mine-mouth power plants in China's north and northwest – is already being implemented, but high demand for cooling water needed by such plants in a region with already serious water deficits will limit the extent of this option.[28]

At least one chronic problem of China's coal industry has finally been solved. In order to make coal readily available for expanding industries, China's Stalinist planners of the early 1950s priced it so low that even the best coal mines working some of the world's richest seams of fine bituminous coal could not make any profit. This irrational underpricing meant that coal mining accounted for only about 2 per cent of China's total industrial output during the early 1990s, and a single oilfield employing several tens of thousands of people could earn greater profits than the country's two million coal miners. The Ministry of Finance introduced a two-tier price system in 1984, and by 1994 the government finally freed all coal prices. In contrast, prices of crude oil and refined oil products are still tightly regulated. So is the price of natural gas, which rose steeply in March 1997 when the State Planning Commission announced a twelvefold increase for fertilizer plants, a near fivefold increase for residential use, and a fourfold increase for other uses.[29] But it is the adequacy of domestic hydrocarbon resources, rather than the pace of price reform, which has become the greatest concern of China's oil and gas planners.

Oil and gas: strategic contradictions

Chinese leaders and Chinese media like to talk and write about contradictions: few such contradictions are as acute as those presented by the country's need for crude oil and natural gas. As already noted, in spite of its large territory, and no shortage of sedimentary basins with clear promise of oil and gas deposits, China is a relatively hydrocarbon-poor place (Figure 2.2). The absence of substantial natural gas reserves is particularly unfortunate. More exploration may eventually modify, if not reverse, this judgment – but so far the most promising new oil and gas region has turned out to be a vast disappointment.

Quite a few enthusiasts had initially envisaged the South China Sea as a new Saudi Arabia – and this promise lured all major multinational oil companies into an unprecedented giveaway of the results of their geophysical exploration to the Chinese.[30] Disappointment came quickly once the drilling licenses were awarded in the early 1980s. Now, after fifteen years of fairly extensive exploratory drilling, the area has one relatively small-size natural gas field in the Yinggehai basin just south of Hainan and a smattering of small oilfields in the Zhu (Pearl) River Basin.[31] Total output from all of China's offshore fields (including about half a dozen oilfields in the Bohai Basin near Tianjin) was less than 7Mt in 1995 – or still less than 5 per cent of China's oil extraction.

And although China is no crude oil production dwarf – in 1996 it extracted 141Mt, enough to be the world's fifth-largest producer – its rapid rate of modernization has already seen demand surpass domestic production. While the country still exports crude oil to Japan and Korea, it has been a net importer of

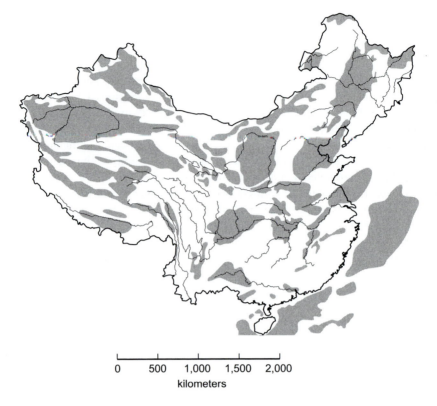

Figure 2.2 China's sedimentary basins

Source: Based on a map in CASP (1999).

liquid fuels since 1993. With exports declining (from 20Mt of crude oil in 1996 to 15Mt in 1997) and imports rising (from just 3Mt in 1990 to 22.6Mt in 1996), China now has a growing trade deficit in its crude oil trade. In addition, its imports of refined products are now approaching the total volume of imported crude. Except for gasoline, China is now a net importer of all refined fuels, with fuel oil accounting for just over half of 15.8Mt bought in 1996.

The potential for further increases in demand is very large as per capita consumption is still only 0.14t/year, or less than 7 per cent of the Japanese mean. Chinese projections have seen the need for at least 50Mt of imported crude oil by the year 2000, and forecasts of annual imports of well over 100Mt a decade later appear conservative.[32] Clearly, times have changed: there is no more boasting about China's imperviousness to the vagaries of the global oil market and to destabilizing threats of oil shocks. Oil security is now among the top concerns of China's energy planners, as rising demand (averaging 5.5 per cent a year for the ten years before 1997), barely increasing domestic extraction (a mere 1 per cent per year for the same period) and fading prospects for discoveries of giant fields combine to create a sense of urgency.[33]

The only way to avert the need for steadily increasing imports would be to discover large hydrocarbon deposits in Xinjiang, China's only remaining great hydrocarbon frontier. The region already produces almost 5 per cent of China's crude oil, but much of it remains to be properly explored. After years of Chinese drilling, Exxon, Agip and several Japanese companies are now active in the area, and recent discoveries of both oil and gas have been fairly encouraging. Still, no supergiant hydrocarbon field has been discovered in the inhospitable deserts of Tarim in central Xinjiang, or the grasslands of Junggar in the region's north. As the Xinjiang experience increasingly mirrors the South China Sea disappoint- ment, the country could find it difficult merely to maintain its current rate of production. Just over half of all Chinese crude comes from two aging fields which have been remarkably successful (mainly due to improved methods of secondary oil recovery) in maintaining a fairly steady output for nearly three decades. Heilongjiang's Daqing oilfields, discovered in 1959, remain by far the largest of the country's nearly 300 fields, producing just over a third of China's crude oil total. Shengli in Shandong, another old field discovered in 1962, has recently been adding about 17 per cent.

That the Chinese oilmen do not have blind faith in Xinjiang's potential has been clear for some time. China now participates in oil extraction in Canada (its first foreign involvement began in 1993), Russia, Mongolia, Thailand, Papua New Guinea, Iraq, Sudan, Peru and Venezuela. These foreign projects were expected to supply up to 5Mt by the year 2000, and at least an additional 15Mt by the year 2010. In addition, China will be negotiating deals for substantial long-term imports of oil and gas from hydrocarbon-rich regions of the former Soviet Union. The first such deal, announced in August 1997, gave the China National Petroleum Corporation the exclusive right to negotiate a contract for developing a giant Uzen oilfield on the eastern shore of the Caspian Sea in Kazakhstan. Even bigger multinational deals involving Russia, China, South Korea and Japan are planned for massive exports of Russian gas from the giant Siberian fields to energy-deficient East Asia.[34] No matter where most of its crude oil will eventually come from, China has a great deal of work to do in order to improve the quality of its liquid fuels. A very important step in that direction was taken in April 1997, when it was announced that only unleaded gasoline would be sold in all of China's major cities by the year 2000. Beijing was to be the first city to convert to lead-free gasoline.[35]

Electricity: doubling decades

A universal feature of the most intensive stages of national economic modern- ization is the demand for electricity growing faster than the total demand for all forms of commercial energy. Historical data show typical annual growth rates of between 6 and 9 per cent for the former, compared to 3–5 per cent for the latter. This means that every decade (or, to be more exact, a period anywhere between 9 and 12 years) sees the demand for electricity double. China conforms closely to this pattern: its installed electricity generating grew by 8.04 per cent between

1980 and 1995, the growth was to average about 7 per cent until the year 2000, and it is projected to remain around 6 per cent until the year 2010.[36] Because of China's already large generating base this has meant a globally unprecedented spell of new power-plant building activity. Annual additions of new capacity are now averaging about 16GW, and China's electricity generation, which in 1980 – at 300TWh – was roughly equal to British electricity production, was to be in the year 2000 (at 1,400TWh) the world's third highest after the Russian and American outputs of 2000.

Inevitably, coal-fired power plants dominate this expansion. Coal combustion now generates about three quarters of China's electricity, with an increasing share coming from large modern plants, mostly equipped with units (combinations of boiler and turbogenerator) rated mostly at 300MW; domestic units of 600 to 1,000MW are now under development. As a result, fuel consumption per unit of electricity has been declining, from about 450 grams of coal equivalent per kilowatt hour (gce/kWh) in 1980 to about 380gce/kWh by 1995.[37] Given the country's huge water power potential it is not surprising that a massive construction program of large hydrostations is another key ingredient of China's long-term plans. The initial goal was to quadruple the installed capacity between 1980 and the year 2000 by putting online some 60GW of new hydro capacity. Actual ratings will fall somewhat short of that goal.

By far the best known, and most controversial, part of this program is the construction of the world's largest hydroproject, the Sanxia (Three Gorges) Dam across the Yangzi in western Hubei.[38] In order to install 18.2GW of generating capacity and to produce 85TWh electricity a year, the reservoir will inundate about 630km² of land and displace at least 1.2 million people. Unprecedented opposition to the construction of Sanxia Dam – both inside and outside China – has been based on a variety of environmental, engineering and economic considerations, but has failed to sway the leadership.[39] Both the USA and Canada, two of the Western world's most experienced builders of large dams, refused to participate in this costly project, as did the World Bank. The official Chinese projection for Sanxia's total cost is 200 billion of 1996 *yuan*, with a quarter of that to be spent on the dam itself and a fifth on the resettlement of one million people.[40] As we have learned from other megaprojects, this cost estimate is almost certainly an underestimate. Sanxia's construction is now well under way: the river was diverted on 8 November 1997 and completion is planned for the year 2009. The second-largest hydroproject now under construction – Ertan on the Yalong River in Sichuan – will have 3GW of capacity.[41]

Nuclear generation is China's distant third choice for large-scale generation of electricity. After years of delays China's first domestically designed nuclear power plant, a 300MW facility at Qinshan near Shanghai, was completed in 1992, and two years later the six-times-larger Daya Bay station in Guangdong, equipped with light-water French reactors based on a US design, began supplying Hong Kong and easing electricity supply shortages in the province. Early nuclear expectations, much like their Western counterparts, were unrealistically high, as were the latest plans calling for the building of four new plants with eight reactors by the year 2001, all in coastal provinces of Zhejiang, Guangdong and Liaoning.[42] Long-term prospects for China's nuclear power were given a major boost by the US decision, announced during Jiang Zemin's American visit in October/November 1997, allowing American companies to sell pressurized and boiling water reactors to China. French and Canadian efforts to sell their reactors will also continue, but forecasting the country's nuclear generating capacity remains a much more precarious effort than foreseeing its coal-fired and hydro capacities.[43]

The magnitude of the task, particularly when combined with China's still limited technical capacities, means that the expansion of the country's modern electricity generating capacity has been, and will continue to be, highly dependent on foreign participation. By 1995, foreign investors had poured almost US$15 billion into China's electricity generation, participating in more than sixty large- and medium-sized thermal and hydroprojects.[44] Foreign expertise has also been important in reducing China's wasteful energy use.

Rationalizing consumption: efficiency gains

The question of meeting rising demand – i.e. the matter of energy supply shortfalls that have reportedly exercised near-chronic checks on the performance of China's economy for the past quarter-century – is more complicated that simple comparisons of official statistics would indicate. In fact, China is using too much energy to satisfy its current demand. Signs of this inefficient energy use abound. There are still too many old Stalinist-style state enterprises whose managers have never been concerned with optimizing energy use. At the same time, China has made some impressive, and too little appreciated, advances. Certainly the most encouraging indicator of its progress toward efficiency has been a rapid decline of the overall energy/GDP intensity. This measure is a powerful marker of two critical trends: lower energy/GDP ratios do not merely indicate a more efficient economy, they also mean that the economy puts, in relative terms, less burden on the environment by reducing the extent of land, water and air pollution.[45]

The long-term decline of energy/GDP intensities is expected with advancing economic modernization, and it has been quite pronounced in both North America and in Western Europe – but the recent Chinese improvements have occurred at an even faster rate. If China's energy/GDP ratio had remained at the 1980 level, the country would have needed to burn twice as much coal in 1995 to produce that year's GDP, and hence also generate a much larger amount of environmental pollution. Using the State Statistical Bureau data on energy consumption and inflation-adjusted values of the GDP, the national average of energy intensity was about 0.7 kilograms of coal equivalent (kgce) per 1 *yuan* of GDP; by 1990 the rate declined to 0.42kgce/1980 *yuan*, and in 1995 it was slightly below 0.35kgce – a bit less than half the value of fifteen years ago.[46] Such a rate of decline is unmatched by any other major modernizing economy.

Industrial efficiencies have improved remarkably, not only because of the introduction of more efficient converters and processes, but also due to the outright closures of many old plants and to a major shift from production previously dominated by inherently less energy-efficient heavy industries to light manufacturing.[47] The performance of China's cement industry, which consumes about 5 per cent of all commercial energy, is a good example of possible efficiency gains. Its output has roughly quintupled since 1980, with more than 500Mt (nearly a quarter of the entire global output) produced in over 7,000 plants. During the same period, average fuel consumption in about sixty of the largest state-run plants using rotary kilns fell from about 6.6MJ per tonne of clinker (which is then ground to cement) to just 4.5MJ/t.[48]

In contrast, too many small local industrial enterprises remain highly inefficient, and major efficiency gains are yet to be made in household energy consumption. Hardly any of today's Chinese apartments are built with wall and ceiling insulation and double-glazed windows, and even fewer have any individual temperature controls – fiberglass and thermostats in millions of newly built apartments would bring energy savings and environmental benefits for decades to come.

The rise in electricity consumption has been driven not only by rapidly growing industrial demand, but also by an even more rapidly spreading ownership of household appliances – and this means that major efficiency gains can greatly influence future demand. Many Western utilities have become increasingly engaged in demand-side management by providing credit or offering more efficient converters at subsidized rates. China's opportunities for this kind of efficiency improvement are immense, as the country now ranks as the world's largest producer of household electric appliances and gadgets. In 1995 its annual production capacity reached 80 million electric fans, 20 million color TVs, 15 million refrigerators, 15 million washing machines, and 8 million room air conditioners. Even small efficiency improvements translate into large-capacity savings when multiplied by tens of millions of various appliances.

These savings could be particularly impressive for such appliances as refrigerators. In 1989, China surpassed the USA to become the world's largest producer of refrigerators, but the insufficient thermal insulation, inefficient compressors and poor-quality gaskets of typical Chinese-made refrigerators makes them up to 50 per cent less efficient than for optimized redesigns which are also chlorofluorocarbon-free.[49] Similarly, better designs could cut electricity demand for a wide variety of smaller gadgets, ranging from electrical fans – now ubiquitous in all affluent urban households – and rice cookers to hair dryers and curlers.

Looking ahead: difficult challenges

Even the most desirable combination of trends reducing the growth of China's energy demand – further industrial restructuring complemented by persistent and aggressive energy conservation campaigns – would not prevent significant increases of China's primary energy consumption and electricity generation. As always with Chinese output statistics, impressive growth rates and huge absolute totals still hide only very modest per capita consumption rates. China's annual per capita consumption of fossil fuels and primary (hydro and nuclear) electricity now averages about 25GJ. This is more than twice as large as the Indian rate, but only about one half of the global mean, and – to indicate the distance separating China from its great East Asian rival – still less than a fifth of Japanese consumption.[50] Numerous national peculiarities – environmental, economic and cultural – make it impossible to offer a definite value of per capita energy use that would indicate a high quality of life in a modernized economy. However, international comparisons show that the promise of economic security, good health care and broadly accessible educational opportunities does not come with annual rates below at least 50GJ/capita.[51]

Consequently, it is easy to make a case for yet another doubling of China's per capita energy use, and because of the expected addition of at least another 250–300 million people during the next two generations the fulfillment of this goal would require a 2.5-fold increase of today's total consumption. Even if no insurmountable extraction and transportation problems accompanied this growth (most unlikely if given, above all, China's deepening involvement in the global oil market), one trend is already causing a great deal of concern. With about one eighth of the global total, China is currently the world's second-largest producer of greenhouse gases. Its emission rates are greater than Russia's and a little over half as large as America's. But while Russian emissions have actually been declining with the post-Soviet collapse of industrial production, and while US emissions are growing only very slowly and, given political will, could be stabilized at current levels or even cut, China's emissions will increase substantially during the coming generation.[52]

Rapid economic expansion and the continuing reliance on coal can be expected to more than double China's current carbon dioxide emissions, and large increases in the other important greenhouse gases are expected as well. As China develops its natural gas reserves, methane losses will rise. In the agricultural sector, more rice will mean more methane from rice paddies, and more nitrous oxide from denitrification of synthetic fertilizers. The question is thus one of when, not if: China will become the world's largest emitter of greenhouse gases, but it may be as early as 2010 or as late as 2025. At this time, official policy offers no hope for remedial action. As expressed in the Beijing Declaration of 1991, China believes that the rich countries are responsible for the rise in greenhouse gases, both in terms of current emissions and in a cumulative sense, and hence it concludes that the developing countries need not do anything to limit their emissions until they reach the developed world's level of per capita emissions, as well as its historical cumulative emissions.[53]

Chinese energy will face many challenges, even if there were no signs of relatively rapid global warming during the coming generation. Judging by the Western experience, dealing with a truly runaway demand for transportation fuels will be particularly problematic. Expected consequences will be rising concentrations of ozone (the most aggressive air pollution oxidant created by complex reactions in photochemical smog), excessive losses of highly productive farmland, huge economic penalties for time wasted idling in stalled traffic, further degradation of urban environments, a rising toll of deaths and injuries in car accidents – and greater dependence on oil imports.[54]

Although it is not yet too late to avoid the worst and follow the *shinkansen* model of transportation by developing a network of efficient rapid train links throughout its densely populated provinces, Chinese planners are most inappropriately bent on following the American example: the official policy is for every family to eventually have a car.[55] This goal is not surprising, as China's leadership follows the Japanese and the South Korean pattern of building up auto industry into the leading manufacturing (and later also presumably export) sector – but its environmental repercussions will be considerable. The two main concerns, already clearly discernible in and around large coastal metropolitan areas, are the effects of photochemical smog on human health and on crop yields.

While China's commercial energy supply is basically adequate, the country's noncommercial rural fuel supply remains precarious: in many areas peasants have barely enough to support minimal existence.[56] The combination of small local coal mines, private fuelwood lots and more efficient stoves has gone a long way toward easing widespread energy shortages in village households. Mass adoption of improved stoves – some 100 million have been installed since the early 1980s – has been particularly helpful,[57] but this alone cannot propel rural populations to modernity. Nor will the role of renewable energies be as helpful as envisaged by many uninformed enthusiasts. Two of China's showcase renewable programs of the 1970s – small-scale hydrostations and biogas digesters – have been reduced to modest proportions, as technical problems and economic realities have made clear their limited utility.[58] China has considerable wind energy (particularly in Inner Mongolia), geothermal energy (in more than a dozen provinces, and especially in Tibet) and solar energy (everywhere in its arid interior) potential but, so far, these sources have made only very limited, local difference, and their future contributions remain highly uncertain.

A quarter-century of frequent long-term energy forecasts has taught us the perils of such exercises. Even when the numbers may click, the realities do not jibe. In my first book on China's energy, written in 1975, my median forecast of the country's primary energy demand had an error of a mere 2 per cent for the year 1985, and only 10 per cent for the year 1990.[59] Yet, although I was certain that major changes were inevitable, I could not have predicted the reality of post-1979 modernization, with all of its complex implications for energy demand, economic expansion and environmental degradation. Inevitably, there are more surprises ahead.

Closer looks at several developments noted in the 1998 retrospective – changing level and composition of traditional energy uses, demise of small-scale energy conversion techniques, expectations and realities of fossil fuel production, and the reduction of energy intensity of China's economy – will take up the remainder of this energy chapter. But before starting these more detailed reviews, I should comment briefly about the latest accomplishments of China's energy production and trade.

As already noted, China's noncommercial energy supply improved during the reform period, but it is far from abundant. A closer look at its absolute levels, composition and changes during the closing decades of the twentieth century reveals more about the realities of everyday life for most of China's population than do the recitals of urban and industrial accomplishments. Traditional, and overwhelmingly (but not exclusively) noncommercial, energy flows and uses are much harder to study than the supplies and conversions of modern commercial energies. But ignoring their contributions and changing patterns results in a very misleading impression of the real state of energy supplies and uses in low-income countries in general, and in the world's most populous Asian countries, still heavily dependent on muscles and phytomass fuels, in particular.

The continuing importance of traditional energies: on muscles, wood and straw

For millennia all societies had derived their kinetic energy from human and animal muscles for their heating and cooking needs from phytomass fuels (mainly wood and crop residues). Gradually, water and wind flows captured by wheels and mills supplied more mechanical energy, but, except for England, coal use remained very limited until the nineteenth century. Although we cannot pinpoint the date, the best possible reconstruction indicates the 1890s as the decade when fossil fuels, mainly coal and some crude oil, began supplying more than half of the world's total primary energy needs (Smil 1994; UNO 1956). The subsequent substitution of animate energies and wood and straws by fossil fuels and primary electricity (hydro, and since the late 1950s also nuclear) proceeded rapidly. By the late 1920s wood and crop residues contained no more than a third of all fuel energy used worldwide, and their share sank below 25 per cent by 1950 (Smil 2003). Unlike with the well-monitored production of fossil fuels and electricity, largely noncommercial uses of biomass fuels cannot be quantified accurately.

The FAO (1999) estimated that about 63 per cent of the 4.4Gm³ of harvested wood was burned as fuel during the late 1990s, implying the thermal equivalent of about 27EJ. Because in many countries a major part, and even more than 50 per cent, of all woody matter for household consumption is gathered outside forests and groves from bushes, tree plantations (rubber, coconut), and from roadside and backyard trees, addition of this non-forest woody biomass raises the total to 30–35EJ. Crop residues (mostly cereal straws) burned by rural households add about 8EJ. The most likely minimum estimate for the year 2000 would be then close to 40EJ of biomass fuels, while more liberal assumptions, higher conversion factors and addition of minor biomass fuels (dry grasses, dry dung) would raise the total closer to 45EJ.

With about 320EJ from fossil fuels and 35EJ from primary electricity, this means that in the year 2000 the global energy supplies from all sources were roughly 410EJ, with biomass energies providing about 10 per cent of the total (Smil 2003). Sub-Saharan Africa, where wood and crop residues continue to supply in excess of 80 per cent of fuel in most of the countries, remains the largest user of biomass in relative terms. China and India are the largest consumers of wood and crop residues in absolute terms, with Brazil and Indonesia ranking next. During the mid-1990s China's annual consumption of these traditional fuels was at least 6.4EJ, India's about 6EJ (Fridley 2001; RWEDP 2000). This means that China still derived close to 15 per cent of its primary energy from phytomass fuels, compared to roughly 30 per cent in India and Indonesia, and about 25 per cent in Brazil (IEA 2001). Obviously, this dependence is much higher when only the total rural energy consumption is considered, and higher still when it is expressed as the share of energy used for heating and cooking by China's peasants.

I became interested in global noncommercial energy supplies almost as soon as I began studying energy systems. I understand that data shortage is the main reason why standard energy analyses pay so little attention to these matters, but – given the critical, indeed truly existential, importance that traditional energy supplies (or their lack of) play in the lives of several billion people in low-income countries – I do not accept this as a valid excuse for marginalizing these concerns. Consequently, as soon as I began working on China's energy I tried, in spite of an extreme shortage of data, to gather, estimate and deduce any information on this important subject.

My earliest work on this topic, done in the mid-1970s, was necessarily based more on general and theoretical considerations rather than on many Chinese specifics. This situation improved rapidly after 1980, and, as the following excerpts from my 1988 and 1993 books will indicate, I used the new information to present both more detailed, and more accurate, appraisals of China's rural energy supplies and needs. More information on China's traditional energy became available during the late 1990s, and I have used it in updating this segment and suggesting some likely future developments.

Energy flows in rural China

Four fifths of the Chinese population living in villages have been until recently only marginally involved in commercial energy flows, relying as they have for millennia on solar energy to produce, via photosynthesis, not only the necessary food and feed but also large amounts of fuel and raw materials. This study of China's rural energy flows (Smil 1979a) thus demands a different approach than the flow analyses used in advanced economies: autotrophic conversions, human energetics, animate power, and traditional phytomass fuels must be the main foci of attention. I have attempted to quantify all of these important sources, conversion, and use for 1974, the twenty-fifth anniversary of the PRC, and choose to present the flows in the form of H.T. Odum's energy circuits (Odum 1971), a very convenient tool for such an analysis.

Insolation and primary production

Average annual radiation without clouds would range from 670kJ/cm^2 in the northernmost Heilongjiang to 980kJ/cm^2 in subtropical Hainan, and China would receive about 8.4×10^{22}J of solar energy annually. Actual duration of sunshine is sharply reduced by high cloudiness associated with summer cyclonic flows over much of the eastern half of the country, and intensity of insolation is attenuated during late winter and spring months by large amounts of sand and dust swept up from the arid northern regions by continental anti-cyclonic winds (Watts 1969). Solar energy received at the surface is thus only between 420 and 585kJ/cm^2 a year for most of China, and the annual total is not higher than 4.8×10^{22}J.

More than half of the solar radiation reaching China's surface is reflected, absorbed and reradiated by barren or very sparsely vegetated areas, mostly in Xinjiang, Tibet, Qinghai, Gansu and Nei Monggol. Net primary production of all of China's land ecosystems totaled about 65EJ in 1974, which means that approximately 0.14 per cent of solar radiation reaching China's surface is being annually converted by autotrophs into new chemical bonds.

Food and human energetics

Conversion of solar radiation by edible plants is, of course, the main source of food energy for China's large population. In 1974 China's harvest reached approximately 4.2PJ of food and industrial crops, and almost twice that energy value was gathered in crop by-products, for a total of 12.5PJ; the largely unharvested roots add another 20 per cent to the annual crop phytomass. Construction of a national food balance sheet for 1974 (for details see the next chapter on food) reveals that out of the total fresh harvest of approximately 470Mt of food crops, no more than 65 per cent actually becomes available for human consumption (Smil 1977a). A comparison of caloric availability and need suggests that China's food production most likely was just sufficient to meet, on the average, the nutritional demand of the population.

Most of the energy input is, of course, spent on the growth and maintenance of body tissues and on thermoregulation, and only a minor portion is converted to useful work. Energy available for activity can be calculated as the residual after subtracting maintenance energy cost (about 1.5 times basal metabolic rate for a given weight) from an average food intake, and this method (WHO 1973) results in an average of 385MJ/year for every economically active Chinese adult. A representative average of about 400MJ of useful energy per adult per year multiplied by 390 million economically active persons in China's villages would then translate into roughly 160PJ in 1974, and would imply a gross rural labor force energy efficiency of about 11 per cent.

Animal energetics

While domestic animals are only a minor source of food energy for an average Chinese, they are of considerable importance in a predominantly solar economy for four principal reasons:

1   they function well on solar energy, eating mostly phytomass unfit for human consumption (grasses, crop residues, crop processing by-products), supplemented, in the Chinese case, with only small amounts of grain;

2   they provide reliable motive power for a variety of farm tasks;

3   their manure production recycles valuable nutrients and improves the quality and the tilth of soils; and

4   they are an essential source of high-quality protein for the population.

Feed requirements for China's domestic animals are supplied predominantly by various roughages; these are obtained by grazing, collection of field weeds, from many crop by-products (mainly cereal straws, legume and vegetable stalks and leaves), and also from specific cultivation. The official Chinese recommendation is to reserve only 6 per cent of the total gross (unmilled) grain harvest, including pulses and tubers, for feeding. The total energy equivalent of China's animal feed amounted to some 8.5EJ in 1974. Some two fifths of this total was consumed by draft animals that remain an indispensable workforce in the countryside. Useful energy expended in a year of animal labor adds up to about 88PJ, implying an average working day efficiency of roughly 9 per cent, an excellent agreement with the best experimental studies of animal energetics (Brody 1964).

For most areas in China recycled organic matter is still the dominant fertilizer, and the breeding of pigs is promoted officially as much for the meat as it is for the wastes. In aggregate, the country's domestic animals produce annually in excess of 1Gt of fresh manure (or about 200Mt of dry solids), and approximately two thirds of this amount is gathered, fermented and returned to the fields.

Traditional fuels

For millennia Chinese civilization has been deriving its kinetic energy from human and animal muscles and its thermal requirements from phytomass. During the 1970s there was no official record of fuelwood use, and no forests were maintained specifically for firewood. The fuel came from scavenging of forest floor debris, lopping of branches, or removal of dead trees, and, unfortunately quite often, from illegal cutting and uprooting of the healthy trees in accessible wooded areas and from pruning (and damaging) of remaining or newly planed roadside tress in deforested regions, where reeds on the stream and canal banks and grass clippings and leaves also are collected.

Richardson (1966) estimated that at least 100 million m³ were used annually in the early 1960s, and the FAO (1975) figures are in excess of 130 million m³ for the early 1970s. Assuming that the annual net primary productivity of the Chinese forests is about 18EJ, area accessibility about 60 per cent, and removal rate about 15 per cent, the 1974 fuelwood consumption would have reached some 1.6EJ, the equivalent of roughly 140 million m³. In deforested regions crop residues always have been the main source of fuel. Although the principal residues – rice, wheat, and millet straw, corn and cotton stalks, and potato, vegetable, and legume vines – have a wide variety of uses as animal feed and bedding, in composting, mulching, thatching, fencing and packing, and as raw materials for the manufacture of hats, sandals, ropes, bags, mats and paper (Tanaka 1973), their consumption as fuel is extremely important throughout China. A conservative accounting yields about 175Mt, the equivalent of some 3EJ, of crop fuel.

Rural energy flows

As the energy-flow analysis makes clear, China's countryside of the mid-1970s consumed annually almost 15EJ of biomass energy in food, feed and fuel (see Figure 2.3). What, on the other hand, were the modern inputs of primary energy – fossil fuels and hydroelectricity? Direct fossil fuel and hydroenergy use in agriculture, predominantly in water pumping and for field machinery, reached no more than 710PJ, and the total rural use of modern energy, including locally mined coal and locally produced hydroelectricity consumed by small village industries and households, did not surpass 2EJ. Using the last figure for comparison, in 1974 China's rural areas used 7.2 times more biomass energy than fossil fuels and primary electricity.

It is thus readily apparent that most of China's population continues to live in solar-dominated ecosystems, largely independent of external energy subsidies. Interestingly enough, even for the nation as a whole biomass energies are still more important than modern inputs: about 17EJ of phytomass was consumed in China in 1974 as food, feed, fuel and raw material, while the aggregated modern primary energy flows reached less than 11.3EJ. For more than a decade the Chinese have been trying to increase the flow of modern energies to the countryside. In 1974, inventories of mechanical pumps and tractors reached, respectively, about 27 and 9.5GW (CIA 1977) and the application of chemical fertilizers almost tripled in comparison with the year 1965 (Erisman 1975).

However, the total 1974 capability of draft animals (at least 25GW), and of the rural labor force (roughly the equivalent of 20GW), was still some 20 per cent greater than the aggregate rating of pumps and tractors. And although the importance of organic fertilizers had been steadily shrinking, in 1974 they were no less important than the synthetic ones: while some 4.3Mt of inorganic nitrogen was available from domestic production and from imports (Erisman 1975), a conservative estimate indicates a roughly equal amount of nitrogen returned to fields from fermented animal and human wastes.

Energy cost of rural modernization

According to the Chinese definition, basic farm mechanization would be achieved when 70 per cent of all current major field, forestry, animal husbandry and fisheries tasks were performed by machines. Energy cost of this endeavor can be estimated on the basis of the flow analysis presented here. Replacing 70 per cent of some 250PJ of the current useful human and animal work by machinery, would call for an annual direct gross energy expense (assuming

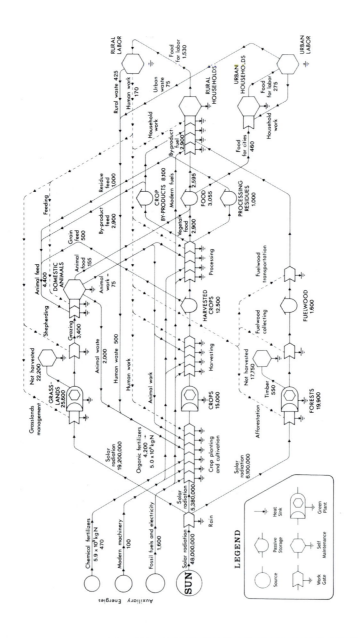

Figure 2.3 Energy flows in China's agroecosystem in 1974. All figures, except those for nitrogen fertilizers, are in PJ (10^15 J)

10–15 per cent conversion efficiency of small machines typically required in the Chinese conditions) of 1.25–1.75EJ of primary energy. This is an equivalent of 40–60Mt of standard coal. Supplanting the manure and night soil by synthetic nitrogenous fertilizers would mean doubling their 1974 production at an energy cost of no less than 5EJ, or some 30Mt of standard coal equivalent. Lowering the still critical dependence on forest fuels and crop residues for household use by 50 per cent would require an additional 60Mt of coal equivalent, even when assuming tripled combustion efficiency of better stoves.

This approximate analysis makes clear the enormous energy cost of merely the most basic rural modernization in the world's most populous nation. Yet to lighten the burden of heavy farm work, to enable easier multicropping (when machinery is essential to perform the field operations speedily), to raise crop yields through fertilization, and to improve rural living standards, the country-side had to become more dependent on nonrenewable energy sources.

And, inevitably, it did. Deng's economic reforms led to many far-reaching changes in China's countryside, and substantial increases in the flow of modern energies to the countryside and higher reliance on synthetic fertilizers were among the key ingredients of this sweeping change. Chinese statistics show that rural energy consumption rose to nearly 10EJ by 1980, and to more than 15EJ by 1990 when commercial energies (coal, liquid fuels and hydroelectricity) began surpassing the total energy content of biomass fuels. During the late 1990s its total rose to nearly 20EJ, or more than three times higher than during the mid-1970s (Zheng 1998; Yuan 2001; Fridley 2001). In terms of mechanical energy, the installed capacity of tractors of all sizes, diesel engines, electrical motors and trucks used in rural transport surpassed 500GW, more than five times higher than before the beginning of economic reforms and roughly ten times higher than the useful power of the still slowly increasing stock of draft animals (NBS 2001). The increase in nitrogen fertilizer applications has been far more impressive, from less than 1Mt in 1978 to about 22Mt by the year 2000 (FAO 2002).

A more open flow of previously suppressed information and studies – inconceivable in Maoist China – revealed severe energy shortages afflicting hundreds of millions of peasants, and also stressed the magnitude of the unfinished task of rural modernization. New Chinese studies and statistics, and my calculations based on these better sources, showed that my original estimate of energy derived from crop residues was almost perfectly on target: I calculated 2.9EJ for 1974; the first Chinese rural energy surveys came up with 3.2EJ for the period 1979–1982. In contrast, my estimate of fuelwood energy (about 1.6EJ) was too low because it referred only to roundwood obtained by felling trees. This cut and stacked roundwood is what passes for fuelwood in Western countries and Russia, but in early 1980s China round-wood for fuel was available only in a few remaining heavily forested regions, and even there it came mostly from felling trees of less than 25cm diameter. The bulk of China's forest fuel was obtained from any accessible woody and non-woody phytomass that was relatively easy to gather.

I evaluated most of the new information on China's rural energy supply in my second book on the country's energy, the first version of which was written as a report for the IDRC (whose revised text was published in 1988), and returned to the topic once again in 1993 in my second book on the Chinese environment. Two fundamental changes began to improve both the supply and the use of China's biomass energy during the 1980s: extensive planting of private fuelwood lots, and the state-sponsored introduction of efficient stoves. In spite of its obvious desirability, the second initiative had a discouraging record by the time China embraced it.

Improved stoves were one of the iconic objects of the appropriate technology movement that arose during the 1970s to provide alternative answers to the modernization requirements of low-income countries. Various programs aimed at designing and diffusing such stoves tried to replace traditional open, or partially enclosed, fires with closed or shielded stoves built mostly with local materials. In spite of a great deal of enthusiasm and interest, the results of these efforts were largely disappointing (Manibog 1984; Kammen 1995). Many designs were still too expensive or were not sufficiently durable or easy to repair. Inadequate training of local craftsmen to build and repair new stoves and, where needed, financial help in their purchase, were other common problems. Moreover, standards efficiency gains were hard to evaluate, given the wide range of actual performances of both traditional and improved cooking arrangements and lack of uniform measurement.

The Chinese tackled these issues fairly systematically, proceeding from design competitions that were governed by a standardized set of efficiency measurements, to demonstration projects in selected counties. They then turned the program into a commercial venture, with households paying more than 85 per cent of the installation cost to rural energy and service companies, and with incentives for government officials whose jurisdictions met the conversion targets. Two decades after the launch of this program the verdict must be largely positive, although there are still many inefficient unvented stoves around (and certainly also many abandoned new designs). The combination of private fuelwood lots, efficient stoves and a rapidly increasing coal output from small rural mines finally began to ease the rural energy shortages and to reduce the relative dependence on phytomass fuels. But more work will have to be done to maintain adequate supplies of traditional fuels during the coming generation.

Energy for the countryside

The following account (Smil 1988) benefitted from the first-ever surveys of China's rural energy supply. Rural energy surveys done in various regions of all provinces in 1979 established the average daily effective energy requirements of only 16.2MJ (Wu and Chen 1982) to 18.7MJ (Deng and Zhou 1981) per family, or a mere 3.25–3.74MJ per day per capita. This means that the nationwide annual need of 800 million villagers would add up to as much as 1.1EJ of effective energy. Practically, this means that a typical Chinese rural household of five people should burn each day at least 12kg of straw (14MJ/kg), or about 11kg of woody matter (16.5MJ/kg), or any mixture of these two fuels dominating the energy consumption in the Chinese countryside, to obtain, with average 10 per cent efficiency, effective energy of nearly 19MJ. The 1979 consumption survey, however, indicated that the actual daily availability of effective energy is only 14.5MJ per family, a difference resulting in an average shortfall of some 22 per cent. Obviously, the supply differs regionally and also fluctuates with the seasons, and different quantitative and temporal appraisals of this deficit are available.

Yang Jike, speaking at the Second National Symposium on Energy Resources in December 1980, stated that 500 million peasants (63 per cent of the total) suffered from a "serious" fuel shortage for at least 3–5 months, and that in the best-off provinces only 25 per cent of all families were so affected, but in the worst-off areas 70 per cent of villagers were short of fuel for up to six months every year. In May 1981 a Xinhua news release estimated that "more than half" of the country's 160 million peasant households were short of firewood, with the share over 60 per cent in Xinjiang, Hebei, Hunan and Sichuan, and with the worst situation in twenty-two counties in the valley of the Yarlung Zangbo, Lhasa and Niamcha rivers in southern Tibet. A year later the same source claimed that "about half" of China's peasant households are short of firewood for "over three months of the year", and in November 1982 an unsigned *Renmin ribao* article put the share of such households at a curiously precise 47.7 per cent.

According to the 1982 edition of *China Agricultural Yearbook*, of the country's 2,133 counties only 397 (19 per cent) in or near the forested mountains have fuelwood supply adequate to meet all household energy demand for more than six months, that is, for the whole heating season, and 915 counties (43 per cent) could cover their basic household energy needs with fuelwood for less than one month. Precise figures must be suspect and are, of course, irrelevant. Without them it is easy enough to appreciate the staggering dimension of China's rural energy shortage: about half a billion people lacking enough fuel just to cook three meals a day for three to six months a year!

The total mass of annually harvested crop residues can be estimated with fair accuracy on the basis of newly available detailed crop output statistics and typical crop/residue ratios. My calculations for the 1983 harvest total 458Mt, a sum identical to a differently derived estimate by Wu and Chen (1982) and very close to Shangguan's (1980) 450Mt. The rural energy use survey put feeding and raw material needs at 220Mt; consequently, I will assume that half of all crop residues are currently used for fuel. These roughly 230Mt of dry residues are (at 14MJ/kg) equivalent to about 110Mt of standard coal, or to about one half of all biomass fuels burned in China's countryside in recent years. Without them over 100 million peasant households of the long-deforested and densely populated plains and lowlands of the eastern third of China, as well as in the barren northwest interior, could not survive.

Using the common term fuelwood would be misleading in the Chinese context. Naturally, villagers in forested regions cut a great deal of roundwood, both from fuelwood lots and from illegally felled trees in protected forests – but the fuel comes literally from any burnable tree and forest biomass: not only branches and twigs, roots and stumps, but also bark off the living trees, needles, leaves and grasses, and carved-out pieces of sod. People carefully raking any organic debris accumulated on the floor of even small groves, peasants drastically pruning the summer growth of trees and shrubs, and children gathering tufts of grass into their back baskets are common sights in China's fuel-short countryside. A 1979 rural energy survey put the total firewood consumption at 181.6Mt a year.

Flows of commercial energies are on the rise throughout the Chinese countryside, but the critical dependence on traditional biomass fuels cannot be shed for decades to come. The best estimates calculated or cited here – 230Mt of straw (110Mtce), 8Mt of dried dung (4Mtce), and 180Mt of forest fuels (104Mtce) – added up to some 220Mtce in 1983. This is roughly 275kgce for every Chinese villager, a total accounting for three fifths of all rural energy inputs.

The existing rural energy shortages are so severe, and the future needs so enormous, that no sensible strategy can abstain from any workable option if it is to succeed eventually. Given the country's extensive coal deposits and hydroenergy resources, both rural coal mining and small-scale electricity generation should keep expanding – and getting larger in size to take advantage of economies of scale. And, as in any other poor country where most of the burned phytomass is wasted in inefficient combustion, improved kitchen stoves could bring impressive aggregate savings. More efficient stoves would also moderate the rates of deforestation and reduce the area of fuelwood plots needed to provide a continuous firewood supply.

Serious Chinese interest in improved stoves dates only to 1979, when a series of tests was done in Shunyi county on the outskirts of the capital to establish the typical combustion efficiencies of various traditional stoves used in northern villages. Predictably, stoves burning crop residues (cornstalks) showed the worst performance, with just 8–14 per cent efficiency; normal firewood stoves averaged around 15 per cent; and their better models with forced ventilation converted 19–21 per cent of wood into useful heat. Average losses of nine tenths of the fuel's heat content were ascribed to five major design inadequacies: combustion chambers were too large, as were stoking inlets, no fire grates and, in some cases, no chimneys resulted in poor air circulation, and lack of insulation contributed to further heat loss.

Eliminating these faults was the objective of two nationwide design competitions sponsored by the Ministry of Agriculture and judged in 1981 in Zhouhou in Henan and in 1982 in Jiangxi. Fourteen winners of the forty-two entries in the 1982 contest had thermal efficiencies between 32–44 per cent for firewood stoves and between 26–31 per cent for stoves burning crop stalks and straw. All of these superior stoves have proper fire grates and chimneys, appropriately sized combustion chambers and fuel inlets, and are designed to operate with 1.5–2.0 volumes of excess air for optimum burn-up; some of the stoves preheat the cold fresh air by leading it along the hot air outlets. The Chinese, ever enamored of numerical labels, would like to see all of their improved stoves meeting the "three 10" challenge: boiling 10 *jin* (5kg) of water by burning no more than 10 *liang* (about 400g) of straw or wood in less than ten minutes. An ambitious plan of large-scale diffusion of improved stoves started in 1982 in ninety selected counties around China. By the end of 1983 some 7 million improved stoves were in use (including 3.9 million stoves in the ninety pilot counties), and the goal was put at 25 million by 1985.

But even with outstanding stoves everywhere, elimination of the current fuel shortages and the addition of at least 160–200 million villagers during the next twenty years will require great increases in biomass availability, and only extensive planting of firewood groves and forests can satisfy this need. Consequently, it is incredible that a regime that was conducting all kinds of mass campaigns kept on forbidding plantings of private fuelwood lots, even in dry and extremely heavily eroded regions of the northwestern interior. Ideological rigidity saw the owner-ship of a small woodlot as one of the "last vestiges of bourgeois mentality", as it forced peasants to cut out in desperation dry sod or to burn animal dung. Reversal of this irrational policy came only in spring 1980, long after other discredited policies had been discarded, when the State Council issued a directive about private tree planting. The critical point of the new regulations is that house-hold ownership of the lot should remain unchanged for decades.

By the beginning of 1983, 25 per cent of China's peasant families were allotted an average of 0.2ha of hilly or odd land for tree planting. The ultimate Chinese goal has been to set aside a firewood grove for three quarters of 170 million rural households, so that by the end of the twentieth century the area with newly planted trees would cover 27–33Mha. Available statistics show, not surprisingly, that the densely populated East and North have, respectively, only about 11 and 13 per cent of all barren land suitable for fuelwood planting, while the Northeast has nearly 18 per cent, the Central South 19 per cent, and the Southwest almost 27 per cent of the total (Huang 1982). Naturally, the best growing conditions for various fast-maturing shrubs and trees are in the South – but there in many areas the warmer climate and greater availability of crop residues and slopeland grasses make the need for additional fuel less pressing than in the devegetated, cold North.

Energy shortfall

As rural modernization was finally lifting millions of Chinese villagers well above the subsistence level, rural energy shortfalls were still common (Smil 1993).

> With a view to a good mess of pottage, all hot,
> The beanstalks, aflame, a fierce heat were begetting,
> The beans in the pot were all fuming and fretting.
> Yet the beans and the stalks were not born to be foes;
> Oh why should these hurry to finish off those?
>
> Cao Zhi, *The Brothers*

The classical gem by Cao Zhi is far from being just cleverly amusing: changing the emphasis, but not forcing the meaning, one can interpret it today as a perceptive insight into the nature of sustainable farming, a revealing comment on the tension between food and energy needs. Indeed, it would be greatly preferable to recycle the stalks – by plowing them directly into the soil, after fermentation with other organic matter, or as a part of animal manure – to improve the harvest of the succeeding crop. That Chinese peasants have been doing this less and less frequently is one of the principal disturbing signs of the country's extensive rural energy shortages.

The magnitude of this shortfall is hard to comprehend for anybody in affluent, fuel-rich societies: every year for several months more than 300 million people have difficulties finding enough fuel just to cook three simple meals a day. In their search for anything combustible they turn to any accessible biomass, causing serious environmental degradation – deforestation, desertification, soil erosion, and loss of nutrients. Obviously, in the worst-off areas where basic food supply continues to be inadequate, these shortages contribute significantly to malnutrition, higher morbidity and higher mortality.

Coal from small mines dominates the rural energy supply in parts of several northern provinces, but elsewhere the cooking and heating needs are still largely covered by inefficient, and insufficient, combustion of traditional biomass energies. Unlike in most other populous developing countries, our knowledge of China's rural energy supplies is based on actual surveys, done in various regions of all provinces, that began in 1979 and continued during the 1980s (Wu and Chen 1982; Deng and Wu 1984). Figures released by the Ministry of Energy in 1989 show that biomass supplied nearly three fifths, and coal (including coke) about one third of all rural energy; household needs claimed three quarters of all fuels and primary electricity; while the expanding rural industries consumed nearly one fifth of the roughly 580Mt total (Figure 2.4).

Household energy use is dominated by inefficient combustion of traditional phytomass fuels for cooking and water heating (Long 1989). Roughly three quarters of China's crop residues, including more than two thirds of cereal straws, are burned in cooking stoves rather than being fed to animals or, most desirably, recycled to maintain high yields. Total combustion of woody biomass was put by the Ministry of Energy at about 230Mt in 1987, with most of this fuel going for cooking and water heating. Rural energy surveys found that nearly 19MJ of useful energy is needed daily to do the basic cooking and water heating for an average peasant family of five to six people.

As the simple stoves convert crop residues and woody biomass to useful heat with efficiencies ranging from less than 10 per cent for straw to 15 per cent for wood (the typical mean would be 10–12 per cent), this demand translates to about 170MJ of fuel a day, or around 350Mtce/year for rural China. Minimum heating of uninsulated northern housing requires about $3.3MJ/m^2$ a day, or close to 20GJ/family for four months of heating for a total of at least 50Mtce/year. Traditionally there has been little house heating south of the Changjiang, in spite of the fact that average January temperatures are just 2–4°C in the northernmost part of the region.

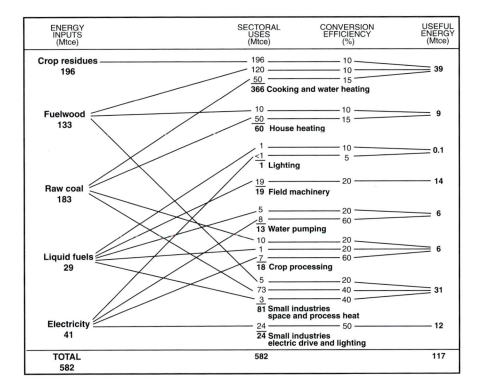

Figure 2.4 China's rural energy consumption

Source: Constructed from consumption data in *China Statistical Yearbook* and Ministry of Energy (1989). Typical conversion efficiencies taken from Wu and Chen (1982) and ITESA (1987).

The actual availability of around 370Mtce of primary energy for household use in 1987 was thus nearly 10 per cent below the minimum annual need of about 400Mtce. Given the great variability of Chinese fuel supply, this shortfall means that large areas experience acute seasonal hardship. Precise figures are not available, but the most frequently cited estimate is that one half of all rural households are short of fuel for three to four months a year. In many dry interior regions the shortage extends to six to eight months, and in many localities it is chronic. In terms of affected population, only the Indian situation comes close to this massive, persistent and genuine energy crisis (CS&T 1985).

Some encouraging news

Extending the story of China's traditional energy use to the very end of the twentieth century entails, fortunately, some encouraging news. As economic modernization has progressed, China's relative dependence on traditional fuels has declined. According to my calculations, crop residues and woody phytomass supplied about 90 per cent of the country's rural energy consumption during the early 1970s; this share fell to below 70 per cent in 1980, below 50 per cent by 1988, and to 33 per cent by 1998 (Zheng 1998; Fridley 2001). But the absolute dependence has remained largely unchanged: while fuelwood harvests declined by nearly 25 per cent from the peak of about 3.8EJ around 1990, China's larger crop harvests have been producing more crop residues, and by 1994 their household combustion was about a third higher than in 1974. As a result, at 6.5EJ China's total consumption of biomass fuels was about as high in 1999 as it was in 1979. In terms of the total primary energy supply, the biomass share fell from more than 30 per cent in the mid-1970s to 15 per cent by 1998.

But this nationwide share both exaggerates and underestimates the importance of biomass fuels in China's energy supply. The exaggeration is due to the fact that combustion efficiencies of these fuels remain considerably below the rapidly improving performance of modern industrial and household converters: although biomass supplies roughly one seventh of the nation's energy it probably delivers no more than one tenth of all useful heat. The underestimate owes to the fact that phytomass fuels are still the dominant providers of energy for cooking and heating in more than 100 million rural households. In spite of the continuing inroads by coal, electricity and liquid fuels, dependence on traditional fuels for household heating and cooking remains high: crop residues continue to provide around a third of all rural residential primary energy consumption, about as much as coal, and fuelwood supplies more than 20 per cent (Fridley 2001).

Household combustion of crop residues peaked in 1993–1994, and a subsequent improvement in the supply of higher-quality commercial fuels reduced the demand for this low-quality fuel by nearly 15 per cent. Unfortunately, this reduced demand for crop residues means that more of them are burned in the field: in 1998 this share was close to 20 per cent, or about 140Mt of straws and stalks (Yuan 2001). Field burning is, of course, the least labor-intensive method of their disposal, but it generates often serious air pollution and it lets nearly all plant nitrogen escape to the atmosphere (Smil 1999a). This is why Chinese researchers are exploring ways to use the residues as feedstock for the production of higher-quality gaseous fuels. As these will not make any early inroads, efficient stoves will remain the main means of reducing the wasteful use of biomass.

Unlike many Maoist campaigns that flared up and failed, the diffusion of improved stoves has been sustained since the early 1980s. Since 1984 their adoption rates ranged rather narrowly between 15 and 20 million units a year, and ten years after launching the campaign the total number of improved stoves reached nearly 143 million by the end of 1991. By the end of 1997 about 180 million units had been disseminated to some 75 per cent of China's rural households (Wang and Ding 1998), and these stoves are credited with annual savings of close to 2EJ of fuelwood and coal (Luo 1998). Details of Chinese stove designs and construction procedures have been readily available for any interested parties in other low-income countries (Wang *et al.* 1993) (Figure 2.5).

The fate of China's expansion of fuelwood forests has not been so satisfactory. The initial spurt of planting new fuelwood plots during the first half of the 1980s resulted in about 5Mha of fuelwood groves and forests and in annual production of 20–25Mt of fuelwood a year by the early 1990s (an equivalent of about 0.5EJ), but then the pace of plantings declined rapidly, from more than 300,000ha in 1991 to just 100,000ha in 1994. Poor monetary returns, reduced state investment and insufficient appreciation of ecosystemic benefits of fuelwood forests, are the main reasons explaining this decline. The official total of fuelwood forests, 4.29Mha in the year 2000, is lower than in 1985, but the State Bureau of Forestry plans to extend their area to 12Mha by the year 2020 (*People's Daily* 2000a).

In the near future we will see a further decline in demand for crop residues in many relatively affluent parts of coastal China, but largely undiminished needs for both straw and wood in many parts of the interior. Consequently, it would be surprising if the country's combustion of biomass fuels were to fall by more than 10 per cent before 2010. And, contrary to some uncritically enthusiastic reports about the potential of new energy conversions, nearly all of these fuels will be burned in household stoves or in small boilers rather than serving as feedstocks for producing liquid and gaseous biofuels.

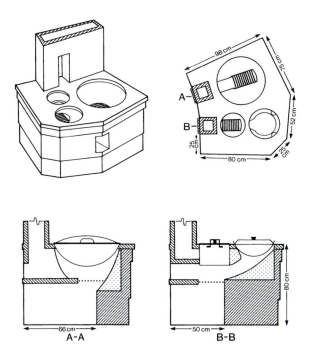

Figure 2.5 View, plan and cross-sections of an efficient stove designed in Shandong's Wenshang county in 1986. The concrete stove can burn wood, crop residues or coal with efficiency of up to 40 per cent

Source: Based on illustrations in Wang *et al.* (1993): 17–18.

A failed strategy: small is not always beautiful

A generation ago it seemed that widespread reliance on small-scale energy production and conversion techniques was emerging as a particular set of developmental strategies that would be of a fundamental importance in modernizing China's countryside. Small coal mines were the dominant ingredient in the first category, small hydrostations in the second. The third notable ingredient was the anaerobic fermentation of organic wastes in biogas digesters. As the campaigns to disseminate these approaches took off during the 1970s they met with a great deal of Western admiration and approbation, because they coincided with a fashionable wave of interest in what was usually called intermediate or appropriate technologies. These invariably small-scale and simple techniques and methods stood in contrast to large-scale, high-tech approaches that were seen as badly mismatched with the enormous and pressing needs of poor, populous countries seeking to satisfy the basic needs of millions of often truly desperate inhabitants.

Consequently, many developmental economists and technical experts were questioning the transfer of advanced, capital-intensive and highly efficient Western technology to low-income countries – and argued in favor of the developmental model combining the modern and the traditional approach as the only sensible way of modernizing poor, populous nations. Ernst F. Schumacher, with his *Small is Beautiful*, became undoubtedly the most influential proponent of this new approach, and for its worshippers a true guru of smallness. Schumacher outlined four fundamental rules to support an economy based not on goods but on people: "1. Make things small where possible. 2. Reduce the capital-intensity because labor wants to be involved. 3. Make the process as simple as you can. 4. Design the process to be nonviolent" (Schumacher 1973).

As I was definitely in favor of appropriate techniques, I thought that China's stress on some small-energy techniques made a great deal of sense. After all, the Chinese were not actually doing anything that would be historically so unusual. Small coal mines were common in Europe of the nineteenth century, and although naive Westerners reading the Maoist propaganda might have believed that peasants with the Chairman's red book in their pockets invented small hydrogeneration, that is how electricity generation using falling water had started everywhere, beginning with the world's first stations in 1881 in Surrey and in 1882 in Wisconsin. During the twentieth century North America, Europe and Japan moved to progressively larger projects but, by coincidence, Western interest in small hydrogeneration increased considerably during the 1970s in the wake of OPEC's series of steep oil price rises.

But three things made me uneasy about the newfound enthusiasm for smallness: I disliked the ideological worship of the scale, because I felt that small techniques can be successful in the long run only if they are as efficient as possible, and I thought it naive to believe that they could be the decisive factor in economic modernization. That is why I resolutely rejected approbation based on scale alone. Depending on circumstances, small may be indeed beautiful – but there is clearly nothing inherently superior about it. And I did not see how those of China's small-scale energy projects that were built so shoddily and operated so inefficiently could have any long-term future. Here is a part of my verdict on small projects in general, and on China's experience in particular, written in 1985 and published two years later (Smil 1987): there is nothing I wish to change. But I should add that the Chinese planners, unlike some Western enthusiasts who argued for a truly Gandhian retrogression, had no plans to abandon large-scale production, and argued that the two modes are complementary.

In the real world there are inherent and predictable, as well as hidden and surprising, advantages and drawbacks to scales small *and* large; judging a technique solely by its scale is neither rational nor useful. Small scale goes too often hand-in-hand with mismanagement, inefficiencies, high energy waste, and uncompetitive costs – as best illustrated by the prodigious Chinese experience with small-scale industrialization between 1958 and 1978.

The Chinese, the world's leading promoters of self-sufficient smallness, concluded that the approach was not only wasteful, but that it was clearly insufficient to provide a foundation for the industrial advancement which is so badly needed by all poor nations. In this respect power output considerations become critical. Most operational techniques based on renewable resources can be, when properly maintained and run, very helpful to a rural household or a small village supply – but they cannot support such basic, modern, energy-efficient industries as iron- and steelmaking, nitrogen fertilizer synthesis, and cement production.

Poor countries need it all: two hot meals a day, higher crop yields, widespread industrialization. Obviously, going "from the ground up" by means of small decentralized energy services would not, costs aside, be without many local benefits, but a prompt and dramatic contribution to world equity would hardly follow. After all, small-scale decentralized energy sources are still an everyday affair for the poor world's peasants, and while replacing today's inefficient rural stoves or open fireplaces with solar cookers and biogas digesters would be an important qualitative gain, it would still be only a partial one, as growing populations, rapid urbanization and higher food production cannot be managed without reliance on large-scale industrial processes.

The following two selections (Smil 1976b, 1988) trace the rise of small energy projects during the 1970s and the changes that took place during the first decade of Deng's reforms: a retreat of small hydrogeneration and biogas digesters, but a rapid increase in the numbers of small coal mines. As I will explain in the last section of this segment on small techniques, a reversal of these fortunes took place during the 1990s, when the construction of larger and better-built small hydrostations embarked on a steady expansion, while the state finally forced the closure of more than four fifths of dangerous and costly small mines.

Expansion during the 1970s

China, the largest and the most populous of all developing countries, has been forced by necessity to adopt the intermediate technology approach based on very similar principles: any effort to modernize her vast and backward countryside is hardly imaginable in any other way. Although the achievements have been mixed, the basic soundness of the approach cannot be doubted. While energy output of large enterprises has increased dramatically since 1949, virtually all of this production has been destined for major industries and urban areas. Production of fuels and electricity by small rural enterprises has thus played the crucial role in rudimentary modernization of the Chinese countryside.

Small coal mines

Massive opening of small outcrop mines had a spectacular, though ill fated, beginning during the years of the Great Leap Forward (1958–1960). The native pit campaign became, together with the erection of small backyard iron furnaces, the chief embodiment of Mao's economic delusions about instantaneous industrialization. Some 110,000 pits were in operation by the end of the first Great Leap year (1958), engaging the incredible number of 20 million Chinese peasants (Wu and Ling 1963). The increase in native pit extraction continued in 1959 – but further expansion was obviously unsustainable. Much of the hastily expanded and badly disorganized pit output, often of appallingly low quality, was wasted; the lifetime of many small mines was ephemeral; a large part of the production was consumed in an equally ephemeral iron-making campaign.

After the collapse of the Great Leap in 1960, the coal industry was thrown back to near the 1957 level, and small mine output declined by about 60 per cent (from over 66Mt claimed in 1960 to about 26Mt in 1961). Production started to climb in the mid-1960s, but most of the new small mine capacity has been added since 1969. This new wave of small mine diffusion has differed substantially from the aborted Great Leap expansion. The basic rationale is, undoubtedly, the same: small mines can be opened up and brought to their full capacity much faster than the large enterprises; they can be run at a relatively low cost, relying on abundantly available labor. However, the actual execution is different. Opening of new small mines is now done in a rather orderly manner, with some essential planning and, if one is to accept official claims, with much more real success: close to one third of China's raw coal output originates in small mines, a higher share than at the height of the Great Leap native pits campaign.

Small hydrostations

Construction of small hydrostations has been perhaps the most meaningful application of an intermediate energy conversion technique in China, especially during the recent past. The program was originally initiated as a part of massive water conservancy work during the Great Leap years. Construction of thousands of small stations with the total capacity of 900MW began in 1958, and a very ambitious plan predicted 1GW total in 1962 and as much as 2.5GW in 1967. The reality was much less impressive. During the year between October 1957 and September 1958, 4,334 small stations with aggregate capacity of 131.5MW were put into operation, and another 200MW were finished in 1959 (Carin 1969). Then the Leap collapsed and the massive construction of small hydrostations was abandoned – to be resurrected only in the latter half of the 1960s.

General guidelines for the development of small hydrostations are quite simple: dependence on local resources, maximum thrift and construction speed. Stations are built with funds accumulated locally. Labor and construction materials are strictly local. Traditional mass methods of construction are used in almost all cases. Small dams are either rock-filled or earth-filled structures, requiring only a minimum of cement, steel and timber. Some 50,000 small and medium hydrostations were in operation in 1973, and over 60,000 in September 1975 (NCNA 1975), concentrated overwhelmingly in the rainy southern half of China. The Yangzi basin has about one third of all stations, approximately four fifths are in the eight southernmost provinces, and Guangdong alone accounts for almost 20 per cent.

Naturally, the typical installed capacities of these stations are very small: available figures for the southern provinces give the weighted average of roughly 48kW per station. Consequently, the total capacity of China's small hydroprojects was around 2GW in 1973 and about 3GW in 1975. Small and medium hydrostations have contributed immensely to the basic electrification of the Chinese countryside. In 1974 they accounted for about one third of the total hydrogeneration.

Biogas generation

Biogas generation has been spreading throughout some of China's rural areas since the early 1970s. The procedure is, at least in principle, rather simple and the processes involved are well known. Animal dung, night soil, pieces of vegetation (crop stalks, straw, grass clippings, leaves), garbage and waste water are sealed up in insulated containers (digesters, pits) and left to decompose. Digestible organic materials are broken down by acid-producing bacteria and the volatile acids are, in turn, converted by anaerobic methanogenic bacteria into a gas which is typically composed of 55–70 per cent methane, 30–45 per cent carbon dioxide and a trace of hydrogen sulfide and nitrogen. Besides the versatile low-pressure medium-energy gas (between 22–$26MJ/m^3$; pure methane has $39MJ/m^3$), the process yields an organic fertilizer of outstanding quality, and can considerably improve the sanitation of rural areas (Fry 1974; Kashkari 1975).

Small-scale, noncommercial production of biogas was tested in India and in Europe in the late 1930s, but it has received greater worldwide attention only during the past decade. The first Chinese attempts date from the Great Leap period, but a massive and apparently well-organized campaign to popularize the technique started only a few years ago in Sichuan. More than 30,000 tanks were built throughout the province by the end of 1973, the total was 209,000 a year later, and twice as many (410,000) digesters were reported to be in operation by the middle of 1975 (NCNA 1975a). About 50,000 digesters were operating outside Sichuan in the summer of 1975. The effort is supported through national conferences, training of technicians (100,000 in Sichuan alone), manufacturing of simple gas stoves and lamps, rubber or plastic pipes and pressure gauges, and by designing differently shaped fermentation pits. Construction of containers is claimed now to be simpler and cheaper, and a typical $10m^3$ digester is, when properly managed, sufficient to supply a South Chinese family of five with enough fuel for cooking and lighting (NCNA 1975b).

Changes during the 1980s

China's small-scale energy operations were clearly a part of the Maoist developmental strategy that prevailed, with ups and downs and modifications, for two decades between 1958 and 1978. As such they had to be profoundly affected by Deng's economic reforms. After 1978 they were no longer subject to ideologically driven promotion and construction campaigns, and as they were increasingly seen in a purely economic perspective they could not remain sheltered under the protective cover of political correctness. Economic realities asserted themselves most rapidly in the case of biogas digesters. In June 1979 their numbers reached a record of 7.1 million units, and there were plans for ten times as many digesters by 1985. In reality, their total fell below 4 million by 1984, and although it rose a bit in subsequent years it has never again surpassed the 1979 total.

The fate of China's small hydrostations has been only superficially alike. Their total had also peaked in 1979, with about 90,000 projects in operation, and fell by 20 per cent by 1985 – but their total installed capacity kept on increasing, as many newly built stations were much larger than the combined capacities of dozens of abandoned mini-projects. As a result, average installed capacity nearly doubled from 70kW in 1979 to 132kW by 1985, as state loans became available even for projects larger than 12MW, formerly the limit for a small hydrostation. First, an excerpt from my second book on China's energy (Smil 1988) will detail why these changes in biogas and small hydro construction took place. In contrast to these two declines and transformations, the development of small mines reached new highs during the 1980s, and their importance continued unabated into the 1990s (Smil 1993). Then, unexpectedly, came their massive post-1997 demise. I will describe these events by drawing on the Chinese information published until the end of the year 2002.

Biogas redux

Chinese came to consider biogas generation to be not only an effective way of solving energy problems in rural areas that are short of coal, fuelwood, or hydroelectricity but, owing to its other benefits – high quality fertilizer, improved hygiene and less air pollution – a most desirable component of rural development throughout China (Smil 1988). Consequently, China's second national biogas conference, held in summer 1978, heard about plans for 20 million digesters in 1980 and 70 million units by 1985. Yet by 1984 there were fewer operating digesters (3.76 million) than in 1977 (4.3 million), and the program was set back especially in Sichuan, the birthplace and main promoter of the technique: the province had nearly two thirds of China's units in 1978, but about two fifths of its peak number of biogas digesters were abandoned by 1982.

While it's still possible to come across some new plans quoting fabulous digester totals by the end of the 1980s, the skepticism must be deep, especially when the statistics of the National Methane Production Leadership Group showed that of the remaining digesters only about 55 per cent can be used normally, and among these "not too many can be used to cook rice three times a day, still less every day for four seasons" (Huang and Zhang 1980). The reasons: the technique, so simple in principle, is rather demanding in practice. Digesters fail for several reasons. Leakage of biogas through the covering dome, cracked walls or bottom, improper feedstock adding and mixing practices, shortage of appropriate fermentation substrates, formation of heavy scum, and inhibition of bacteria by low temperatures were the leading causes.

Unless the digesters are well built (the slightest water and gas leaks ruin the process) and convenient to feed and clean; unless careful attention is paid to proper temperature, C/N ratios of feedstocks and pH of the fermenting mixture; and unless the digester is frequently fed with the right kind of degradable materials, the units can turn quickly into costly waste pits and are abandoned. Not surprisingly, failures in the second year of operation were common, and for millions of peasants digesters were a burden and a costly loss. In many instances a small family digester was simply of no great benefit compared with the time, effort, and investment put into producing woven baskets, tobacco, eggs or pork. The long overdue demise of command farming, which led to more food, resulted in the disappearance of many mass campaigns, including the "enthusiastic" building of digesters. More fundamentally, inherent limitations on the efficiency and expansion of the process would keep the contribution of biogas to China's rural energy supply surprisingly low, even under the best circumstances.

If half of China's rural families owned a small digester there would be a staggering 80–90 million units for which to find proper feedstocks. Even assuming that enough animal, human and crop wastes were available, the digesters could properly operate for seven to eight months only in southernmost China, just three to five months north of the Changjiang; the nationwide weighted average based on Chinese data is seven months. With an average digester volume of $8m^3$ and mean generation rate of $0.2m^3$ of biogas per m^3 of digester, this would translate to some $29Gm^3$ of biogas a year, equivalent to just 25Mt of coal equivalent, or some 8 per cent of China's current biomass energy use! Even when considering the fact that biogas could burn more efficiently than straw or wood, the best imaginable contribution would not surpass 15 per cent of today's inadequate rural biomass energy consumption.

Still, this is a worthwhile approach – but only at a slow and voluntary pace, not in hasty campaigns leaving behind useless expense of labor and materials. And only in locations well suited for sustained generation, that is, throughout the warmer southern provinces where the biogas production can go on, although diminished, even in winter months. In such locations it may also make sense to build larger village-size digesters, where the gas can be used for local electricity generation.

Larger small-scale projects

Widespread construction of small hydrostations has been perhaps the most successful innovation transforming China's rural energy consumption, the most realistic and the most sensible choice for the basic electrification of large areas of isolated Chinese countryside. Its growth during the 1970s was impressive, from about 26,000 in 1970 to almost 90,000 in December 1979. In terms of installed capacity the growth was even more rapid, from 900MW in 1970 to 6.33GW in 1979.

Post-1978 changes affected the development of small-scale hydrostations in several important ways, none being more notable than the abandonment of a large number of hastily built, inefficient projects. It is not difficult to see the reasons for this decline. Drastic lowering of water storage or a complete desiccation of reservoirs during the severe droughts that afflicted large parts of China in the late 1970s and early 1980s wiped out numerous small projects in several northern, eastern, and south-central provinces. Accelerated silting destroyed the usefulness of many reservoirs, and poor engineering, so common in projects built during the past mass campaigns, has been responsible for the demise of others.

Although the numbers were declining, total installed capacity and mean size kept rising: at the end of 1985, 72,000 stations had 9.5GW, which is an average of 132kW per station. However, the average size of newly completed stations rose to 218kW in 1981 and 232kW in 1982, and the 1,150 stations completed during 1983 averaged about 250kW, with projects of several megawatts becoming relatively common. Consequently, the Chinese definition of a small hydrostation has shifted considerably: in the 1950s it included only projects below 500kW; in the 1960s the limit went up to 3MW; and the current definition of a small hydrostation embraces all single-generator projects not exceeding 6MW and group (cascade) installations up to 12MW. Moreover, at a January 1980 meeting the Bank of China and the Farmers' Bank of China recommended that in all suitable places (i.e. in locations with rich water resources, adequate investment funds, equipment, materials and skills) the limit of 12MW should be lifted and loans be made available to build larger small stations. China's newfound appreciation of costs and rational economic management are clearly responsible for these moves.

Small as these stations are, many have rated capacities much beyond the generation potential: "a big horse pulling a small cart" is an apt Chinese description of this phenomenon (Yu 1983). An average load factor of about 25 per cent (roughly 2,200 hours a year), and the nationwide mean of around 2,000 hours annually during drier years, 2,500 hours during the rainier ones, compares unfavorably to means of 4,000–4,500 hours available for generation in larger power plants. As for the cost, the Chinese are emphatic in stressing the economic viability of small stations, although their capital cost is mostly higher or at best roughly the same as in large hydroprojects. Generating costs are, however, somewhat lower. Clearly, small hydros are in China to stay – and to grow larger. Their importance goes beyond the fact that they have been producing roughly every twentieth kWh in China: in most cases these stations have been the first source of electricity for the villages, and have served as the foundation of the rudimentary electrification of China's countryside.

Continued expansion of small coal mines

Post-1978 large-scale modernization plans could have been expected to de-emphasize the importance of small mines, but the household responsibility system gave them an excellent boost. Of the 50,000 small mines operating in early 1985, about 10,000 were run by individuals in yet another demonstration of flourishing rural industrialization that has been taking villagers from the fields. No less importantly, economies of scale are making themselves felt: 2,000 mines now have capacities of over 30,000t of raw coal a year, and the largest ones are extracting more than ten times as much.

Most of these small mines are as simple an operation as could be imagined: open pits or shallow shafts where coal is dug out and removed without any special mining equipment and without even rudimentary safety rules and precautions. During the early 1980s many small underground mines did away with the single exit, installed some kind of ventilation, and banned open-flame illumination and sparking blasting fuses. A Chinese coal industry journal may not be wrong for seeing in these changes the beginning of a transformation to normal small-scale production mines, but the task may not be completed for decades and the inefficiencies, waste and appalling working conditions will remain the mark of small rural mining for a long time to come.

This assessment is inevitable in view of the 1983 decision to end the state monopoly on coal mining, aimed at relieving the country's chronic energy short-ages. On 22 April 1983 the State Council approved the Ministry of Coal Industry's recommendations to base China's long-term coal expansion once again on "two legs": "While emphasizing development of the country's uniform allocation coal mines, to develop local state-owned coal mines and small coal mines as well". The new regulations permit private – individual or group – ownership of small mines while forbidding "reckless mining and indiscriminate digging" and "requiring the establishment of 'minimal safety conditions'". Perhaps most significantly, "coal mines and the masses are to be allowed to use various kinds of transportation equipment for the shipment of coal", and they may haul coal over long distances for sale without interference from any jurisdiction. Predictably, these regulations resulted in a coal rush surpassed only by the Great Leap mania. In March 1985, more than one million villagers were working in 50,000 small pits.

The rush is not completely unregulated: the Ministry of Coal Industry set aside large areas with reserves amounting to 35Gt just for small-scale production.

Peasants must apply to provincial coal resources commissions for permission to start extraction, and local authorities should see to the application of essential technical standards. Still, there is little doubt that indiscriminate, wasteful and dangerous extraction is the norm rather than an exception in thousands of cases. The state readily closes one eye: the new capacities and tens of millions of tonnes of new output need very little money from its treasury. In 1984 *Zhongguo meitan bao* reported that during the 1970s it cost 47 *yuan* to develop one tonne of new capacity in state-run local mines, while Shanxi peasants boosted the annual output of their small mines by 40Mt at a cost of a mere 7 *yuan*/t. Shanxi's peasant mining has been extolled as a great success story. In 1984 about 40Mt (of 70.6Mt produced) of their output was shipped out of the province, mainly to fuel-short Jiangsu and Zhejiang.

China's future plans are critically dependent on small-mine extraction, and the recent Chinese writings profess no concerns about the desirability of its rapid expansion. According to China's leading coal-mining journal, local pit extraction is to grow by more than 20Mt a year "to reach 450Mt by 1990, with limitless prospects". In 1986 the Chinese press carried stories of things that should not be happening anymore: mining accidents with numerous casualties as farmers rush to work in unsafe pits, and open plundering of the resources as mines continue to be set up indiscriminately. That fundamental question about Chinese intentions returns here once again: is it the quality (economically mined, cleaned, and sorted coal suitable for a wide variety of efficient final uses) or quantity (fuel seemingly cheap but burdened with a large proportion of uncombustibles precluding efficient utilization) that the planners are after?

The answer to that question remained predictably orthodox for another decade after I asked it in 1988. Extraction of poor-quality raw coal – and coal could be really a misnomer in numerous instances when the material contained more rocks and clay than carbon – in tens of thousands of small mines continued to grow during the first half of the 1990s. But, starting in 1998, there came a sudden reversal: this process, which had seen the number of China's small coal mines reduced by more than 80 per cent by the end of 2002, may continue, albeit at a gentler pace, for a few more years. During the same time there have been some signs of reviving a nationwide biogas program but, even if relatively successful, such development would have little impact on China's overall energy supply. In contrast, the construction of small hydrostations continues at a fairly steady pace, and these are the only valuable survivors of China's infatuation with small energy systems.

A new era

Extraction in China's small coal mines doubled its share of overall production during the 1980s (from 17 to 38 per cent), and then went on to surpass half of the country's huge coal production by 1996 (Fridley 2001; Thomson 2003). And nothing had changed about its original circumstances and consequences. A very large share of small mines (by some claims up to 80 per cent) operated illegally;

indiscriminate exploitation of accessible seams resulting in extensive environmental degradation, above all in significant local losses of farmland taken up by mushrooming numbers of outcrop or pit mines, and by mine wastes and access roads, was the norm; and wherever the coal from small mines fuel was burned, unwashed and unsorted, it only added to the country's already excessive particulate and sulfurous air pollution.

But, most tragically, casual neglect of even basic safety rules was responsible for accident rates that would be intolerable in any other industrial undertaking, indeed even in China's own large mines. According to China's official statistics, between 1994 and 1998 deaths in China's large, state-owned coal mines averaged 1.24/Mt of coal mined, while in small mines the mean for the same five years was a staggering 8.64 (Fridley 2001). For comparison, twenty-nine coal mining fatalities recorded in the USA in 1998 prorated to 0.03 deaths per million tonnes of extracted coal (MSHA 2000), a difference of two orders of magnitude. In absolute terms, the death toll in China's small coal mines was surpassing 5,000 people a year since 1994, and this unacceptable record became finally one of the two key reasons for the state's drastic curtailment of rural coal-mining enterprises. But clearly not the most important one, because by that time extraordinary, albeit somewhat lower, rates of fatality were tolerated for more than a decade.

The most important reason for the drastic campaign of small-mine closures was the excessive production of coal. China's raw coal extraction doubled between 1980 and 1994, from 620 to 1,230Mt; it peaked at about 1.375Gt in 1996; and it remained above 1.3Gt in 1997. At the same time, the improving energy intensity of China's economy (to be appraised in the last segment of this chapter) and growing supplies of hydroelectricity, natural gas and imported liquid fuels, made much of this rising fuel production superfluous. Given the fact that small collieries were responsible for about half (the peak rate was 52 per cent in 1996) of all coal output, and that their poor productivity and dismal safety record should have sufficed on their own as reasons for closing down most of them, it did not come as a surprise that the decision to reduce China's coal extraction was executed largely by eliminating tens of thousands of small mines.

As China's coal production fell by 25 per cent between 1997 and 2000 – from 1,325 to 989Mt – the total number of small coal mines was reduced by more than 50 per cent, from 82,000 in 1997 to about 36,000 by the end of 2000; more than 10,000 mines were shut down during 2001. About 23,000 mines were still in operation as of May 2002, but the plan called for closing 8,000 more operations during the remainder of the year, to bring the total to no more than 15,000 mines (*People's Daily* 2002). With China's coal extraction rising once again (up by almost 11 per cent in 2002, to 1,110Mt) it is impossible to say if further cuts in small mine operations and their natural attrition will lower this total even further, or if this may be a new longer-term bottom. In any case, it appears most unlikely that China would resort once more – as it did during the Great Leap years and then, unexpectedly, for more than fifteen years during the time of economic reforms – to an exceptionally high reliance on such inefficient, environmentally damaging and dangerous means of producing a low-quality fuel.

During the 1990s I would have said that "most unlikely" is also the best verdict about any comeback of China's biogas generation – but there are apparently plans for its revival. The *People's Daily* (2000b) cited a Vice-Minister of Agriculture promising that "China will speed up the research and application of biogas technology under the system of market-oriented economy". This article also claimed that there were 7.6 million biogas digesters in operation, while Yuan (2001) put the total at 6.88 million units. Setting aside the usual unreliability of Chinese data, what matters is the actual contribution these units could make to China's energy supply.

Even when crediting them with 50 per cent improved efficiency compared to the units built during the late 1970s (an average of 0.15 rather than $0.1m^3/m^3$ of digester a day), seven million digesters would produce (assuming, liberally, 250 days of full operation) about $2Gm^3$ of biogas. This would be equal to about 50PJ, or less than 0.15 per cent of China's total primary energy supply in the year 2001, and to no more than 0.25 per cent of the country's rural energy consumption. Clearly, even an unlikely doubling of the current biogas generation would not make any noticeable difference to China's energy use.

And so small hydrostations are the only enduring component of the original triad of energy techniques embraced during the Maoist period because of their scale, that is worthy of further expansion. This makes sense particularly because the projects are now larger in size (averaging almost 600kW), better designed and better built. After all, China has the world's largest hydroenergy potential, and a significant share of it (at least 100GW) can be tapped only by small (or relatively small) stations. Official statistics put the aggregate installed capacity of some 43,000 projects at 24.85GW in the year 2000 when another 1.5GW were put online (IN-SHP 2002). One third of this capacity is in stations smaller than 500kW, three fifths in projects rated at less than 10MW. Four southern provinces (Sichuan, Guangdong, Fujian and Yunnan) account for nearly 60 per cent of the overall capacity.

Given the facts that 75 million people still have no access to electricity and that its rural per capita consumption averages just 280kWh (that is an equivalent of just three 60W lightbulbs lit for about four hours a day), it is a rational strategy to nearly double this low consumption before 2010 by building more small hydrostations: continuation of the recent pace (at least 1.5GW of new capacity a year) would bring the total capacity of China's small hydroprojects to about 40GW by the year 2010, or nearly as much as Russia had installed in 1999 in all of its hydrostations.

From a new Saudi Arabia to concerns about oil security: the ups and downs of China's oil industry

Crude oil prices were fairly steady during the first half of the twentieth century and between 1945 and 1969 they actually declined in real terms. OPEC's first round of crude oil price increases abruptly reversed that trend as the prices nearly quadrupled between October and December 1973, from $3.01 to $11.64/barrel (Smil 1987). Resulting temporary supply shortages panicked not only politicians but also many energy experts: they should have known better than to tell the world that the OPEC action was an unmistakable sign that the world was running out of oil and that the lights were going out on Western civilization.

I belong to the minority that did not join this Cassandric chorus, and our views have been amply confirmed by history. More than a quarter-century later, global crude oil production is nearly 40 per cent above the 1973 level, oil prices adjusted for inflation are lower, and the reserve/production ratio is about forty years, compared to just thirty-one years in 1973 (BP 2002). This means that even without any new discoveries the world could produce crude oil at the 2001 rate until the year 2041 – but the oil industry is always diligently searching for oil, and there is little doubt that the fuel will retain a critical, albeit declining share of the world's primary energy supply until well past the year 2050 (Smil 2003).

But OPEC's ascent was undoubtedly China's luck: the OPEC-induced crisis arrived just as the country began its opening to the world, and one of its first important economic acts was to offer crude oil to Japan. The Japanese, heavily dependent on the Middle East, jumped at this opportunity, and then let wishful thinking take over as they claimed that imports of first tens, and then hundreds of millions of tonnes of China's petroleum, were just a matter of years. That did not, indeed could not, happen.

But the idea of China as a new Saudi Arabia came back to life just a few years later, as the country opened its offshore waters for foreign oil and gas exploration. Stratigraphy of the South China Sea bed off Guangdong and Hainan was seen by some experts as resembling closely that of the Persian Gulf, a promise that attracted every major Western oil company into competitive bidding for the rights to explore it. Again, the Chinese timing was extremely fortuitous, as the entry of multinationals into China coincided with OPEC's second round of oil price increases in 1979–1980, a hike triggered by the fall of the Iranian monarchy and the return of Ayatollah Khomeini to claim the country for his theocracy of medieval mullahs. That dream, too, was short-lived, as the South China Sea proved to be a valuable, but definitely not a major, oil province. While definitely worthy of further exploration and certain to yield a number of small- to medium-size oil and gas structures that will contribute to China's hydrocarbon supply for decades to come, the Nanhai is no North Sea containing a number of giant oil and gas fields.

More than a decade after the Nanhai story began, the basin was producing less than 2 per cent of China's crude oil. By 1993 the location of the dream had shifted far inland, into the extremely inhospitable deserts of Xinjiang's Tarim Basin. Incredibly enough, the story of Western involvement repeated itself. As Paik (1997: 2) noted, "China decided to let the foreigners in, but gave them the least desirable tracts". As with the Nanhai, exploration in the no less geologically complicated Tarim basin began producing oil and gas finds from medium- and small-scale oil reservoirs – but after more than a decade of searching there is no sign of any supergiant fields of the Middle Eastern class.

And so a reversal took place by 1993, as China became a net importer of oil and refined products. Declining amounts of crude oil were shipped from China, mainly to Japan, during the rest of the 1990s, but the net imports nearly tripled between 1993 and 2000, and a new fashion in oil trade forecasting is now to predict when China will surpass Japan to become the world's second-largest consumer of oil and, eventually, its second-largest importer behind the USA. Not surprisingly, this has brought a new kind of worry stemming from China's growing dependence on imports: what this will do to the country's perception of economic and political security, to its role in Middle Eastern affairs, and to world oil prices (Troush 1999; Soligo and Jaffe 1999; IEA 2000)?

As the following excerpts show, I counseled caution when the country was seen as a new fabulous source of oil for the first time during the mid-1970s (Smil 1975, 1976c), as well as a decade later when its offshore oil potential attracted a new wave of exaggerated expectation (Smil 1988): it was always highly unlikely that China could become a new Saudi Arabia. And I still counsel caution when the reverse view is now the fashion of the day, that is when the country's increasing oil imports are seen as one of the key reasons for accelerating competition for the world's diminishing oil supplies and for driving up the world price of oil: I believe that China's oil imports will not rise as steeply as many experts now fear.

Export dreams and realities

Mr Ryutaro Hasegawa, chairman of the Japan–China Oil Import Council, staged an airport press conference on his return from the PRC on 15 August 1974, and announced that the country's annual crude oil output is expected to reach 400Mt in the near future – and that one quarter of this vast amount could be supplied to Japan. This has been, so far, the most enthusiastic assessment of Peking's oil industry and its export potential, perhaps the culmination of two years of increasingly optimistic reports emanating from the official sources and from a growing number of Peking's visitors and suitors. The PRC has been portrayed as an emerging oil giant rivaling the Middle East with her resources and with her future exports, and providing a principal alternative source of hydrocarbons to the advanced nations in exchange for Western and Japanese technology. Considering this state of abundant superlatives and rising expectations, the need for critical evaluation of Peking's oil export capability is imperative. It would seem prudent to conclude that the PRC, to build up her technology and to increase her food production, might become a major crude oil exporter (of the order of several tens of millions of tonnes annually) for a short, intermediate period of time in the near future.

But it took some time before this cautious assessment was generally accepted. Beginning in the latter half of 1974 and during 1975 many Japanese businessmen, the world press and quite a few Western China scholars kept conjuring up the image of the PRC as an emerging new "Middle East", a country on the verge of exerting far-reaching political influence and reaping vast economic benefits through fabulously growing exports of oil. Japan, which bought 1.12Mt in 1973, 4Mt in 1974 and 8Mt in 1975, was expected to import up to 18Mt in 1976, 40–50Mt well before the end of the 1970s, as much as 100Mt in 1980 and about 200Mt in 1985.

These figures – based on the uncritical predictions of some Japanese experts, whose wishful thinking was mistaken for a genuine critical forecasting – have been disseminated by many press agencies and reprinted in scores of newspaper articles around the world. Unfortunately, they have even found their way into influential scholarly publications: the PRC's growing oil potential was seen as a "time bomb in East Asia" and its exports as an "oil weapon". However, recent realities have turned to be much more prosaic – and certainly quite disappointing for the forecasters of the PRC's new role as an international oil giant. What could be dismissed by many as overly pessimistic in spring 1975 had to be grudgingly accepted by spring 1976: the PRC is not potentially another Iran or Saudi Arabia – and its future oil exports will be restricted to much more modest totals.

The best proof has been, of course, offered by the failure of Japanese importers to conclude any long-term oil export agreement with Peking and by a sharp decline in Japanese oil purchases in 1976. Vice-Premier Li Xiannian told the Keidanren's President Toshio Doko in October 1975 that "China could not supply as much crude oil as Japan wanted" and advised him, astonishingly enough, that Japan should buy instead "more silk and other traditional Chinese products" (Kyodo 1975). On 3 March 1976, Ryutaro Hasegawa signed a contract for imports of 2.1Mt of Daqing crude in 1976 – a total identical to the original 1975 quota (Kyodo 1976).

While it is clearly impossible to predict actual annual shipments and destinations of the PRC's crude oil in the years ahead, reasonable attempts can be made to evaluate the country's future export potential by considering the likely rates of extraction and China's growing domestic demand. The PRC may have exportable surpluses equal, respectively, to 60 and 80Mt of coal equivalent in 1980 and 1985. The PRC's share of the global oil market – probably somewhere between 30 and 70Mt – will constitute barely 1.5–3 per cent of the total. "Time bomb" ticking in East Asia is hardly going to send shock waves around the continent.

And it did not. China's exports of crude oil rose to 36Mt in 1985, when they accounted for nearly 3 per cent of the world's market. Total coal and oil exports reached the 60Mtce level in 1985, rather than in 1980, and they have remained near, or above, that rate ever since. But the proportion of exports has shifted as China became first a small net importer (in 1993) and then an increasingly important buyer of crude oil and petroleum products (nearly 60Mt in 1999), while its coal exports rose from less than 10Mt in 1985 to nearly 50Mt by 1999. But wishful thinking is a powerful addiction and, contrary to my conclusion, even the world's largest multinational oil companies nursed their hopes that the PRC might yet be another Iran or Saudi Arabia. This belief led to one of the more astonishing episodes in the modern history of oil exploration (Smil 1988).

Offshore hopes and disappointments

During the last years of the 1970s, the Chinese were facing several frustrating realities concerning their oil industry. Output at their two largest oilfields (Daqing and Shengli, producing 70 per cent of the total extraction) was stagnating. With the exception of the conveniently located and relatively rich Zhongyuan oilfield, all other discoveries were yielding only smallish additions of new production capacity, moreover, mostly in difficult-to-develop reservoirs. The geologically most promising unexplored onshore oil-bearing basins appeared to be in Xinjiang, thousands of kilometers from the industrialized coastal regions. Sedimentary basins offshore were even more promising, but Chinese capacities to explore them and then to develop them were wholly inadequate.

The way out was by breaking with the long-standing proscription of foreigners developing China's natural resources, and letting the Western and Japanese oil companies find the offshore hydrocarbons and bring them to market. The first stage of this marriage of convenience was richly rewarding to the Chinese, who lured in the multinationals – eager to have a try at what was perceived by many oilmen as one of the last remaining big plays in relatively easy waters – not by contracts but merely by promises.

By July 1979, sixteen groups of foreign oil companies signed agreements to provide geophysical surveys – bearing the entire cost, letting the Chinese sample and learn advanced techniques, and turning over to them all results with the hope of being invited back later for exploratory drilling and production. About 420,000km^2 of the South China Sea and the southern part of the Yellow Sea were explored by 110,000km of seismic linear surveys, and after completion of exploration in six of the eight contract areas in April 1980, forty-six companies from twelve countries were invited to submit exploration tenders. A model exploration contract was revealed in May 1982, and of the forty-six companies that started the dealing in 1979, thirty-three decided to take the plunge and twenty-five opted for risk sharing in the form of twelve consortia. Finally, during 1983, the awarding of exploration blocks got under way.

These contracts required the holders to drill 120 exploratory wells within three years at a cost of roughly US$1 billion. During 1983 came also the first news of foreign hydrocarbon discoveries. Total China found crude oil and natural gas in the Weizhou 10-3-3 well, and did even better at a nearby site in the Beibu Gulf with Weizhou 10-3-4. Clearly, 1984, the first full year of extensive offshore drilling, looked very promising – although the persistent and deepening glut on the global oil market was making foreign companies less enthusiastic about the whole Chinese adventure. The Chinese, as always fond of military similes, saw the year as "the eve of a massive battle", and the general manager of the Nanhai Western Petroleum Corporation assured a *Beijing Review* reporter that "we have found another battlefield in the South and we are not going to lose. D-day is not far away."

The analogy was grotesquely inaccurate: large offshore oilfields are not explored and developed by rapid, concentrated, mass assaults – but by a prolonged, incremental process. The Chinese talked often about the South China Sea as another North Sea. In that case they should have kept in mind that no less than thirteen years elapsed from the first geophysical confirmation of the undersea hydrocarbons to the time when Britain and Norway started to land more than 50Mt of crude annually. The realities of 1984 brought a different perspective: after a year of wildcatting in the Zhujiang basin there were no worthwhile discoveries. Perhaps most disappointing was BP's failure after spending $55 million on six wells in the Nanhai's most promising offshore structures. As the best prospects yielded no commercial finds, many Western oilmen came to share a feeling that the complex stratigraphy of the Nanhai makes the discovery of a huge oilfiled fairly unlikely, and that the prospects lie in a multitude of smaller and deeper structures.

In these changed circumstances the China National Offshore Oil Corporation announced the second round of bidding for offshore contract areas on 21 November 1984. Eventually twenty-three oil companies decided to participate, and by the time the first contracts came up for signing in late 1985 the Nanhai prospect brightened, owing both to agreements on development of two previous discoveries and to a couple of new, promising finds. But there are other important considerations complicating development of the Nanhai's hydrocarbons. First, the South China Sea play started to unfold as the global oil market reposed on huge production reserves with soft crude oil prices and few signs that economic recovery in the West will push oil demand soon again to its pre-1991 levels. Put simply, the Chinese are trying to enter the big league when most paying spectators are leaving the bleachers – and when many managers are having second thoughts about the enduring frustrations and costs of joint business with the Chinese, while less daunting options beckon elsewhere.

In the coming years there will be more to follow than the still open fate of the Nanhai and orderly, unexciting development of the Bohai: foreign companies are moving onshore. How successful the Nanhai exploration and other offshore and onshore searches will eventually be nobody can tell, but by the mid-1990s it should be possible to say with confidence which way the country's long-term oil fortunes will tilt: a true superpower in the class of the United States (if not of Russia or Saudi Arabia), a durable major producer (with extraction at least double the current level supportable for decades), or a minor player, at, or even below, the recent flows?

China's oil imports and security

Interestingly enough, the answer to the above question turned out to be, at least partially, all of the above: China's crude oil reserves put the country firmly among the group of second-echelon petroleum powers; increased production will not double the current output within 10–15 years, while rising domestic demand will make China a larger buyer on the international market, but not one to destabilize it. An unspectacular but fairly steady stream of new offshore discoveries, both in the Nanhai and in Bohai, and the first phase of intensive exploratory drilling in the Tarim Basin, have added to China's crude oil reserves. Their total at the end of 2001 was about 3.3Gt, just ahead of Nigeria's 3.2Gt, and not far behind the three big oil powers of Mexico, Libya, each with 3.8Gt, and the US with 3.7Gt (BP 2002). Reserves almost in the US class are, of course, still very far behind the four Persian Gulf leaders, Saudi Arabia (36Gt) and Iraq, Kuwait and Iran (all of them having reserves of more than 10Gt).

China ranks even higher on the production list: it has the world's eleventh place in crude oil reserves, but in 2001 it was the eighth-largest producer, less than 10 per cent behind Norway, Venezuela and Mexico, about 10 per cent behind Iran, but still with less than half of Russia's or the US rate, and about 30 per cent of the Saudi extraction. Although the growth of its production, up by about 17 per cent since 1991, has been a bit faster than the global mean (14 per cent between 1991 and 2001), its domestic demand has been running ahead of this supply, and China's net imports of crude oil and refined oil products have increased from an equivalent of about 10Mt of crude oil in 1993 (the year China became a net importer) to about 23Mt in 1997, and Chinese forecasts were for shipments of 50Mt by the year 2000. These forecasts proved to be too conservative. Net imports rose to 30Mt in 1999, and then, in a big jump, reached 69.6Mt in 2000, while the 2001 total of 64.9Mt was only about 7 per cent lower.

Consequently, China is now buying about 30 per cent of its oil consumption, and it has suddenly become the world's sixth-largest importer of liquid fuels, still far behind the USA and Japan, but closing rapidly on Germany, France and Italy. Times have changed. China does not boast any more about its imperviousness to the ups and downs of the global oil market; securing enough foreign oil has become one of the major preoccupations of its energy planners – and, in a development little noticed beyond expert energy circles, the country is now putting in place an extensive infrastructure needed to make it the world's second-largest importer of hydrocarbons. After the disappointments in Nanhai and Tarim exploration, Chinese planners could have reverted to the rationing of liquid fuels in order to maintain maximum possible self-sufficiency – but they decided to abandon that Maoist policy and go for large-scale imports.

Following the Japanese precedent, they opted for reducing the purchases of refined oil products and concentrating on imports of crude oil, a decision that will require building new oil ports and refineries that will have to include desulfurization facilities required to handle Middle Eastern crudes with relatively high sulfur content (otherwise South China's already serious acid rain problem from coal combustion would get even worse). Immediate plans are for building four new terminals (eleven are in service now) able to handle 150,000-t tankers and 70Mt of crude oil a year. Recent plans range from negotiating long-term joint-production agreements for crude oil to purchasing the most expensive fossil fuel, liquefied natural gas (LNG). To be sure, the China National Petroleum Corporation (CNPC) is no Exxon, but through shareholding, joint ventures and operational and leasing rights the country now participates in oil extraction in Canada, Thailand, Papua New Guinea, Iraq, Iran, Kuwait, Peru, Sudan, Venezuela, Azerbaijan and Russia.

The first shipment of Chinese-drilled overseas oil arrived in Qinhuangdao from Peru in September 1997, and foreign projects are expected to secure an annual production capacity of 50Mt by the year 2010. By that time they could be rivaled by planned deals for long-term imports of oil and gas from hydro-carbon-rich regions of the former Soviet Union. In 1997 CNPC contracted for further development of two Kazakh oilfields, and even bigger multinational deals involving Russia, China, South Korea and Japan are planned for massive exports of Russian gas from Siberian fields. Kazakhstan has been particularly eager to break its dependence on Russian-controlled pipelines by exporting its oil eastward – but such hopes will take a long time to materialize.

And just before the end of 1999 the State Council approved the construction of China's first LNG terminal, to be completed by the year 2005 in Shenzhen, and in August 2002 China announced two large LNG contracts. The larger one was to Australia's North West Shelf consortium for a twenty-five-year, US$13.5 billion contract to supply Guangdong and Hong Kong, the smaller one to a joint BP-Pertamina operation at Indonesia's Tangguh field to supply Fujian. China will thus join the USA and Japan in importing this expensive fuel, and further contracts are likely to follow, as the Chinese planners are aiming to double the 2001 share of natural gas (a mere 3 per cent) in the country's primary supply within a decade.

Chinese forecasts of 100Mt of crude oil imported by the year 2010 that looked bold just a few years ago now appear distinctly low. More than 100Mt of crude oil may be bought even before 2005, but if the Tarim fields bring bigger discoveries, and if the necessary construction of a long and expensive pipeline proceeds according to plan, these imports may stabilize at least for a number of years. The potential for much higher shipments is easy to appreciate, as China's per capita consumption of all liquid fuels is still less than one tenth of the Japanese mean, and as coal still dominates the country's primary energy consumption. The International Energy Agency forecasts that China may buy as much as 400Mt of oil in 2020, more than a tenth of the world's current oil extraction (IEA 2000).

Whatever the actual annual totals will be, it is now highly likely that China will become the world's third-largest importer of crude oil before 2010. Will it then go on to surpass Japanese imports to stand only behind the USA in its foreign oil purchases? Inevitably, such development would have many international repercussions, particularly as US oil output, now second in the world after Saudi Arabia and just ahead of Russia, keeps declining (it fell by 17 per cent during the 1990s), as the North Sea extraction is nearing its peak, and as the global oil market shows recurrent tightenings, with prices spiking above $30/barrel.

As always, it is easy to construct some scary scenarios. China will have to depend largely, as does the rest of the oil-importing world, on shipments from the member states of OPEC. Larger Chinese purchases will help to increase that cartel's share of global crude oil sales in general, and the importance of Muslim Middle Eastern exporters in particular. China has already given moral and military support both to Iraq and Iran, and its growing economic, diplomatic and military presence in the Middle East is bound to create more friction with the United States, if not with the entire West. This would set the stage for yet another world oil supply crisis and its unpredictable economic and geopolitical consequences, this time with China being an unpredictable part of the mix.

In contrast, one can foresee relatively early progress on major imports from Russia (whose oil companies have made a number of offers to sell) and/or Kazakhstan. Even more importantly, one can see China taking advantage of Siberia's enormous natural gas resources and becoming more of an importer of gas rather than of oil, a shift that would further help to lower the energy intensity of its economy. And it is to the country's post-1980 achievements in this particular area that I will turn next, looking closer at some surprising gains in China's energy conversion efficiency.

A remarkable shift in energy intensities: a closer look at an unexpected achievement

The energy intensity of a nation's economy is simply a ratio of the annual total primary energy supply (converted to a common denominator) and the gross domestic products (for convenience I will use the respective abbreviations EI, TPES and GDP). National energy intensities can be calculated by using fuel and electricity statistics issued annually by UNO (2001), IEA (2001), EIA (2001) and BP (2001), and GDP data summarized by UNDP (2001) and the World Bank (2001). Standardized EI values in constant US$ are now also available for all OECD countries (OECD 2001), and the US EIA publishes the latest annual values, as well as historical retrospectives, for most of the world's countries (EIA 2001). Energy intensities are used as revealing indicators of national economic development. The heuristic appeal of this aggregate measure is obvious, as nations with relatively low EI should enjoy several important economic, social and environmental advantages.

A relatively low EI will help to lower total production costs, make exports more competitive and, for countries dependent on foreign fuel, imports less costly. Low EI is also a good indicator of the prevalence of advanced extraction, processing and manufacturing techniques, and of efficient use of raw materials. And because production, processing, transportation and final uses of energy constitute the world's largest source of atmospheric emissions and are a major cause of water pollution and ecosystemic degradation, low EI will minimize many inevitable environmental impacts and help maintain a good quality of life.

Historical trends of national EI show some basic similarities, with the measure rising during the early stages of industrialization and then, after reaching an often sharp peak, declining significantly as modern economies use their inputs more efficiently. The US EI conforms to this pattern, with a sharp peak around 1920 followed by a near 60 per cent decline by the year 2000, but the Japanese trend shows much more modest changes and an extended plateau (Figure 2.6). Different timing of EI peaks and different rates of ascent and decline of national lines reflect the differences in the onset of intensive industrialization and the country-specific tempo of economic development and technical innovation.

During the 1950s China's EI displayed an entirely predictable rapid rise caused by the Stalinist-type modernization that was predicated on the expansion of energy-intensive heavy industries (Figure 2.7). The subsequent rapid decline of EI did not reflect any gains in efficiency but rather the collapse of the Great Leap Forward and, shortly afterwards, the turmoil of the early Cultural Revolution years. Once the political situation had largely stabilized, China's EI resumed its rise at a rate very similar to the pre-1958 trend. In 1978 nobody could have known that China's EI had peaked in 1977 and that it would embark on a fairly rapid and sustained decline. During the last six years of Mao's rule China's EI rose by 14 per cent – but during the first full six years of Deng Xiaoping's reforms (1979–1985) the country's EI fell by nearly 30 per cent. In 1985 this could have been seen as a one-time effect of closing down the most inefficient enterprises and bringing in advanced foreign techniques to modernize many large-scale energy-intensive processes.

But by the end of the 1980s China's EI was down by an additional 18 per cent, after which the decline unexpectedly accelerated as EI fell by 25 per cent during the first half of the 1990s. These developments lowered China's EI by 54 per cent since 1978 – and an even more incredible decline was yet to come: between 1995 and 2000 the measure fell by an additional 45 per cent, and by 18 per cent in the year 2000 alone, bringing the aggregate reductions of China's EI

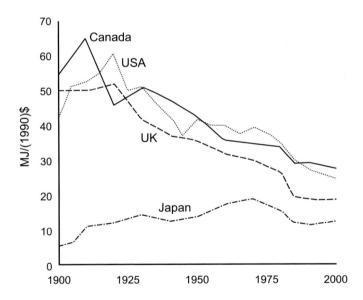

Figure 2.6 Long-term trends of energy intensities in the USA, Canada, UK and Japan, 1900–2000

Source: Smil (2003).

to about 75 per cent in twenty-two years (see Figure 2.7). A naive reaction would be to gape at yet another Chinese first: no other country in modern economic history has come even close to such a rate of improvement. A critical response would be to deconstruct the measure in general, and look much closer at the peculiarities of China's EI in particular.

Problems with calculating EI

EI reveals and clouds at the same time. A simple division is needed to calculate it, but both numerator and denominator contain aggregate measures whose real values are not easy to determine. There are three major problems with the numerator. To begin with, EI is invariably calculated by using only the statistically well-documented inputs of fossil fuels and primary electricity and excluding entirely all uses of traditional biomass fuels. This makes hardly any difference for calculating the EI for the USA or France, but in all countries with a significant biomass energy component the adjustment for wood and crop residues consumption would boost the TPES and, everything else being equal, increase EI. Conversions of fossil fuels to a common denominator (Joules, coal or oil equivalents) are usually a matter of straightforward multiplications, but inadequate information on the changing quality of fuel may lead to far-from-negligible conversion errors.

Finally, there is an intractable conversion problem with the primary, that is mostly hydro and nuclear, electricity. When the primary electricity is converted by using straight thermal equivalent ($1\text{kWh} = 3.6\text{MJ}$), countries relying heavily on hydro or nuclear generation will appear to be much more energy efficient

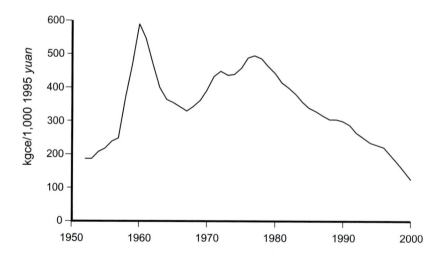

Figure 2.7 Energy intensity of China's economy, 1952–2000

Source: Based on data from *China Statistical Yearbook* and Fridley (2001).

than nations generating electricity from fossil fuels. Equating primary electricity with the heat content of fossil fuels used to generate a nation's thermal electricity solves that undercount, but it introduces another problem. Conversion ratios must be adjusted annually with improving efficiency of thermal generating stations – but then the fuel equivalent of hydroelectricity would be declining even if its generated total remained steady.

Complications with the denominator are, if anything, even more intractable even when leaving aside the fundamental problem of what is really measured: after all, GDP grows even as the quality of life may be declining (e.g. greater air pollution leads to higher incidence of respiratory diseases which, in turn, leads to more money spent on medical examinations, drugs and hospital admissions); it increases even as irreplaceable natural resources (old-growth forests, wetlands) and services (e.g. the water-retention capacity of eroding soils) are being destroyed (Daly and Cobb 1989). Standard national accounts do not include the value of essential subsistence production and barter, and nor do they capture black market transactions whose inclusion may raise the real GDPs of even the least corrupt Western nations by anything between 5 and 25 per cent (Mattera 1985; Thomas 1999). The second fundamental problem arises from conversions of national GDP values to a common denominator in order to make revealing international comparisons of EI.

Using official exchange rates is an unsatisfactory approach, as these rates reflect primarily the prices of widely traded commodities and may have few links with those parts of a country's economy that are not involved in foreign exchange. Consequently, conversions with official exchange rates almost always increase the real economic disparity between the rich and poor nations: in other words, poor countries are not as poor as they appear when their GDPs are converted by using nominal value of the US dollar (the World Bank's highly misleading, but endlessly repeated, claim about hundreds of millions of people in low-income countries forced to live on US$1 a day is perhaps the most obvious misuse of this conversion). Conversion to a common currency by using purchasing power parity (PPP) avoids the errors of relying on nominal exchange rates, but it can result in exaggerations whose errors may be relatively even larger, albeit in the opposite direction, than those arising from the use of market exchange rates.

Chinese circumstances

All of these problems must be considered when appraising China's EI. To begin with, during the late 1990s China still derived about 15 per cent of its primary energy consumption from biomass, and hence its TPES in the year 2000 was at least 41EJ rather than just 35EJ, a reality that would increase China's EI. However, as biomass supplied a substantially higher portion of the nation's total energy use during the earliest period of the economic reforms (roughly a quarter in 1980), its inclusion would actually slightly accentuate the decline of China's EI since 1980. China's high dependence on poor quality coal presents a conversion problem: in the Chinese official statistics raw coal output is multiplied by 0.71 to get the hard coal equivalent (i.e. fuel containing 29GJ/t). But, as already explained in this chapter, during the 1990s as much as half of China's coal extraction originated from small local pits, and less than 20 per cent of all raw coal output was washed and sorted (Fridley 2001). Consequently, the real conversion factor to standard fuel could be as much as 10 per cent lower than the official value, an adjustment that would reduce China's TPES.

On the other hand, unreported output from illegal small coal mines would raise the official TPES total, as would the reported smuggling of foreign crude oil into southern provinces. In addition, slightly different conversion procedures result in an appreciable overall difference. For example, China's official TPES in the year 2000 amounted to 1,071.7Mt of coal equivalent, or 31.1EJ, while BP (2002) puts it at 804.7Mt of oil equivalent, or 33.8EJ, or nearly 9 per cent higher. On the money side, subsistence production and barter still represent a significant part of economic activity in China's countryside (although clearly much less than a generation ago), and quantification of black market transactions (whose total volume is almost certainly much larger than twenty years ago) is impossible in such an extraordinarily corrupt economy. Inclusion of these transactions would increase China's GDP and, everything else being equal, further lower EI. In contrast, there is widespread agreement that China's official GDP is significantly overestimated, and its downward adjustment, with TPES remaining the same, would, naturally, increase the EI level.

Official statistics claim that between 1980 and 1999 GDP grew annually by an average of 9.8 per cent, with four consecutive years of double-digit expansion (as high as 14.2 per cent) between 1992 and 1995. Maddison (1997) argues that the actual average expansion for the period 1978–1994 was more than 2 per cent lower, 7.5 rather than 9.8 per cent. This makes a huge cumulative difference: official GDP for the 1990s comes to about 56 trillion in constant 1995 *yuan*, the revised total is about 40 trillion *yuan*. Relative difference is nearly 30 per cent. Absolute difference is more than 15 trillion of 1995 *yuan*, the total equal to China's GDP in 1996, 1997 and 1998! Standard and Poor revisions of China's GDP during 1990 indicate a similar gap between official claims and the real performance.

Perhaps the only certainties here are that China's GDP and TPES are not what the NBS claims they are – and that there is no unequivocal procedure with which to bring these suspect figures closer to reality. The least arguable thing to do is to revise China's GDP estimates along Maddison's (1997) lines: this brings the total GDP for the year 2000 to 5.75 trillion *yuan*, rather than the officially claimed 8.6 trillion. This adjustment raises China's EI from about 3.6 to about 5.4GJ/1,000 *yuan* in the year 2000, and it results in the overall 1980–2000 EI decline of 58 per cent, rather than 72 per cent. But I would argue that the period per cent between 1997 and 2000 should not be used for EI calculations that are to reveal long-term trends in China's energy use. Official Chinese data show that between 1997 and 2000 the country's TPES fell by 22 per cent while its GDP rose by nearly 24 per cent. One does not have to be an energy economist to suspect the integrity of the statistical information that implies the expansion of GDP by nearly a quarter – while eliminating about 9EJ of energy consumption, or nearly as much as the UK uses every year. Alternatively, it is possible to argue that an improvement close to the claimed EI drop did actually take place, but that such an event was a singularity that arose from a unique combination of macroeconomic policies, above all from the aggressive reduction of coal extraction in small mines and a rapid expansion of low-energy intensity (high value-added) manufacturing.

Consequently, it may be more meaningful to base any international comparisons on the years 1980–1997 before the abrupt state intervention that closed down tens of thousands of small mines. China's EI for that period, calculated with adjusted GDP values, declined by 36 per cent, or at an annual rate of −2.6 per cent. This is still an impressive performance, but one closer to the achievements of other countries. For example, the EI of the Japanese economy was declining at an even faster rate of 2.8 per cent for fifteen years (1974–1989) between the time of OPEC's price shock and the peak year of the Nikkei index (EDMC 2000). This feat was much harder to achieve because Japan's EI in 1974 was already very low by international standards, and the country was at a level of economic development that was far ahead of the conditions in post-1980 China. And even the US economy, the world's largest (and an order of magnitude bigger than China), matched China's performance as it reduced its EI by an average 2.6 per cent a year between the OPEC's price rise and the collapse of high crude oil prices in 1985.

Consequently, the post-1980 reduction of China's EI is obviously a most welcome development and the overall achievement is impressive – but it is not unprecedented. Moreover, as Sinton and Fridley (2000) stress, the electricity intensity of China's economy (kWh/*yuan*) has not improved since 1980. Using, once again, adjusted GDP values, China's economy needed about 220kWh/1,000 *yuan* in 1980 and the rate was approximately 230kWh/1,000 *yuan* in 2000. In this sense China behaves as any other rapidly modernizing country where the demand of electricity – driven by all sectors of the economy as well as by rising household requirements for lighting, refrigeration and air conditioning – commonly grows by 7–10 per cent a year, far outstripping the growth of the TPES.

Although secular reductions of EI are the norm in all rationally run economies, China's post-1980 record has received so much attention because of its implications for the generation of greenhouse gases (Streets *et al.* 2001). Most of the long-range energy consumption forecasts published during the 1980s and the early 1990s did not factor-in China's substantial efficiency gains, or at least greatly underestimated their pace, and hence they overestimated the country's future energy consumption and its generation of CO_2. And, of course, it was impossible to anticipate the sudden post-1997 drop in China's TPES that lowered the country's consumption by 22 per cent in three years, and that was reversed only in 2001.

As a result, it is now highly unlikely that, as commonly predicted as late as the year 2000 (EIA 2000), China's CO_2 emissions from fossil fuel combustion will surpass the US output before 2020, or shortly thereafter. Some conservative projections now foresee the difference between China's and US carbon generation to be actually slightly larger in 2020 than it was in 2000. This development would leave the USA as the undisputed, and in the absence of any effective reductions, the even more reviled, number-one producer of CO_2 for most of the first half of the twenty-first century. But caution is in order. China's energy use has been returning to normal: although the TPES for 2001 was still below the level reached in 1994, it increased by 8.4 per cent, well above the 1987–1997 mean of 4.7 per cent a year. Similarly high rates would soon bring the long-term trend closer to the pre-1997 trajectory. Given China's murky statistics, we may never know the real extent of the 1998–2000 TPES decline, but whatever it was, it is not going to be repeated: no modernizing economy can support an annual 7 per cent GDP growth and accommodate another 250 million people during the coming generation by having very large periodical dips in its TPES.

International comparisons

Interpreting EI gets even more difficult when trying to answer an obvious question: given its impressive achievements in lowering its EI, how does China's current performance compare with the world's major economies? When the country's GDP is converted from *yuan* to US$ by using the official fixed exchange rate the value is just short of $800/capita in the year 2000 – while the PPP value used by UNDP (2001) gives about $3,600/capita, a 4.6-fold difference. The first rate would yield, with China's 2000 TPES at about 31EJ (without biomass), EI of about 33GJ/$1,000, the other one would result in EI of less than 7GJ/$1,000. For comparison, conversions with official exchange rates produce EI of less than 5MJ/$1,000 for Japan, more than 11MJ for the USA, about 19MJ/$1,000 for Canada, about 26MJ/$1,000 for India, more than 80MJ for Russia, and an incredible 200MJ/$1,000 for the Ukraine. When using PPP the intensities (all in MJ/$1,000) change to about 7 for Japan, 11 for the USA, 13 for Canada, 10 for India and 25 for Russia.

There is something wrong with either set of conversions. In the first case, the numbers immediately signal the dubious value of market exchange rates: Russia and Ukraine are not that inefficient, Canada cannot be that different from the USA – and it is most unlikely that China's energy intensity is about 30 per cent higher than India's. In the PPP case, the values for all affluent countries come, as expected, closer together – but China would be performing better than does Sweden or the Netherlands, a most unlikely conclusion. China's EI is obviously somewhere between these two extremes, but until we stop relying on many clearly misleading market exchange rates, and until we come up with a much more reliable way to calculate truly representative PPP, we will be unable to offer realistic international comparisons of national EI.

Reasons for EI decline

But no matter how accurate or misleading, the measure does not tell us why it has been changing and why the countries rank as they do. Not surprisingly, China's rapidly declining EI attracted the attention of economists who tried to identify the sources of this improvement. Several studies that tried to measure the relative contributions of sectoral shift (i.e. away from energy-intensive processes) and subsector productivity change, concluded that the latter was the single largest contributor to China's falling EI (Sinton and Levine 1994; Lin and Polenske 1995; Garbaccio *et al.* 1999). These studies looked at various periods between 1981 and 1992, and Zhang (2001) extended this kind of analysis to 1996 by looking at twenty-nine industrial subsectors. His conclusion was that 93 per cent of the post-1990 cumulative energy savings in the industrial sector should be attributed to real EI change, and that the efficiency improvements in just four subsectors (machinery, nonmetal minerals, ferrous metals and chemicals) accounted for nearly 80 per cent of the total gain.

Fisher-Vanden *et al.* (2002) confirmed the marginal importance of changes in industry composition by analyzing a unique set of data for about 2,500 large and medium-size industrial enterprises, working at a much greater level of disaggregation than used by the studies cited in the previous paragraph. They found that changing energy prices and R&D expenditures have been the drivers of declining EI, and that Chinese firms are now responding to prices. That a major share of China's EI decline is attributable to improvements in conversion efficiency is not surprising. Before 1978 China had, by any measure, one of the world's least efficient energy systems, and hence its modernization had to bring some impressive results. The combination of energy price reforms and state-driven measures to reduce the use of energy explains most of these gains.

Subsidies on energy use were gradually lowered and then entirely eliminated, coal prices were deregulated, crude oil subsidies fell from 55 per cent in 1990 to 2 per cent in 1995, and oil prices are now set by the world market; and in 1993 electricity prices were raised for the first time since 1976, with other increases following during the remainder of the 1990s. Energy conservation policies and measures have included some thirty laws (capped by the Energy Conservation Law of 1 January 1998), financial incentives (low interest rates for efficiency loans, reduced taxes on purchases of energy-efficient products), stepped-up management in factories (monitoring energy use, consumption quotas), funding of demonstration projects, and setting up information networks and service centers at several administrative levels.

Some of these measures have been recently discontinued or weakened, but it is both desirable and realistic to maintain the reduction of China's EI at a rate of at least 2 per cent for another decade, and then to maintain a slightly lower rate of at least 1.5 per cent a year. For comparison, in its long-term forecast of global energy demand, the US Department of Energy assumes that the EI of the world's low-income economies will keep improving at a rate averaging 1.4 per cent between 2002 and 2020 (EIA 2002). Fortunately, the country still has enormous opportunities, be they in its industrial enterprises, fields or households, to use energy more efficiently. My estimate of China's PPP-adjusted GDP (based largely on a basket of basic foodstuffs) is about US$2,000/capita in the year 2001. At that rate China's EI (calculated, as other national means with BP's TPES, i.e. about 35EJ in 2001) would be approximately 14GJ/$1,000, about 30 per cent above the US level, and twice the Japanese rate, leaving plenty of space for future improvements.

Notes

1 A good example of this widespread genre is the latest World Bank review of the Chinese economy: *China 2020: The Development Challenges in the New Century* (Washington DC: World Bank, 1997).

2 For details on this inertia and on gradual transitions, see Cesare Marchetti and Nebojsa Nakicenovic, *The Dynamics of Energy Systems and the Logistic Substitution Model* (Laxenburg: IIASA, 1979); Vaclav Smil, *General Energetics* (New York: Wiley, 1991).

3 Most notably, when expressed in constant monies, the average world crude oil price in the late 1990s is no higher than it was a century ago. See British Petroleum, *BP Statistical Review of Energy 1997* (London: British Petroleum, 1997) 14.

4 A resource category comprises the total mass of a particular commodity present in the earth's crust, regardless of the technical means to recover it or the economic viability doing so. While total resources can be only estimated, reserves are the accurately known fraction of resources that can be recovered at a known price by using commercial techniques. A combination of technical innovation and higher prices constantly creates reserves out of resources.

5 The best hard (black, bituminous) coals have a heating content of between 27 and 29 megajoules (MJ) per kilogram (MJ/kg); typical steam coals used in electricity generation have around 22MJ/kg, with the poorest lignites (brown coals) being below 15MJ/kg. Most of China's coal resources have an energy density between 22 and 29MJ/kg. For more details see Vaclav Smil, *Energy in China's Modernization* (Armonk: M.E. Sharpe, 1988) 31–35.

6 Mistakenly, this reserve/production (R/P) ratio is often seen as an indicator of the time a country, or the world, will run out of a particular mineral. This would be the case only for resource/production ratio, a quotient we cannot reliably calculate because of the uncertain nature of the numerator. Higher prices and better techniques can raise R/P ratios quite rapidly: for example, the global R/P ratio for crude oil was well below 30 during the time of low oil prices in the early 1970s – but recently it has stood above 40, higher than at any time since 1945. For the latest estimates of coal reserves, and coal R/P ratios, see British Petroleum, *BP Statistical Review*, 30.

7 *Ibid.*, 4.

8 *Ibid.*, 20.

9 Crude oil contains 42MJ/kg, 1 cubic meter (m^3) of natural gas averages around 35MJ, and it has a mass of about 720 grams (g); consequently, energy density of natural gas is nearly 49MJ/kg.

10 This is a particularly important concern for China, the world's largest producer of nitrogenous fertilizers. Synthesis of ammonia needs about 50MJ of natural gas per kg of nitrogen, and China has been recently using almost 30 per cent of its total natural gas production for ammonia synthesis.

11 For example, burning typical heating coal (energy content of 22MJ/kg, with carbon making up 70 per cent of the mass) in a fairly efficient (35 per cent) stove will release about 90g of carbon (C) for every MJ of useful energy; in contrast, burning natural gas (75 per cent C) in a high-performance (90 per cent efficient) household gas furnace will release a mere 17g C/MJ.

12 China's total of about 380 billion watts (GW) of exploitable power is well ahead of potential capacities in Russia, Brazil and the USA, but the more even flow of great Siberian rivers could eventually generate more electricity.

13 Capital costs per unit of installed generating capacity are commonly only half as much in coal-fired stations. High-voltage direct-current links are the best way to minimize transmission losses.

14 For comparison, coal has a roughly 25 per cent share in the US primary energy consumption, and it supplies 20 per cent of all commercial energy in both Russia and Japan.

15 Because of many readily available statistical sources I will not reference individual output numbers. Standard Chinese sources are *Zhongguo tongji nianjian* (Beijing: China Statistics Publishing, annually), and *Zhongguo nengyuan* containing monthly production statistics. By far the most comprehensive source in English is: Jonathan E. Sinton (ed.) *China Energy Databook* (Berkeley: Lawrence Berkeley National Laboratory, 1996).

16 For a review of recent reforms of the industry, see Elspeth Thomson, "Reforming China's coal industry", *The China Quarterly* 147 (September 1996): 727–750.

17 Eventual combined capacity of these mines was to surpass 200Mt/year. Shanxi's Pingshuo (Antaibao) mine involved a much publicized personal deal between Armand Hammer, the late CEO of Occidental Petroleum, and Deng Xiaoping.

18 The worst accidents in large mines are caused by coal dust explosions due to inadequate ventilation and poor safety practices. According to the Public Works Ministry 9,974 people died in all mining accidents in 1996. With coal mining accounting for about two thirds of all deaths, Chinese fatalities would average about 5.0 deaths/Mt of coal, compared to 0.15/Mt in the USA.

19 In contrast, basic coal cleaning, involving washing and sizing, is standard in Western mining; some coal also undergoes specialized cleaning aimed at reducing coal's sulfur content in order to meet air emission standards.

20 Besides reducing biodiversity, deforestation contributes to higher erosion rates and straw burning deprives soils of nitrogen which would be otherwise recycled. For a discussion of the extent and implications of these problems, see Vaclav Smil, *China's Environmental Crisis* (Armonk: M.E. Sharpe, 1993).

21 Published estimates have ranged from 8.5 to 23 fatalities per million tonnes of extracted coal. Rates above 20 would clearly represent one of the riskiest occupations anywhere in the world.

22 Wei Hu and Robert Evans, "The impacts of coal mining in Shenmu county, the Loess Plateau, China", *Ambio* 26(6) (September 1997): 405–406.

23 The capital's mean annual total suspended particulate levels are between 400 and $500\mu g/m^3$ – while the WHO's daily maximum of $150–230\mu g/m^3$ can be exceeded only 2 per cent of the days in a year.

24 Dai Hewu and Chen Wenmin, "Characterization and utilization of Chinese high-sulfur coal", *Meitan kexue jishu* (*Coal Science and Technology*) no. 5 (May 1989): 30–35.

25 Mao Yushi and Li Dazheng, *Spontaneous Combustion of Coal in China and its Environmental Impact* (Beijing: China Institute of Mining Technology, 1994).

26 Vaclav Smil, *Environmental Problems in China: Estimates of Economic Costs* (Honolulu: East–West Center, 1996) 19–20.

27 Desulfurization increases both capital and operating costs by at least 20 per cent. Japanese aid offers a perfect opportunity to channel sizable amounts of money through the country's large chemical companies which produce and install modern flue gas desulfurization plants.

28 Smil, *China's Environmental Crisis*, 116.

29 "SPC hikes natural gas price", *China OGP* no. 5 (15 May 1997): 10.

30 For details see Smil, *Energy in China's Modernization*, 162–171.

31 China OGP, *China Petroleum Investment Guide* (Beijing: China OGP, 1994) 91–140.

32 Chinese imports will help to bring closer the date when OPEC will become once again the supplier of last resort – and when the world will have to pay higher crude oil prices. Will China's greater involvement in Middle Eastern affairs be a stabilizing or destabilizing influence? Plausible arguments can be made for both outcomes.

33 Xihe Yu, "Oil security risk, wolf at door?", *China OGP* no. 10 (15 May 1997): 1–3. With rising oil imports, China will also have to build sufficient storage capacity (generally, it should equal 25 per cent of annual imports).

34 The Kazakh deal would involve not only a 3,000-km pipeline to move some 8Mt of crude a year to Xinjiang, but perhaps also trans-shipment through Iran. Detailed discussion of large-scale international oil and gas projects involving Russia, China, Korea and Japan can be found in: Keun-Wook Paik, *Gas and Oil in Northeast Asia* (London: The Royal Institute of International Affairs, 1995).

35 *China News Digest*, 10 April 1997 (http://www.cnd.org).

36 Institute of Techno-economics and Energy System Analysis, *Global Electrification: The Next Decades* (Beijing: Qinghua University, 1997) 1–3.

37 *Ibid.*

38 For comparison, Itaipu, currently the world's largest hydroproject on the Parana between Brazil and Paraguay, has 12.6GW, and Grand Coulee, the largest US hydro-station, rates 10.83GW.

39 For detailed analyses of what is wrong about Sanxia, see Grainne Ryder (ed.) *Damming the Three Gorges* (Toronto: Probe International, 1990); Dai Qing (ed.) *Yangtze! Yangtze!* (London: Earthscan, 1994).

40 *China News Digest*, 8 April 1996 (http://www.cnd.org).

41 China's long-term hydrogeneration plans are outlined in: Smil, *Energy in China's Modernization*, 171–180.

42 *China News Digest*, 16 October 1996 (http://www.cnd.org).

43 Sales of Russian nuclear power plants to China are particularly uncertain.

44 This is about 40 per cent of the total foreign direct investment China received by the end of 1995: World Bank, *China 2020*, 90.

45 For problems with determining and comparing China's energy intensity see Smil, *China's Environmental Crisis*, 72–75, 126–128.

46 Vaclav Smil, "China's environment and security: simple myths and complex realities", *SAIS Review* 17 (winter–spring 1997): 107–126.

47 Lin demonstrated that energy conservation measures rather than structural changes were the leading cause of post-1980 efficiency gains: Xiannuan Lin, *China's Energy Strategy: Economic Structure, Technological Choices, and Energy Consumption* (Westport CT: Praeger, 1996).

48 F. Liu, M. Ross and S. Wang, "Energy efficiency in China's cement industry", *Energy – The International Journal* 20 (1995): 669–681.

49 David G. Fridley, "U.S.–China super-efficient CFC-free refrigerator project", in *LBNL Energy Analysis Program 1995 Annual Report* (Berkeley: Lawrence Berkeley National Laboratory, 1996) 24–25.

50 The gap is even wider for average annual electricity use: China's 1995 rate of about 800kWh/capita was only a tenth of the Japanese mean, and only 10 per cent of that low total was accounted for by household use.

51 Vaclav Smil, "Elusive links: energy, value, economic growth and quality of life", *OPEC Review* 16(1) (spring 1992): 1–21.

52 Vaclav Smil, "China's greenhouse gas emissions", *Global Environmental Change* 4(4) (1994): 279–286.

53 Although China strongly objects to any imposition of binding obligations on developing countries, it is now prepared to make an (unspecified) effort to reduce greenhouse gas emissions: *China News Digest*, 5 November 1997 (http://www.cnd.org).

54 The effects of ozone on China's food-production capacity may be the most worrisome long-term problem: Vaclav Smil, *Energy and the Environment Challenges for the Pacific Rim* (Vancouver: Asia Pacific Foundation of Canada, 1996).

55 This unwise goal would eventually mean between 300 and 400 million vehicles – compared to about 500 million cars registered worldwide in 1995: American Automobile Manufacturers Association, *Motor Vehicle 1996 Facts & Figures* (Detroit: AAMA, 1996) 44. Even if the average fuel consumption of Chinese cars were just one half of the current US mean, China would need about 300Mt of gasoline a year, roughly twice its present annual crude oil consumption.
56 For basic numbers see Smil, *China's Environmental Crisis*, 101–110.
57 R. Kirk Smith, G. Shuhua, K. Huang and Q. Daxiong, "One hundred million improved cookstoves in China: how was it done?", *World Development* 21 (1993): 941–961.
58 For details on these programs, see Smil, *Energy in China's Modernization*, 54–69.
59 Smil 1976a.

3   Food

Traditional Chinese farming has been widely seen as a paragon of organic agriculture, relying on close integration of crops and domestic animals, on recycling of organic wastes and on often-complex crop rotations. While its achievements made it possible for China to be the world's first nation to surpass the 500 million population mark (perhaps as early as the late 1920s), its performance remained vulnerable to natural catastrophes and to productivity dips caused by wars and other conflicts. China entered the twentieth century with the ever-present threat of another sweeping food shortage. In the 1920s, J.L. Buck (1937) found that Chinese peasants recalled an average of three crop failures during their lifetime that were serious enough to cause famines. These famines lasted on average about ten months, and they led up to a quarter of the affected population to eat grasses and strip bark from trees, and forced nearly one seventh of all people to leave their hungry villages in search of food.

During the first eight years of Communist control it appeared that such terrible experiences would be, finally, left to history. But then, unexpectedly and rapidly, the tide of the slowly improving food supply turned, and within months, perhaps already during the last days of 1958 and then increasingly in 1959, people were dying of hunger in more than a dozen provinces. As I will demonstrate in the first section of this chapter, "The world's greatest famine", this was an overwhelmingly man-made (Mao-made, to be exact) famine, and by the time it ended in 1961 it left behind about 30 million dead. The second section, "From subsistence to satiety", will first document the persistence of barely adequate diets during the 1970s and then a transformation that was as unexpected, and no less rapid than, the ill-fated experiment of the late 1950s: the diffusion of the household responsibility system. Deng Xiaoping understood that food production had to be drastically reformed, hence his first step toward modernization was a *de facto* privatization of farming.

This decision moved the country, in conjunction with market resurgence and relaxation of population and capital controls, from subsistence to satiety (at least in terms of statistical averages – by no means for everyone). The chapter's third section will detail China's rapid post-1979 dietary transitions as the developments that elsewhere took decades to unfold – multiple increases in per capita consumption of meats, fish, fruits, oils, sugars and alcohol – were accomplished in less than one generation. Naturally, this impressive gain in China's food-producing capacity is the result of a complex, multifactored process, but one input stands out because of its biochemical uniqueness and indispensability: the abundant supply of inexpensive nitrogen applied to China's fields since the late 1970s. China could not have reached its present (relatively enviable) nutritional status without first becoming the world's largest producer and user of nitrogenous fertilizers.

The continuous success of China's farming is now inextricably bound to very intensive use of synthetic nitrogen fertilizers. That is why in the fourth segment of this food chapter I will take an unorthodox view of China's history by looking at nitrogen in China's agriculture. Finally, an inevitable question intrudes: can this progress be maintained, can China feed itself? In the last section I will give a reasoned affirmative answer to this question.

The world's greatest famine: its origins, toll and inexplicable neglect

On 6 April 1958 Mao Zedong invoked the most beloved, and the most unruly, character of China's popular mythology as he implored his comrades: "The Monkey King disregarded the laws and the Heavens. Why don't we all emulate him?" (Mao 1969: 89). The Chairman of the Chinese Communist Party had no small shake-ups in mind. Two weeks later he asserted that "the destruction of balance constitutes leaping forward and such destruction is better than balance. Imbalance and headache are good things" (Mao 1969: 112). Mao wanted to imbalance the whole nation in order to trump Nikita Khrushchev – the de-Stalinizing Soviet leader who refused to share Soviet nuclear weapons with China – and, in the process, to achieve a feat unprecedented in human history: the modernization of the world's most populous nation in one enormous economic leap.

Yet in order to do so he advocated only a more intensive version of the very method used by his Russian adversary. As Khrushchev was traveling around the world and making speeches outlining how the Soviet Union would soon catch up even with the USA and then go on to surpass America's economic performance (the attitude summed up in his famous boast that "We will bury you"), Mao devised a much bolder version of catching up and surpassing. Starting from a position greatly inferior to that of the already much more industrialized Soviet empire, he envisaged an astonishing Great Leap Forward, first passing the UK and then the USA as China dashed toward global supremacy.

His obsession with this task became delusionary. He did not (indeed his almost nonexistent understanding of modern economies could not allow him to) conceive the daunting goal in its multifaceted complexity, and caricatured it as merely a specific quest for producing more steel. This Stalin-despising Stalinist was mesmerized by the metal. In late May 1958 he was sure that "with 11 million tons of steel next year and 17 million tons a year after the world will be shaken" (Mao 1969: 123). But the country had only a handful of modern iron and steel mills designed by Soviet engineers and built with Soviet help during China's just-completed first five-year plan – and no prospect of getting more from the same source as the dispute between Mao and Khrushchev worsened. The only way Mao could act on his delusions was to order China's peasants to make the Leap work. They faced an impossible task.

Leaping into famine

Tens of millions of people began digging up local deposits of low-quality iron ore and limestone, destroying not just the remainders of China's scarce forests, but also cutting down orchards and groves in order to make charcoal. All of these ingredients were charged into simple clay "backyard" furnaces built by peasants and by commandeered groups of city workers and students. But such primitive metallurgy cannot produce steel, an alloy with just a trace of carbon whose great tensile strength makes it such an excellent material for myriad uses (Bolton 1989). China's "backyard" furnaces yielded merely lumpy cast iron, a metal full of carbon, and hence brittle, and not even fit for a simple field hoe.

Urban populations were mobilized to contribute to this frenzied effort, but most of the work was done by peasants, who instead of cultivating their fields wasted their labor on the futile smelting. This was a catastrophic misallocation of human energy. In 1958 China's farming was still energized almost solely by human and animal labor: machines began to make a difference only when oil started to flow from the country's first sizeable oilfield a decade later (Smil 1976a). At the same time, the area planted to grain, the source of more than four fifths of China's food energy, was shrinking.

Grain yields kept rising even during the early years of collectivization, which began in 1955, not because of the success of command farming but because until 1958 everyday communal production was still largely organized on a household basis (Kung and Putterman 1997). But the party leaders believed that this trend meant that another Great Leap was shaping up, this time in the fields. They called for planting less and harvesting more, a feat to be achieved by relying on yet another item of Stalinist dogma, Lysenkoist practices of close seeding and deep plowing. As a result, the total area sown to grain declined by 5 per cent in 1958, and by a further 10 per cent in 1959 (Crook 1988). Eager to prove that these policies had worked, party bureaucrats began fabricating ludicrously exaggerated reports of record harvests. They announced first that the country had harvested an incredible 375Mt of grain in 1958, then lowered this to a still-excessive 250Mt (compared to 190Mt in 1957) while the real harvest was no higher than 194Mt; similarly, the initial claim for 1959 was 270Mt while the actual crop was just 165Mt (Crook 1988).

These grossly inflated claims were the basis for expropriating higher shares of produced grain for the urban supply: peasants had to surrender 29 per cent of their harvest in 1958 and up to 40 per cent in 1959. Inflated figures were also used to prove the superiority of command farming, and hence to adopt further centralization of food production in giant communes. And in a step toward a truly communal living, the party decided that the peasants should eat free meals in village mess halls. Inevitably, this led both to a sharply higher demand for food and to unprecedented waste, as the peasants had no incentive to economize their food intakes, and as a peculiar (and historically unprecedented) variant of the tragedy of commons gripped the nation. Continuation of any one of these changes alone – wasting labor on iron smelting, abandoning fields, reducing the area planted to grain, relying on dubious agronomic practices, taking more grain away from peasants, offering free communal meals – would have been sufficient to imperil China's food supply.

As I will show in some detail in the next section of this chapter, my careful reconstructions of the country's average food energy availability and needs in 1957, the last pre-Leap year, show a very close fit between supply and demand (Smil 1977a). Per capita supply averaged between 2,100 and 2,200kcal/day, while the age- and sex-adjusted needs of the overwhelmingly rural population engaged in moderate-to-heavy unmechanized fieldwork were about 2,200kcal/day. Consequently, only a highly equitable distribution of food could have prevented massive malnutrition. Such a distribution was largely achieved only in cities, through the strict food rationing imposed in 1953, although there was an urban hierarchy with respect to availability of fine grain (highly milled rice and wheat). In the pre-1958 countryside malnutrition was widespread, and there was always the possibility of seasonal hunger or starvation following poor or failed harvests in the most vulnerable areas, as the country had at that time only a limited capacity for moving large amounts of grain from better-off provinces (particularly from the Northeast) to food-short regions.

Quantifying the toll

Given the fact that China's food supply was precarious even in normal times, the sudden combination of irrational changes was bound to result in a tragedy. Piazza's (1983) reconstruction of average food availabilities shows a 16 per cent drop between 1958 and 1959, from 2,053 to 1,722kcal/capita, followed by an identical percentage drop in 1960 to 1,453kcal when the countrywide grain harvest fell to below 140Mt (Figure 3.1). As in all previous large-scale famines, peasants in the worst affected provinces – including the populous Sichuan and Hunan in the South and the three North China Plain provinces of Anhui, Henan and Shandong – tried to cope by first limiting their physical activity, gathering traditional famine foods (wild seeds and roots, grasses, eventually even tree bark), and deliberately under-feeding girls and old people, the most dispensable members of their households.

In some counties the weakened survivors tried walking away from villages where a quarter or a third of all people were dying, but because of police controls and the food rationing that was tied to places of permanent residence, there was apparently no mass exodus from the countryside to preferentially supplied cities. And as in all such famines, people died in predictable ways: first the most vulnerable (infants and the very old) due to age, aggravation of their chronic conditions, or loss of immunity; and eventually even many of those who survived for months and then succumbed to prolonged wasting. One of the most remarkable facts is that the famine ended while the average food supply was still very low: the nationwide mean for 1962 was still a few per cent below the 1959 level, and the 1963 mean was just a few per cent higher. This clearly demonstrates that even just a partial return to socio-economic normality (including the abolishment of communal kitchens and the restitution of private plots and local markets) was more important than a specific per capita supply, and that an early intervention – be it reduced grain transfers from the countryside, grain shipments from better-off provinces, or a request for foreign food assistance – could have limited the famine's extent and converted the event just to a large-scale outbreak of serious malnutrition.

Subsequently, the disruptions of the Cultural Revolution prevented any sustained improvement of food supply: in 1966 its per capita availability finally

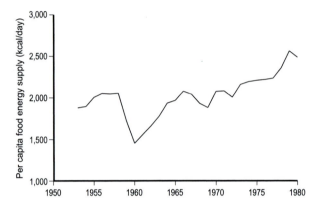

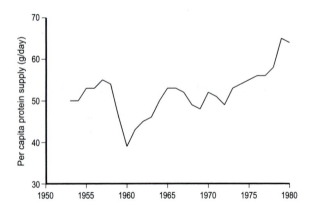

Figure 3.1 Average per capita availability of food energy and dietary protein, 1950–1980

Source: Plotted from data in Piazza (1983).

reached the 1958 level, but then it fell once again, and did not permanently surpass the 1958 level until 1974 (Piazza 1983; FAO 2002). Two generations after the catastrophe, China's Communist Party still toes the original exculpatory line: three years of natural catastrophes caused the suffering. China's own official statistics make this argument untenable (SSB 1980). In 1959 the area affected by drought and flood (with grain yields 30 per cent below the expected mean) was nearly 10 per cent less than in 1957, the year of the previous record grain harvest (see Figure 3.2). The situation got worse in 1960 and 1961 with, respectively, 18 and 20 per cent of agricultural land affected by natural disasters – but three decades later, in 1991 and again in 1994, with drought and floods reaching their highest extent in modern China's history, there was only a marginal effect on overall food supply, as the 1994 grain harvest was less than 3 per cent below the 1993 record (NBS 2000) (Figure 3.2).

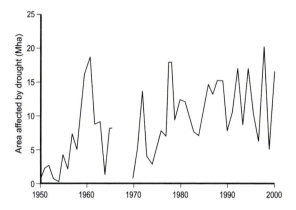

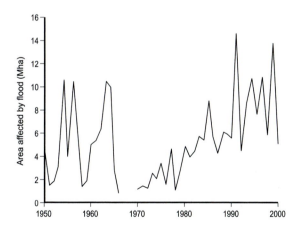

Figure 3.2 Areas annually affected by drought and flood in China, 1950–2000

Source: Plotted from data regularly published in *China Statistical Yearbook*.

There is no doubt that given the much weaker production capacity during the late 1950s (hardly any mechanization of field tasks, almost no chemical fertilizers or pesticides) the natural disasters of 1960–1961 would have caused much more widespread chronic malnutrition and more acute seasonal hunger than would the similarly widespread droughts and floods of the 1990s. But they alone would have caused only a small fraction of the eventual toll – and most of that could have been prevented by an early appeal for international food donations. But in their ultimate disdain for tens of millions of starving people, the government continued to export grain, and the famine remained publicly unacknowledged by the rulers.

This made it so much easier for outsiders to discount eyewitness reports of Chinese refugees reaching Hong Kong, and of Tibetans fleeing to India and Nepal, and it helped Western apologists for Mao's warped social experiment to deny the famine's very existence or to denigrate its impact. Wes Pedersen, at that time a US foreign service officer in Hong Kong, wrote in 1960 a report entitled *Famine: Grim Specter over China* for the US Information Agency, where it was rejected as irresponsible speculation (Pedersen 2000). Cheng's (1961) report on famine and its repercussions was published in Taiwan, but it was ignored in the West. Instead, Werner Klatt, writing in *The China Quarterly*, estimated that the average daily per capita food energy supply in China in 1960–1961 was 1,850–1,900kcal, and that only "certain cases of malnutrition in deficit areas…have given currency to the erroneous view that the whole of China is suffering from conditions of starvation. There is no evidence to support such a contention" (Klatt 1961a: 69). And in the journal's next issue he reiterated that "malnutrition is not a general feature of the Chinese scene", and argued that "it would be prudent" not to overestimate the impact of "mediocre harvests" of the past two years (Klatt 1961b: 126). What a commendable prudence, indeed!

More than a decade after the famine's end, a Harvard nutrition expert wrote, after a brief visit to China, that famine was avoided even during the bad harvests from 1956 to 1961 because of a careful distribution of food to the neediest groups (Timmer 1976). The great famine was revealed to the world in its horrific extent only during the 1980s. First, in 1980, China finally published the basic results of its 1964 population census, which could be compared with the more accurate 1953 census. But only when single-year age distributions from the country's first highly reliable census taken in 1982 became available, and when adjustments were made to official fertility and mortality rates, was it possible to estimate the total number of excess deaths (Coale 1981; Aird 1982; Ashton *et al.* 1984). Explicitly derived estimates of excess deaths range from 16.5 million (Coale 1981) to about 30 million (Ashton *et al.* 1984; Banister 1987). In contrast, the retrospectively reported, and undoubtedly grossly underestimated, official mortalities result in a total of 15 million deaths, while some undocumented Chinese estimates offer totals in excess of 40 million.

Unless the still inaccessible Chinese archives contain convincing evidence whose free scrutiny could settle the matter, it is most unlikely that we will ever know the actual death toll of the famine. This is hardly surprising, given the well-known uncertainties in using secondary information to quantify mortality during many past famines. And two recent African famines show how difficult it is to come up with consensus figures, even when first-hand information is available. There were many independent observers present in the Sahel between 1972 and 1975, as the region experienced a major famine whose toll was initially estimated at well over a million but was eventually put at about 600,000 people (Comité Information Sahel 1975; Franke and Chasin 1980). Even more remarkably, when several Western agencies actually undertook field studies of prevailing mortality during the height of the Somalian famine in 1991–1992, their crude mortality rates for the total population ranged from 7.3–23.4 per 10,000 per day, and age-specific mortalities for children younger than five years ranged even more widely, from 16.4 to 81 per 10,000 per day (Boss *et al.* 1994).

What is surprising is that even after the extent of the famine's toll became known, and after a great deal of previously guarded information about China's Maoist past became available during the most liberal spells of Deng's modernization, the world has paid inexplicably little attention to the event whose death toll stands out even against the background of the massive man-made mortality of the twentieth century. A truly astonishing example of this indifference is the 1997 edition of *Encyclopedia Britannica*. All its entry on *Famine* has to say about modern China is this: "famine also continued to plague China into the 20th century: more than 3,000,000 persons starved to death in 1928–29" (Encyclopedia Britannica 1997: 674). And, on the following page, the encyclopedia claims that the "tabulation below is relatively complete for the last 200 years" – yet the table does not contain *any* mention of the world's greatest famine!

Moreover, China's great famine received only marginal attention from both students of famines and Sinologists. This is particularly clear in comparison with relatively well-studied nineteenth- and twentieth-century Indian famines, especially the Bengal famine of 1943–1944 (India Famine Inquiry Commission 1945; Gangrade 1973; Uppal 1984). Incredibly, *Agricola*, the most extensive index summarizing publications on food production and nutrition, does not contain a single entry on China's famine for the period 1970–2002. Carl Riskin was the first Western Sinologist to review the event, in a chapter on China's food and development written for a book about hunger in history (Riskin 1990). In the same year Lin published his explanation of China's "agricultural crisis", arguing that it was due primarily to the changed nature of collectivization whereby the self-enforcing contract that prevailed before 1958 could not be sustained and productivity collapsed (Lin 1990). A year later Friedman *et al.* (1991) took a closer look at the famine as part of their revealing history of a Hebei village, stressing that "death toll was not a sudden, one-time error resulting from unique policy blunders", but rather "the culmination of institutionalized processses, values, and interests that had previously generated frightening consequences".

In contrast, Chang and Wen (1997) blamed communal dining as the key causal factor of the famine. Yang (1996) devoted about a third of his book on calamity and reform in China to description and analysis of the famine. And the only compendium of articles written by Sinologists and devoted solely to the famine was published as a special issue of *China Economic Review* in the fall of 1998 (Johnson 1998; Riskin 1998; Lin and Yang 1998; Yang and Su 1998; Chang and Wen 1998). There is also a Chinese-language famine website containing a few dozen reproductions of various public documents from the late 1950s and the early 1960s, and a slowly growing number of post-1980 publications, as well as a collection of (poor quality) images reproduced from newspapers and posters (Chinafamine.org 2002).

As the fortieth anniversary of the famine approached I felt that a much broader dissemination of some basic facts and questions regarding the world's most devastating, and overwhelmingly man-made, famine was in order. And because I agree with Rhodes (1988) that ideologically motivated man-made death is probably the most overlooked cause of modern mortality, I welcomed the opportunity to publish such a paper in the world's leading medical journal, whose pages have been consistently open to writings and ideas far beyond the traditional medical confines (Smil 1999b).

China's great famine: 40 years later

Summary points

The largest famine in human history took place in China during 1959–1961.

Although drought was a contributory factor, this was largely a man-made catastrophe for which Mao Zedong bears the greatest responsibility.

We will never know the precise number of casualties, but the best demographic reconstructions indicate about 30 million dead.

Two generations later, China has yet to openly examine the causes and consequences of the famine.

Forty years ago China was in the middle of the world's largest famine: between the spring of 1959 and the end of 1961 some 30 million Chinese starved to death and about the same number of births were lost or postponed. The famine had overwhelmingly ideological causes, rating alongside the two world wars as a prime example of what Richard Rhodes labeled public man-made death, perhaps the most overlooked cause of twentieth-century mortality.[1] Two generations later China, which has been rapidly modernizing since the early 1980s, is economically successful and producing adequate amounts of food. Yet it has still not undertaken an open, critical examination of this unprecedented tragedy.

Origins of famine

The origins of the famine can be traced to Mao Zedong's decision, supported by the leadership of the Chinese Communist Party, to launch the Great Leap Forward. This mass mobilization of the country's huge population was to achieve in just a few years economic advances that had taken other nations many decades to accomplish.[2] Mao, beholden to Stalinist ideology that stressed the key role of heavy industry, made steel production the centerpiece of this deluded effort. Instead of working in the fields, tens of millions of peasants were ordered to mine local deposits of iron ore and limestone, to cut trees for charcoal, to build simple clay furnaces, and to smelt metal. This frenzied enterprise did not produce steel, but mostly lumps of brittle cast iron unfit for even simple tools. Peasants were forced to abandon all private food production, and newly formed agricultural communes planted less land to grain, which at that time was the source of more than 80 per cent of China's food energy.[3]

At the same time, fabricated reports of record grain harvests were issued to demonstrate the superiority of communal farming. These gross exaggerations were then used to justify the expropriation of higher shares of grain for cities and the establishment of wasteful communal mess halls serving free meals.[4] In reality, the grain harvest plummeted (Figure 3.3); and since supply and demand of food before 1958 were almost equal, by the spring of 1959 there was famine in a third of China's provinces.

As an essentially social catastrophe, the famine showed clear marks of omission, commission, and provision. These three attributes recur in all modern man-made famines.[5] The greatest omission was the failure of China's rulers to acknowledge the famine and promptly to secure foreign food aid. Studies of famines show how easily they can be ended (or prevented) once the government decides to act, but the Chinese government took nearly three years to act. Taking away all means of private food production (in some places even cooking utensils), forcing peasants into mismanaged communes, and continuing food exports were the worst acts of commission. Preferential supply of food to cities and to the ruling elite was the deliberate act of selective provision.

These actions are perfect illustrations of Sen's thesis about the critical link in the political alienation of the governors from the governed:

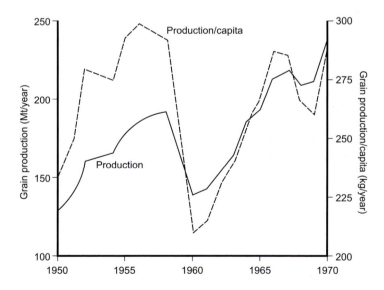

Figure 3.3 Total and per capita grain production in China, 1950–1970

The direct penalties of a famine are borne by one group of people and political decisions are taken by another. The rulers never starve. But when a government is accountable to the local populace it too has good reasons to do its best to eradicate famines. Democracy, via electoral politics, passes on the price of famines to the rulers as well.[6]

There was no such link in Mao's China.

Weather only exacerbated the suffering. Official accounts still blame the natural catastrophes for the suffering but China's own statistics belie this explanation.[7] Undoubtedly, the drought of 1960–1961 would have lowered grain supply in the worst affected provinces, but by itself it would have caused only a small fraction of the eventual nationwide death toll. During the 1990s the worst droughts and floods in China's modern history had only a marginal effect on the country's adequate food supply. Only a return to more rational economic policies after 1961, including imports of grain, ended the famine.

China's opening up to the world made a key difference. The first business deal signed after US president Nixon's visit to Beijing in 1972 was an order for thirteen of the world's largest and most modern, American-designed, nitrogen fertilizer plants. More purchases of such plant followed, and China became the world's largest producer of nitrogenous fertilizers. The first major change initiated by the reformist faction of the Communist Party in 1979, less than three years after Mao's death, was to dissolve agricultural communes and free farm prices. By 1984 all food rationing was lifted in the cities, and China's average per capita food supply rose to within 5 per cent of Japan's comfortable mean.[8]

The extent of the famine

The true extent of the famine was not revealed to the world until the publication of single-year age distributions from the country's first highly reliable population census in 1982. These data made it possible to estimate the total number of excess deaths between 1959 and 1961, and the first calculations by American demographers put the toll at between 16.5 and 23 million.[9] More detailed later studies came up with 23 to 30 million excess deaths, and unpublished Chinese materials hint at totals closer to 40 million.[10–12] We will never know the actual toll, because the official Chinese figures for the three famine years greatly underestimate both the fall in fertility and the rise in mortality, and because we cannot accurately reconstruct these vital statistics (Figure 3.4).

The lack of accuracy is as expected. All death tolls cited for major famines have large margins of error. This is true even for events unfolding amid unprecedented publicity. An attempt to discern a coherent picture of morbidity, mortality and nutritional status during the 1991–1992 famine in Somalia, an effort based on twenty-three separate field studies, ended in failure.[13] Similar controversies surround the recent estimates of the excess deaths in Iraq attributable to economic sanctions after the first Gulf War.[14]

The need for open discussion

But no amount of additional information and no new and more sophisticated demographic analyses can change the fundamental conclusion: Mao's delusionary policies caused by far the largest famine in human history. Yet in contrast to other great famines of the twentieth century (Ukraine 1932–1933, Bengal 1943–1944), the causes of the Chinese famine and an attribution of responsibility for its depth and duration have never been openly discussed in the afflicted nation. Beyond a narrow circle of China experts, the famine has also been virtually ignored by Western scholars and politicians. The need for moral examination and historical closure is obvious. Eventually the country will have to examine the causes and consequences of the tragedy, whose magnitude surpasses the combined toll of all other famines China has experienced during the past two centuries.

How could this famine have lasted so long? How tenable is it to excuse the actions of so many people throughout the party and state bureaucracy by blaming solely their leader? Had they no other choice but to follow orders and to carry out, often against resistance, mindless collectivization and reduced planting of grain, to falsify harvest statistics, and to forcibly take grain away from evidently starving peasants? Germany has spent two generations trying to under-stand the horrors of the Third Reich and to atone for its transgressions. Russia

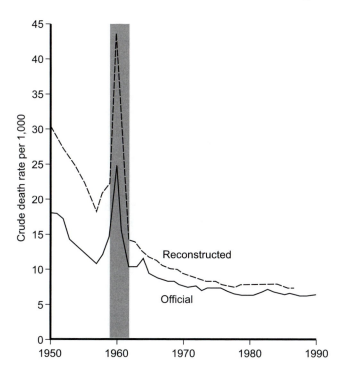

Figure 3.4 Officially reported and reconstructed mortality in China, 1950–1990 (famine period is shaded)

began to face its dark past soon after Stalin's death, when Khrushchev opened the gates of the gulag and had the dictator's embalmed corpse removed from the Red Square mausoleum. China's turn is yet to come.

If, as is likely, such an accounting does not happen soon, the direct memories of survivors will be lost. Of course, the archives of the Chinese Communist Party and of its enormous secret police apparatus will eventually be opened and yield, much like the party and KGB archives in Russia since 1991, some of their long-hidden secrets. Many facts we will never know. A leading Chinese demographer found that even casual surveys of villages in areas that experienced the worst starvation show an unusually high extent of mental impairment among adults born during the famine years (Xizhe Peng, personal communication). Given the importance of nutrition for the development of mental capacities during infancy and early childhood, this was a predictable tragedy.[15] We will never know how many millions of survivors throughout China have had their lives twisted in this terrible way.

Finally, what are we to make of the Western indifference to the great famine? Eyewitness stories of refugees who fled to Hong Kong were widely dismissed and rarely reported during the famine years. Two generations later, a journalistic account is the only fairly comprehensive volume on the famine published in the West.[16] Incredibly, the 1997 edition of the *New Encyclopedia Britannica* does not even list the catastrophe in its tabulation of famines of the past 200 years.[17] An in-depth scholarly history of the famine has yet to be written.

Unanswered questions

Little has changed regarding our understanding of famines in general, and of China's great famine in particular, since the *BMJ* paper was published in 1999. Recent attempts to evaluate the toll of Asia's latest famine, one on China's very border, confirm how difficult it is to come up with any consensus when the offending regime remains (although in this case not completely) in a non-cooperative denial. Estimates of North Korea's famine-related deaths in the period between 1995 and 2000 (based on a variety of evidence, including refugee surveys and some assessments of child nutrition carried out by the World Food Programme inside the country) range over an order of magnitude from less than 300,000 to 3.5 million, with the most likely total of 0.6–1 million (Goodkind and West 2001).

And I found a new book by Davis (2001) – which identifies the combination of a series of El Niño-Southern Oscillation (ENSO) episodes and a deliberately murderous conspiracy of "liberal capitalists" as the cause of large-scale famines that swept late nineteenth-century India and China – relevant not for what it wholesales (a simplistic ideological zeal), but for what it omits. Namely that the right policies are more important in determining the outcome of food production than even relatively severe natural catastrophes. In closing my review of Davis' book I used the Chinese example to illustrate what such measures can do to combat climatic teleconnections, or any other natural disasters, in the modern world (Smil 2001a: 645):

In 1980, after decades of Maoist misery, China began disbanding the communes and privatizing the farming. Does Davis know that just a few years later, when the powerful 1982–1983 El Niño was affecting its climate, the country had two years of record grain harvests, which made it possible to abolish the food rationing that had lasted since 1954? Anybody out there willing to credit this to a Wall Street conspiracy?

As for the great famine itself, it remains one of the least studied, and certainly one of the least known, catastrophes in modern history. Beijing's unending Communist gerontocracy has no interest in opening party and secret police archives and giving permission for nationwide research that could still salvage some of the steadily disappearing evidence of that terrible catastrophe. Western moral judgment, so demanding of Germans, so critical of Russian and Japanese transgressions, remains almost completely suspended, or exceedingly muted, where the inhumanity of the Maoist regime *vis-à-vis* its own people, and the apologetics of the current Chinese rulers is concerned. I believe that the magnitude of the suffering (in this respect it is clearly irrelevant if the toll was 40 or "just" 15 million) demands that we see this entire matter in clear moral terms. That is why I am both disappointed and surprised that the few scholarly contributions devoted to the better understanding of the event have been so preoccupied with searching for the purported primary cause.

I feel it is both counterproductive and distracting to argue about the famine's primary cause. Attempting to elevate a single, albeit very important, factor to the primary causal role is to do disservice to a patently complex historical reality. This is not to deny that the search for the primary cause has been often ingenious and painstaking – but ultimately all such calls disappoint. Several studies of total factor productivity of China's agriculture show convincingly the sudden drop of the measure in 1959. But it is one thing to agree with Lin's (1990) hypothesis that the removal of the exit right from communes enacted in that year triggered this productivity drop – and another to conclude that this productivity drop was the cause of the famine. After all, a comparison of total productivity indices calculated by five different researchers, and included in Lin's paper, shows little difference between values for 1960, the peak famine year, and 1962–1964. Moreover, three of these series put the productivities of the early 1970s *below* the values prevailing during the three famine years, and much below the performance during the years of the pre-1958 voluntary collectivization.

Communal dining, with participation rates as high as 95–98 per cent in the most radically governed provinces (including Henan and Sichuan), clearly led to an immense waste of food, but Chang and Wen's (1997) thesis, that this "consumption inefficiency" caused the famine, and that it led to its onset already in the fall of 1958 after a record autumn harvest, is difficult to accept. As Lin and Yang (1998) rightly point out, it is most unlikely that food that would normally last six months would be uniformly consumed everywhere in just two months to cause the first famine deaths before the end of 1958. A variant of this explanation is Yang's (1996) "loyalty compensation" hypothesis restated two years later by Yang and Su (1998). This hypothesis states that the communal dining reached its highest levels in provinces with lower shares of party members because those who aspired to join the party would demonstrate their loyalty to the central government by becoming excessively radical. But as the rural membership shares were very low everywhere (on the average less than 1.5 per cent) this explanation is not persuasive.

Riskin (1998: 116), who looked critically at the attempts to find the famine's cause, summed up the failure of these efforts well by noting that any closer examination leads us back "to a general set of extreme policies, rather than to any one key component, as cause of famine". New research will hardly add new causes to a long list of major factors whose dynamic interaction triggered and sustained the famine: mistaken belief in the existence of large grain surpluses; the resulting reduction in the area planted to staple grains; massive and prolonged transfers of rural labor into dubious industrial undertakings in the countryside; temporary large-scale migration of peasants to cities; strong urban bias of the leadership leading to excessive procurement of grain for the cities (nearly 25 per cent higher in 1959 than in 1958); continuing grain exports (net shipments reached a record of 4.2Mt in 1959 and were still 2.7Mt in 1960, the year of the severest death rate); clearly above-average rates of natural disasters, particularly of drought; and the absence of normal civil society with free and rapid reporting of food shortages and first signs of famine.

Climate aside, all of these factors have, of course, a common denominator: the ruling party whose policies triggered the crisis, whose initial denial of mass deaths deepened it, whose inexcusably belated response prolonged the suffering, and whose refusal to admit responsibility even more than forty years after the famine ended prevents any historic closure. Even if all the proposed causal hypotheses outlined above were true, a normal society would move rapidly to correct either the sudden onset of indolence caused by forced collectivization or a runaway tragedy of commons induced by unlimited access to food. A bad policy could generate a problem, even a crisis, but it alone would not suffice to perpetuate such an extraordinary, prolonged and widespread spell of dying, as a determined and timely response would limit both the extent and the severity of suffering.

The undeniable fact that these normal corrective processes took such an inordinately long time to make the difference is clearly the responsibility of the ruling Communist regime, and as at that time that dictatorship was under the near-total command of a single man, the most fundamental cause of the famine is clear enough: Mao's delusions, which could be acted out due to his near-imperial command of power (Li 1994). This is not a simplistic personification of a complex event, merely a recognition of historical reality. Productivity slumps and communal kitchens were no more the real causes of China's great famine than the KGB, kolkhozes and the gulag were the causes of Russia's post-1929 suffering. As in so many other cases in history, a pupil who despised his teacher still learned the lessons well enough to surpass him. Accurate quantification of the victims of the Stalinist and the Maoist terror is impossible, but their kindred genesis is all too clear.

From subsistence to satiety: food supply and agricultural transformation

More than a decade after China recovered from the world's greatest famine and began its opening-up to the West, we still did not know the country's real nutritional status. Official propaganda and naively uncritical visitors were supplying a predictable stream of encouraging reports, but they did not support those claims with any representative figures. My first contributions to a better understanding of China's food situation attempted to quantify the basics. My quantifications of the country's average per capita food supply and its basic composition in 1957, the last "normal" pre-Leap year, and in 1974, the twenty-fifth year of Communist China's existence, were to show the lack of progress in feeding China's people over a course of nearly one generation. And a comparison of the most likely supply rate with an estimate of approximate average food requirements of the mid-1970s indicated the virtual absence of any nutritional surplus.

As in the case of my early energy work, these were ambitious goals given the paucity of available data, but in retrospect my calculations of average food supply and requirements turned out to be very representative of the actual situation in the mid-1970s. They clearly indicated the precarious nature of China's food supply, and hence the need for its fundamental improvement. One thing I would have never predicted at that time is how rapidly such an improvement would come. Being acutely aware of the fact that only a very thin, and regionally much tattered, safety cushion separated China of the 1970s from massive malnutrition, I watched the *de facto* privatization of China's farming – the birth of *baogan daohu* (household responsibility system) in Sichuan and Anhui and its diffusion throughout the country – first with much hope and later with a great deal of satisfaction.

As soon as the first new statistics were published during the late 1970s I began to evaluate them and to use them in tracing the rising supply of food. Subsequently, as China's average per capita food energy availability approached that of Japan and stabilized at this fairly comfortable level, I kept returning to this important topic regularly, and published papers or book chapters dealing exclusively with China's food supply and requirements, or pieces that set these matters in a wider context, every two or three years for the next two decades. Selections from these writings (Smil 1977a, 1978) trace China's road from nutritional subsistence to levels of food supply unprecedented in the country's long history.

Food availability in 1957 and 1974

During the past few years food production in the People's Republic of China (PRC) has been portrayed in impressive terms. The leader of the PRC's delegation to the 1974 United Nations World Food Conference in Rome informed the plenary session that the country had "ensured the supply of basic means of subsistence, stable food prices and adequate food for everyone" (Hao 1974). Numerous dispatches of the New China News Agency, radio broadcasts, newspaper and journal articles repeat the stories of record harvests, high stable yields, grain self-sufficiency and food abundance.

Many Westerners admitted for a quick guided tour of the country concur with these judgments. Remarks on healthy, well-nourished and content people crowding the streets of the large cities and cultivating the verdant countryside have become a trademark of visitors' reports (Galbraith 1973; MacLaine 1975). However, there is relatively little quantitative evidence cited to support these statements and impressions. Information on the per capita availability of food energy – the most essential indicator of a country's nutritional status – is particularly rare.

Persistent scarcity of reliable primary statistics is, of course, the main reason for this paucity of quantitative evidence. Yet a quantification of the PRC's food availability and per capita consumption, though difficult, is possible and a range of reasonably representative values can be obtained by incorporating plausible alternative input estimates. The process entails the preparation of food balance sheets and their comparison with population totals.

Food balance sheets

Construction of a food balance sheet starts with production figures for all-important edible crops, with total counts of domestic animals and total fish catches; these figures are then corrected for trade in raw and processed foodstuffs to establish the gross domestic food availability. Domestic utilization of crops is subdivided into food and non-food uses (seed, feed, industrial manufacture), quantities wasted during storage and transportation are subtracted and appropriate extraction rates are used to convert the raw products into processed foods; average slaughter rates, carcass weights and output rates are applied to animal counts in order to derive meat, milk and egg production.

Balance sheets provide estimates of food supplies available for human consumption at the retail level, that is either as the food leaves retail shops or otherwise enters the household – in China's villages mostly from communal allotment or from a private plot. Balance sheets do not account for losses during household storage, preparation and cooking and for any leftovers fed to domestic animals and pets or thrown away (Schulte *et al.* 1973); they give no indication of seasonal variations, diet differences in various population groups (socio-economic, regional, religious) and consumption differences within a household (den Hartog 1972). In general, a food balance sheet is thus to be considered as a good, and a rather liberal, approximation, as a revealing summary of a nation's nutritional status.

To enable a time comparison of per capita food availability in the PRC, the comprehensive food balance sheets were prepared for the years 1957 and 1974. The first year marked the end of the first Five Year Plan – and it was also the last year for which a relative abundance of reasonable statistics is available; 1974 was, of course, the twenty-fifth year of the PRC's existence, a convenient time to assess the country's progress.

Per capita food availability

Complete food balance sheets give the country some 200Mt of plant and 13Mt of animal food in 1957; in 1974 these totals increased to just over 300Mt and to 25Mt respectively. Depending on which of the two sets of consistent population estimates – by L. Orleans or J.S. Aird (Orleans 1975) – is used, these aggregates translate into 2,073–2,102kcal per day per capita in 1957 and 2,070–2,256kcal in 1974. These differences in per capita consumption grow even larger (1,966–2,211kcal in 1957, and 2,079–2,256kcal in 1974) when the food energy availability is considered in terms of a range bracketed by values ±5 per cent around the calculated figures.

It is quite interesting to compare these per capita values with available pre-war averages. J.L. Buck's (1937) rural surveys resulted in average daily supply of 2,537kcal/person. Liu and Yeh (1965) argued persuasively that a 10 per cent reduction of this figure (i.e. to 2,283kcal) would bring it nearer to the actual nationwide average. They themselves calculated daily supply of energy at 2,130kcal/person in 1933.

And it is also interesting to compare my mid-1970s calculations with the best possible retrospective reconstruction of China's food balance sheet undertaken by the FAO once the revised official Chinese statistics for the 1970s became available during the 1980s. FAO (2002) now credits China with average daily supply of 2,073kcal/capita in 1974, compared to the range of 2,070–2,256kcal/capita I published in 1976. The relatively high value of the upper rate is due entirely to the fact that in 1974 there was a gap of 76 million (844–920 million) in the best available estimates of China's population, and the use of a low population total in the denominator naturally boosted the average rate.

Absolute values of food availability that I was able to calculate in 1974 were virtually identical with FAO's later reconstruction, and if I had known the actual population total for that year (908.6 million) my calculation of average daily per capita supply (2,096kcal/capita) would have differed from FAO's rate by a mere 1 per cent. As for the basic breakdown, the two estimates are, once again, identical: FAO attributes 94 per cent of all available food energy coming from plant foods; my calculation showed 93.5 per cent. This proves that even at a time when only very limited, and in addition often highly distorted, information was coming from China it was possible to use it in a critical way and to derive revealing conclusions.

Notwithstanding the inevitable errors in any calculations of this type, as well as the necessity to operate with value ranges rather than with single figures, the quantitative evidence presented demands the conclusion that very little – if any – improvement has taken place in average Chinese per capita food consumption between 1957 and 1974. Average food availabilities in 1957 and 1974 certainly do not indicate any chronic, massive malnutrition – but neither do they reflect any substantial advances in the country's nutrition during the past two decades or in comparison with the prewar levels.

Food requirements

For many generations the average per capita food supply in affluent countries has been surpassing any conceivable dietary requirements of largely sedentary populations. In contrast, in subsistence economies where food supply is nearly always limited and where physical exertion is the norm for a large share of the population, it is not enough to know the average per capita energy availability in order to appraise a country's food status. In all such cases food supply must be compared with energy needs that are a function of age, sex, weight and physical activity (FAO/WHO/UNU 1985). None of this information was available for China of the mid-1970s, but I tried my best to reconstruct these needs.

I started with standard physiological accounts based on the standard assumption of moderate physical activity. Then I took into consideration large shares of China's population engaged in tasks that required heavy, rather than moderate, energy expenditure: most field chores, from plowing and hoeing to mowing, loading and canal-digging, belong to this category. This reconstruction strongly suggested a food energy deficit in 1957, while the slightly better nutritional situation by 1974 was probably just sufficient to cover food energy demand. The composition of the average diet (plant vs. animal origin) did not change significantly, and "any improvement in Chinese nutrition that took place is probably the result of more equitable food allocation rather than of increases in farm output which have not significantly outpaced population growth" (Smil 1977a: 13).

Ruling elites aside, uniformly low incomes – the shared poverty of Maoist China – precluded any major differences in access to food, but the most important reason for the relatively equitable food sharing was the nationwide rationing of all staple, as well as many minor, foodstuffs. This is how I described the situation in 1978, the twenty-fifth year of China's food rationing.

Food rationing

For foreign visitors, the country has the best Peking duck and repeated ten-course banquets with lean pork, poultry, seafood and *maotai* (Smil 1978). For the "revolutionary masses" – when things go well – there are ubiquitous ration tickets (tied, and tying their bearers, to the place of their permanent residence), fluctuating allocations of grain, standing in line – pots in hand – for bean curd when available, one egg per person per week, the black market – and an anticipation of the New Year festival, with its special supply of glutinous rice, melon seeds, black mushrooms and red dates.

Rationing of all major foodstuffs has been in force since November 1953. Tickets are issued for all staple grains, meat and sugar – and for vegetal oil, soybean sauce, bean curd (three kinds – fresh, spiced and dried), bean sprouts, mushrooms, water chestnuts, fish (fresh and salted), string beans, potatoes and liquor (Ch'en 1978). Ration tickets have thus become China's second currency, more important than money itself, and as such they are offered for good prices on the black market, traded in streets, stolen and forged. Rules of the involved rationing system – quantities and restrictions of the purchase – change in response to local economic and political conditions, and actual amounts of allotted food may be far below the standard levels.

Grain rationing is complex. The urban population is divided into nine categories (according to age and labor exertion) and receives four different certificates and two kinds of ration coupons. Rural rations are structured differently (there is so-called "basic grain" and additional "work point grain", purchasable with accumulated commune work points), and can be changed into urban rations only with a special permit that acts as a very efficient check on migration. It is also much more difficult to exchange rural rations for provincial or national grain ration coupons, which are necessary to buy meals in restaurants or any grain products while traveling.

Monthly rations

The standardized average monthly ration for the general public and children over ten years of age is 12.5 kilograms of rice in the south and 13.75kg of grain products (mainly wheat flour) in the north; light laborers should receive 16–17.5kg and hard laborers 20–22kg of grain or grain products each month. In the north, an increasing portion of this allotment has been in coarse grain rather than in preferred wheat flour; a recent report mentions that while the privileged Beijing rations are composed of 50 per cent wheat flour, 30 per cent rice and 20 per cent millet, kaoliang and corn, Shenyang residents receive the same cereals in the far less palatable proportion of 20:10:70 (Broyelle and Broyelle 1978).

Meat tickets and fish tickets are issued only for urban residents. Each month, Communist party cadres get 1.5kg of pork, people in Beijing, undoubtedly the best supplied city in China, may purchase as much as 1kg, while the rations in remote provincial centers are only a half or a quarter of this amount. In many places, people eat meat only during the New Year and Qing Ming festivals or at the time of family celebrations. Sugar rations fluctuate considerably with availability, up to no more than 0.5kg per capita per month. Vegetal oil, so essential for deep-frying and stir-frying, is rationed in truly meager amounts: although the privileged cadres may get as much as 1kg each month, the normal Peking rate is only 0.5kg monthly; in most other cities, the ration is a mere 100–200 grams, and in rural areas as little as 50g! Drastic oil shortages are also illustrated by the fact that oil tickets are issued for quantities as small as 10 and 25g.

A comparison in easy-to-visualize units for those who have never stir-fried a Chinese dish, indeed never cooked at all: 25g represents two scant tablespoons of oil, while about three tablespoons are needed just to stir-fry properly one dish of vegetables for a small family meal, and normally at least 2–3 such dishes would be prepared. A no-less-revealing comparison can be made in annual per capita terms. In 1978 even Beijing's privileged rate of 6kg/capita was, for example, less than a third of Italy's average supply of cooking oil.

Rations are loosened or temporarily removed only to stock up for festivals. For the 1977 New Year festival, Tianjin had 45 per cent more liquor than in 1976 (normal festival rate: 150–400g per adult); there were more candies, cakes and fresh vegetables in Beijing; and each Shanghai family could buy ten preserved eggs, half a kilogram of salted jellyfish and shelled peanuts, and unrestricted amounts of pork and frozen shrimp, whose exports were temporarily diverted for home consumption. After the festival, it was back to staples.

As I was writing these lines in the summer of 1978, the tide was just about to turn. In December of that year Deng Xiaoping accomplished his final return to power and, to the surprise of most experts abroad and to the deep gratitude of hundreds of millions of people inside China, began his sweeping economic reforms with the most urgent shift, the abolition of communal farming. The man who a quarter century earlier was a leading executor of Mao's ruthless campaign against landlords and rich peasants (that brought death to hundreds of thousands and that laid the foundations for the communization of China's farming) decided that to "get rich is glorious". But these rural reforms actually started even before they were sanctioned and promoted by a new regime. Yang (1996) is undoubtedly correct when he argues that profound disillusionment with the communal farming produced by the suffering of the Great Leap Famine provided a powerful impetus for the rapid dismantling of command farming, and he demonstrates that the first steps in this direction were taken well before the policy became official in the very provinces (Anhui, Sichuan) that suffered most during the great famine of 1959–1961.

Agricultural reforms and improved food supply

The results of this agricultural transformation were unexpectedly rapid. Between 1978 and 1984 the average annual growth rate of agricultural output rose to 7.7 from 2.9 per cent for the years 1952–1978, and decollectivization accounted for about half of this jump and the increase in state procurement prices for most of the rest: other factors played only a small role (Lin 1992). I have felt many times during the past two decades that the importance of this fundamental shift has not been sufficiently appreciated, both inside China and abroad, both as it was taking place as well as in retrospect: a better life is so easily taken for granted. In 1981 I concluded that "new farming policies are already bringing in a greater supply of non-staple foods and, given political stability, they should appreciably improve Chinese diets during the next generation" (Smil 1981: 67). At the same time, I had to reiterate that "the quantitative evidence shows an uncomfortably small difference between availability and need". Just a few years later I could say with some confidence that, on the average, the Chinese had, finally, enough to eat but I also had to point out that the adequate nationwide mean conceals major, and widening, regional and socio-economic disparities (Smil 1985).

In 1986 I prepared a new food balance sheet for the year 1983, compared it with a slightly higher new set of nutritional figures published by the State Statistical Bureau, and found that even my conservative calculations put China's average per capita food supply less than 10 per cent behind Japan's comfortable mean (Smil 1986). The following excerpts and comments trace these shifts over a period of two decades, beginning with the food balance for the late 1970s (Smil 1981).

The food balance for China in 1978

Average per capita food supply amounted to 2,130kcal/day in 1978, and it provided 57g of protein and 25g of lipids. The cost of this plain diet to urban consumers is quite high. A typical urban working-class family of five spends about 60 per cent of its income on food, and for lower-income families the share is as much as 75 per cent. A typical worker's hourly wage will buy 3–4kg of cabbage in season, 0.75–1kg of medium-quality rice, 3–4 eggs, or 100–200g of pork.

By 1985 food claimed about 52 per cent of all household spending by an average urban family, and by 2000 the share was down to 42 per cent (NBS 2000), compared to 22 per cent in Japan (SB 2002). Food balance sheets show that no improvement of average individual consumption took place in the past two decades. In most of the intervening years the position was worse than during 1955–1958 and 1977–1979. Moreover, the mean food supply in 1977, or 1957, was no higher than during the good harvest years before the Japanese invasion in 1937: average Chinese food availability has thus remained virtually static for at least half a century (see Table 3.1).

Table 3.1　China's average daily food per capita availability, 1930s–1970s[a]

Year	Plant foods	Animal foods	Total
1929–1933[b]	2070	210	2280
1933[c]	1940	190	2130
1931–1937[d]	2073	153	2226
1949–1958[e]	–	–	2017
1957[f]	1962	113	2075
1964–1966[g]	1863	182	2045
1974[f]	1910	135	2045
1978[g]	1850	86	1936
1977–1978	1995	105	2130

Notes:

[a] Owing to the slightly different assumptions in constructing individual balance sheets and to the use of non-uniform energy equivalents in conversions, values in this table are not strictly comparable. They are just the best available quantitative appraisals of average food availability.

[b] J.L. Buck's (1937) figures, originally expressed in adult-male intake units, are based on a survey of 17,351 persons in 2,727 rural families in twenty-one provinces; as Liu and Yeh (1965) argue, Buck's values were reduced by 10 per cent to bring them closer to the national average.

[c] Liu and Yeh (1965).

[d] Shen (1951).

[e] Buck (1966).

[f] Smil (1977).

[g] FAO (1971).

[h] CIA (1979).

Major regional and temporal differences in food availability are perhaps best illustrated by the situation in Sichuan, China's most populous province: in 1976 there was a famine in the relatively rich Sichuan Basin, and only large grain transfers from other provinces prevented further starvation. Starvation in Sichuan in 1976 was confirmed by, at that time, Vice-Chairman Deng Xiaoping, himself a Sichuanese, in an interview with Han Suyin published in 1977 (Deng 1977). In 1980 the Chinese released the 1976 grain consumption figure for the province: just 180kg of unmilled grain per head (Xinhua 1980)

Many places in China's southwest and northwest appear to be especially poorly off. In Guizhou province, average peasant grain rations were only 76.8 per cent of the country's mean in 1976, implying an average daily food consumption per head of around 1,700kcal, clear evidence of malnutrition (Guizhou Provincial Service 1976). In northwestern loess areas of Gansu and Ningxia, peasants in some counties harvested only 100kg of grain per head and, by official admissions, are fed worse than during the war against Japan four decades ago (Tong and Tong 1978). A document of the Central Committee of the Chinese Communist Party (1979) admitted that in 1977 "more than 100 million people in rural areas suffered from a lack of grain". The country is a mosaic of regions where the population is fairly well-off, consuming little more than their essential energy requirements, and areas of either chronic (e.g. some parts of loess highland) or recurrent (e.g. frequently drought-stricken provinces of Henan and Anhui) shortages where food intake is, at best, sufficient to cover basic metabolic and activity needs but is hardly compatible with a vigorous and healthy life. These areas have had spells of famine and major malnutrition.

In spite of inevitable inaccuracies and approximations, the quantitative evidence shows an uncomfortably small difference between availability and need. This must be the cause of serious concern in a nation that cannot afford to rely on massive purchases of foreign food, and that is beset by many economic, social and environmental problems.

And this concern was fortunately uppermost in Deng Xiaoping's mind as he began reforming Maoist China. His new household responsibility system was used to dismantle communes, and while the peasants still could not own the land, they could now begin to increase agricultural productivity by using the comparative advantage of their soils or their skills rather than trying to fit them into a rigid muster of the Maoist grain-first policy. In less than five years, Deng Xiaoping's radical solution brought no less radically encouraging results (Smil 1985).

Benefits of the reform

Because "food and eating are central to the Chinese way of life and part of the Chinese ethos" (Chang 1977), the misery of Chinese life during the two decades between the late 1950s and the late 1970s is easy to understand. Steel output was rising, nuclear weapons and intercontinental ballistic missiles were tested, the Soviet Union turned from an eternal friend to an aggressive hegemonist, President Richard Nixon, the paragon of despicable American imperialism, was regaled in Qiang Jing's presence by revolutionary ballet, and Chinese leader Deng Xiaoping disappeared, reappeared, disappeared and reappeared again.

But all these momentous developments did nothing to sweeten the thin breakfast gruels, to bring in more fine wheat flour to steam tasty *mantou*, to make a flavorful chicken dish more than a once-a-year delicacy for hundreds of millions of people. Per capita consumption in 1976 or 1977 was virtually the same as it had been in 1956–1958, and was just marginally higher than average food availability during the years immediately preceding the start of the Sino-Japanese War in 1937. The record looked impressive only when compared to the depths of the massive 1959–1961 famine. And the outlook, after two decades of campaigns, exhortations, slogans and boastful unrealistic goals, was hardly promising.

Only a fundamental move could change those prospects. Such a move, sustained during its early faltering years and then intensified, was by far the most important development in China after Mao. The widespread diffusion of the household responsibility system (*baogan daohu*) has brought unprecedented average food availabilities, and has assured nutrition adequate to cover basic growth and activity needs of a larger share of the population than at any time since 1949. The key to this revolutionary change (the obvious question: would Soviet leaders dare to move so boldly and so rapidly to return common sense to farming?) was the spectacular increase in productivity; not infrequently a few people in a specialized household now produce in a few months the equivalent of the annual communal command farming products of dozens of peasants.

Specialized households started with relatively small-scale, short-term contracting for grains, oil or sugar crops, pork, poultry or fish, but both the scale and the variety of their operations expanded rapidly after 1982, and by now it might be hard to come up with a task that cannot be contracted or a service that is not offered to satisfy huge pent-up rural demand.

Deng's policy of "letting peasants produce what they can do best" has been an overwhelming success but, expectedly, its implementation was not without problems. Most obvious is the inevitability of increasing income disparities and, perhaps even more importantly, the "class" distribution of these benefits. Living standards are rising across the board but the formerly privileged household (commune leaders, managers of local enterprises, educated cadres) are benefiting even more.

And in spite of all the rapid diversification, typical Chinese diets remain monotonous, grain-dominated, and relatively rather expensive. But unlike very recent diets, today's diets appear to supply, on the average, enough energy and protein for normal growth and healthy life. As for average daily food energy, protein and lipid availabilities, these values are calculated at 2,700kcal and 85g and 40g, respectively, with plant foods supplying 95, 85 and 55 per cent of the totals.

The differences between food balance sheet averages and the value of actual daily intakes determined by periodical dietary surveys are at least 25 per cent and as much as 40 per cent in industrialized countries. In China one would expect less of a difference between the two values, and the results of a 1983 nutritional survey of 7,605 people in Beijing municipality (Xinhua 1983) indicate that the gap is between 8 and 15 per cent. Chinese publications have repeatedly mentioned that 2,600kcal are needed to satisfy average dietary requirements, but my calculations, based on the age–sex and occupational distributions from the 1982 census and on new measurements of energy expenditure levels, indicate that the most likely mean should be around 2,300kcal. By 1983, if not by 1982, the Chinese had, finally, enough to eat.

This is, of course, *baogan's* greatest achievement. But there are at least 90 million people, mostly in the northwest and the southwest, who, according to an official appraisal cited by Deng Xiaoping, still do not have enough to eat. While the average diet was still of a relatively poor quality, its magnitude was rapidly approaching the level of Japan's supply (Smil 1986).

Closing on Japan and continuing shortfalls

By 1984 per capita availability of rice was about 30 per cent above the 1977 level, the harvest of wheat doubled, that of oilseeds nearly tripled, per capita meat production rose by almost 89 per cent and sugar refining nearly doubled (Smil 1986). Such changes in a mere six years would have been remarkable anywhere; in China, coming after a generation of stagnation at levels of bare subsistence, they were truly revolutionary.

This greatly improved performance has put China into a new category. As shown in the comparison of principal food availability trends in China, India and Japan since 1950, the three countries were at a surprisingly similar level in the early 1950s, and Chinese and Japanese availabilities were virtually identical by 1957 (Figure 3.5). Afterwards, Japan's rapidly rising affluence and China's two decades of turmoil made a difference of nearly 800kcal per capita per day by 1977, and for most of that period China's average food availability was just marginally ahead of India's (20-year means for 1958–1977 are about 1,950kcal for China and 1,900kcal for India).

But after 1977 India, in spite of its recently improving performance, was left behind, as China pulled to within about 250kcal of Japan and – as a quick look at FAO's global listing of food availabilities will indicate – reached the levels of Mongolia, Malaysia and Brunei (FAO 1985). Even in terms of protein availability, China's performance is similarly impressive, surpassed in East Asia only by Japan, South Korea, and Mongolia.

A simple comparison of the most likely intakes (2,200–2,400kcal) and requirements (2,100–2,400kcal) shows a nearly perfect overlap. Were Chinese food supplies distributed according to need, everybody would have enough. Not equally but according to need, because the hilly and mountainous terrain of inland provinces and the virtually nonexistent or very low levels of mechanization in the poorest regions mean higher metabolic expenditures than in the much more modernized coastal lowlands.

Since 1979 the Chinese have increasingly acknowledged the existence of these regional disparities. Deng Xiaoping stated that (in 1984) "there are still some tens of millions of peasants in the countryside who do not yet have enough food" (Deng 1985: 15), and Liu (1984: 6) put their number at 11 per cent of the rural population. Can this total, equivalent roughly to the population of Nigeria, be verified using the recently published results of rural consumption surveys? From sample surveys we now have provincial averages for per capita consumption of unprocessed grain ranging from a mere 205.5kg in Xinjiang to 329.5kg in Jiangxi. The countrywide mean is 260kg. Because cereals are such a decisive portion of Chinese diets, it is logical to prorate total energy intakes according to the grain consumption means. About 225kg of unmilled grain consumption corresponds to 2,100kcal of actual food intake, which should be seen as the minimum daily food energy requirement under conditions existing in China.

From provincial grain means and rural population totals, it is easy to calculate that almost exactly 200 million people in the nine worst-supplied provinces have average consumption equal to this minimum. If consumption had a normal (Gaussian) distribution, 100 million people would be below that level, an excellent confirmation of Liu's figure of 11 per cent. Raising the minimum requirement to 2,200kcal, an intake corresponding to about 470kg of unmilled grain, would mean that as many as 210 million could be below that level.

There is a fundamental difference between these two requirements. Those 90–100 million peasants consuming on the average less than 2,100kcal per

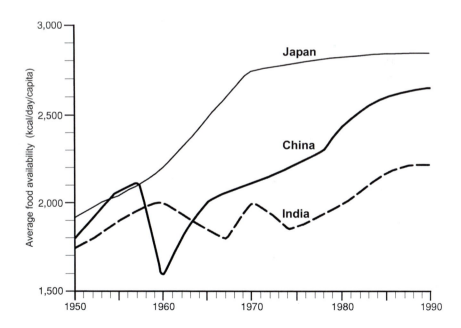

Figure 3.5 Trends in average supply of food energy in China, India and Japan, 1950–1983

Source: Plotted from data in Piazza (1983) and from various volumes of FAO's *Food Balance Sheets*.

capita per day are undoubtedly short of food: in Liu's words, they "still have not resolved the problem of dressing warmly and getting enough to eat" and their lives are certainly "still extremely bitter" (Liu 1984: 6). For the additional 100 million villagers whose average consumption may be below 2,200 but above 2,100kcal, their diet may meet most but not all of the normal growth needs and fall short of the activity requirements of demanding rural work: they may not have enough for a healthy *and* vigorous life. Smaller birth weights, slower growth, greater susceptibility to diseases, a slower pace of field work, and a shorter life expectation will be their lot in comparison with the better-fed villagers.

In retrospect, few developments in modern nutritional history have been so rapid, so far-reaching and so impressive as China's post-1978 achievements. Until Deng's return to power China's food consumption pattern was one of bare subsistence – but only a few years later there was, on average, a growing margin of nutritional comfort. Perhaps the best illustration of the pre-1978 misery is that the direct rural grain consumption kept steadily increasing for years after rice and wheat flour availability became higher; indeed, it did not level off until 1985, at about 260kg per capita. The higher supply of grain was, of course, the most important result of China's radical post-1978 turn away from communal command farming to the family contract system. With privatization, the nation's total grain output jumped from 304.77Mt in 1978 to 407.31Mt in 1984, an astonishing 33 per cent increase in just six years. While between 1952 and 1978 the average nationwide grain consumption actually declined from 197.7kg to 195.5kg, by 1988 it was up to 259.1kg.

These gains pushed China's average per capita food availability to within less than 10 per cent of the Japanese mean: in 1984–1986 the Chinese supply averaged about 2,630kcal a day per capita, compared with the Japanese mean of 2,680kcal (FAO 2002). China's shift from a precarious subsistence (pre-1978) to basic adequacy of average food supply (1984–1986) was accomplished in less than a decade. Subsequent improvements proceeded at a slower but fairly persistent rate, and the country has been able to reduce, but not to eliminate, a significant share of undernourished people. FAO (1996) estimated that in the early 1990s, 15 per cent of China's population (or at least 170 million people) were undernourished, the second highest national total after India (21 per cent or 180 million).

The latest FAO (2002) report on global undernutrition puts the estimate of undernourished people at 840 million, or about 14 per cent of the world's population, during the years 1998–2000. China, with about 9 per cent, or about 120 million, of its people undernoursihed, accounted for 14 per cent of the world's total. Consequently, China's impressive food production achievement continues to mask consumption disparities whose extent is unparalleled among the countries with average per capita availabilities in excess of 3,000kcal/day. Perhaps only one post-1978 development has been more remarkable than the nearly 50 per cent increase in average food supply and the 63 per cent reduction (from about 210 to 120 million) in the total of undernourished people: rapid qualitative transformation of China's average diet. This unprecedented, and very well-documented, dietary transition will be the topic of the next section of this food chapter.

Dietary transitions: eating better, wasting more

The diets of most pre-industrial populations were highly monotonous, not very palatable and barely adequate in terms of basic nutrients. China was no exception (Simoons 1991), and its traditional food consumption pattern persevered during the first half of the twentieth century, and was little changed as the country began to emerge from nearly three decades of Maoist deprivations just before the end of the 1970s. In the late 1960s and throughout the 1970s, about 95 per cent of all food energy in an average diet originated in plant foods, with 75 per cent of that share coming from just the three staple grains: rice, wheat and corn. As soon as it got under way, the privatization of farming began to improve the quality of available foodstuffs and to diversify previously monotonous diets. Increased consumption of animal foodstuffs has been the most obvious marker of this change: by 1986 their share of the total food energy in typical diets surpassed 10 per cent; it topped 15 per cent by 1995 and was nearly 20 per cent by the year 2000 (FAO 2002).

Although actual shares of animal foodstuffs may be somewhat lower (the cited percentages are derived from FAO's food balance which, as I will explain below, almost certainly overestimate the average meat supply), all other measures of China's dietary transition, be it higher intakes of fruits or greater availability of lean meat, confirm that both the pace of the process and its extent have been definitely impressive. The following selections from my writings (Smil 1985, 1995a) trace the main advances of this transformation, and I will conclude this section with a new assessment of potential changes during the coming generation.

Eating better

In the countryside, where heavy work demands higher food inputs, peasants increased their average grain consumption by about 5 per cent from (in unprocessed weight) 248kg in 1978 to 260kg in 1983, while in the better-supplied cities grain consumption actually declined. However, in both cases the most important change has been qualitative. The Chinese have always preferred well-milled rice and wheat flour; this means at least a 70 per cent milling rate for rice and 85 per cent for wheat, but for the country as a whole the proportion of these fine grains did not change between 1957 and 1978. Except for the famine years of 1959–1961, when coarse grains supplied an even larger share, about 60 per cent of nationwide grain output was in rice and wheat, often milled less than the preferred norm, and among peasants the ratio of fine-to-coarse grain in actual consumption averaged just 50:50 by 1978.

The subsequent change was so rapid that by 1982 even an average peasant family consumed 75 per cent of its grain as milled rice or wheat flour, a ratio available only with privileged urban cadre rations a few years earlier. The move from brown rice, cornmeal, millet and potatoes has been the most far-reaching dietary change of post-1978 China. Coarse grains and tubers now supply just 20 per cent of all food energy, and it is safe to predict that if the reforms continue this proportion will keep falling.

A welcome post-1978 food supply improvement has seen a more than twofold increase in the availability of edible plant oils. For decades, the meager ration of cooking oils meant that urban per capita consumption remained mostly below 300g a month even during good years, while rural consumption was negligible and lard remained the leading source of fat. But once the Maoist grain-first policy gave way to more balanced farming, areas planted in oilseeds zoomed and the total harvest of rapeseed, peanuts, sunflower seeds, sesame seeds, linseeds and castor beans grew from just 4Mt in 1977 to 11.8Mt in 1982. This means that, together with oil from soybeans, about 4.5Mt of vegetal oils are now available per year.

The sugar story is very similar. With cultivation of beets and cane suppressed by the grain-first command farming, China's 1977 sugar output was 1.9Mt lower than in 1965 and just marginally higher than it had been in 1957 so that, even with imports, per capita supply stayed below 2.5kg a year. But by 1983 the northeast's sugarbeets and, more importantly, Guangdong's and Fujian's sugarcane brought in 3.7Mt of sugar, so that with imports of 1.4Mt (primarily from Cuba and Australia) the per capita availability rose to almost exactly 5kg a year.

The other important food whose consumption had made an impressive jump by the mid-1980s is meat (aquacultural expansion came later). Poultry production went up especially rapidly, but it still remains very small in comparison with red meat, whose output continues to be dominated by pork (about 94 per cent of the total, with mutton supplying about two thirds and beef one third of the rest). In 1977, pork output was just 7.3Mt but by 1980, 210 million pigs with an average live weight of 89kg were slaughtered and for the first time production surpassed 10Mt. By the spring of 1981, the Chinese media were reporting the end of pork supply shortages as the output kept increasing. In the following years, as the average per capita availability surpassed 12kg a year and approached 20kg in large cities, pork rationing was gradually abandoned, only to be reinstated in early 1985, in the wake of the country's record grain harvest.

This incongruity tells much about the fundamental deficiencies of China's food production, especially its irrational pricing. The state-fixed prices made it unprofitable for farmers to breed and feed pigs because higher and easier profits could be realized by growing grain, keeping a flock of hens, weaving baskets or selling rabbit hair. Only where the pricing was more sensible, as in Sichuan, was there no need to return to rationing. And although China has the world's largest number of pigs, they are poor performers. In 1978 their nationwide take-off rate (the share of animals slaughtered in one year) was a mere 54 per cent; recently it rose close to 70 per cent, but even this means that an average Chinese pig needs about seventeen months to reach slaughter weight, compared to just 6–7 months for a typical Western hog. A large part of this huge difference can be explained by the energy loss sustained by tens of millions of rural Chinese pigs running around the villages and more or less fending for themselves – but even those confined to modern suburban piggeries perform poorly, because there is little properly formulated concentrate feed to turn them into efficient meat converters.

Although the production of compound feed has been growing rapidly – from a mere 1.1Mt in 1980 to 4.5Mt by 1983 (for comparison, American output in the early 1980s was about 200Mt a year) – its share in 1983 was still only slightly more than 10 per cent of all grain fed to livestock (Whitton 1984). Moreover, of about 10Mt of high-protein oilseed cakes more than half are used as a fertilizer instead of as feed. Current plans include the continued rapid expansion of the feed industry, with capacities up to 120Mt by the year 2000, but this will be a most challenging goal.

Finally, better, meaty breeds must be introduced to supplant the dominant fatty breeds. Even before the reimposition of pork rationing in twenty-one large cities in February 1985, supplies of lean pork were far below demand – in privileged Beijing they made up a mere 1.4 per cent of total sales – in spite of a large price difference. While a kilogram of standard pork – that is, an indiscriminately hacked-off piece of lardy carcass – cost around 2 *yuan*, lean pork retailed in private markets at up to 3.8 *yuan* (and a limited quantity of it is now available with coupons at 2.92 *yuan*).

Development of a large-scale feed industry and the introduction of high-performance breeds are also the two critical requirements for expanding poultry production. The first-ever official disclosure of the Chinese poultry inventory put the total at 1 billion birds at the beginning of 1983 and average meat consumption at a mere 1.2kg per capita a year (compared to about 30kg in the USA). Nationwide production of milk rose 2.4 times between 1978 and 1983 (cow milk now accounts for 80 per cent of the total), but this rapid expansion started from such a low base that it would take a further fifteenfold increase to reach the current Japanese per capita consumption level.

Comparison with the Japanese milk-drinking pattern is most appropriate, because the Chinese could never aspire to European or North American levels of dairy consumption. In reality, hundreds of millions of Chinese never drink milk, sales of which are heavily concentrated in large cities, where the per capita average is now around 10kg a year and where the potential demand is far from covered. And as with pigs and poultry, feed conversion efficiencies and the performance of dairy cows will have to improve if increased dairy production is to be economical. The output of aquatic products went up by less than 20 per cent between 1978 and 1984, reflecting the substantial increase of freshwater fish breeding and coastal mariculture, and the stagnation and even decline of high sea catches in badly overfished waters, especially in the East China Sea. Annual per capita fish consumption of around 4kg conceals very large regional differences, ranging from once-a-year tasting of a few tidbits to sales of almost 30kg a year in Guangzhou, a total not far from Japan's uncommonly high average.

But neither fish nor poultry are, after pork, the second most important source of food energy and protein from animal foods: eggs are now ahead of both. Actual per capita consumption averages just 3kg a year, that is about one large egg a week (American consumption is now about 15kg of eggs a year), which is more than three times as much as in 1977. It is here that the private market has made a rapid and large difference.

There is one notable exception to the rising trends among basic foodstuffs: soybean consumption is now far below the level of not only the late 1950s but even that of half a century ago. In 1936 China had, at 11.3Mt, the still unsurpassed record harvest of soybeans, which prorated to some 22kg per capita. During most of the 1950s soybean per capita output stayed above 15kg but once it dropped below 10kg during the 1959–1961 famine it never rebounded: in 1977 it was a mere 7.5kg, in 1983 it rose to 9.5kg but in 1984 it fell again to 9.4kg. Moreover, the Chinese stopped importing soybeans (largely from the USA) by 1983, when they more than doubled their exports (mostly to Japan); and because nearly half of the soybean crop has recently been used for oil, the actual availability of this high-protein legume as food is now a mere 5kg a year per capita, a negligible 13g a day.

With two-income, one-child families becoming the norm in cities, there is more need and more money for a wide range of traditional and modern convenience foods, with the current demand vastly surpassing the meager offerings. For instance, less than 40,000t of instant noodles were produced nationwide in 1983 (that is, a mere 40g a year per capita), and shortages of sweet and salty biscuits, and crackers, dried fruits, dried and pickled vegetables, processed meats, instant soups and various traditional ready-to-eat snacks and meal accompaniments – crullers (*youbing*), sesame biscuits (*shaobing*), twisted fried cakes (*mahuar*), steamed meat-filled buns (*baozi*), and fried rice flour cakes with sweet filling (*zhagao*) – remain widespread.

There has been a revival of snack shops and teahouses and restaurants, but Beijing still has less than 5 per cent of Tokyo's eateries. In cooperation with the French, the Chinese are making a table wine for export (*Great Wall* brand) but beer production for the huge domestic market remains pitifully small. True, it has taken off, from 690,000t in 1980 to the planned total of 2Mt in 1985, with most of the increase coming from many expanded and newly established local breweries. But the per capita average is just short of two liters a year, an order of magnitude below the European average.

When measured as a share of disposable income, the cost of food in China has declined since 1978, but it remains very high. In 1964, a survey by the State Statistical Bureau found that urban families spent 69.4 per cent of their income on food; in 1980 the first survey in sixteen years put the share at 60.6 per cent (Xinhua 1981). Since then, the Chinese have published more information indicating similarly high expenditures in 1983: 59.3 per cent for rural families, down from 67.7 per cent in 1978, and 59.2 per cent for urban families (SSB 1984). A 1983 survey showed that of all the money spent on food among worker families, 55 per cent goes to purchase meat, vegetables, fruits and eggs, 21 per cent is spent on grain, and the rest on beverages, tea and sugar. An average Chinese worker must still labor about twice as long as his Taiwanese counterpart for the same amount of rice and pork; in comparison with Japan, these differentials rise to, respectively, four and six times.

But expensive as Chinese foods (and above all, animal protein) are, they would cost much more if billions in state subsidies were removed. While the state purchasing prices for farm products rose about 50 per cent since 1978 to spur *baogan*'s productivity, retail prices for basic foodstuffs are now only about 25 per cent above the level of the mid-1960s. Obviously, the arrangement of buying high and selling low must eventually end. The first round of price increases in May 1985 affected the twenty largest cities and applied to pork (up by over 30 per cent), chicken (almost 50 per cent higher), fish (for some species doubling, even tripling, the price), and vegetables. At the same time, subsidies of up to 7.50 *yuan* (roughly a tenth of the average monthly urban wage) were issued to cover the higher cost. Further price rises will follow, but the government has promised to keep some subsidies for grains and oils indefinitely.

A new Chinese diet

Since the beginning of the economic reforms, the Chinese have followed the near-universal pattern of nutritional shifts that accompany industrialization and urbanization (Smil 1995a). Major staple grains have become less important as legume consumption has decreased and consumption of animal foods, oil, fruits and sugar has increased. In specific Chinese terms, this means that rice is becoming an inferior food; that the consumption of pork and plant oils used in stir-frying has risen rapidly; and that the domestic production of sugar cannot meet the growing demand.

The level of meat consumption will have the greatest impact on China's future food self-sufficiency. So far the demand for meat has been rising faster than anticipated. Average per capita annual consumption almost tripled between 1978 and 1994, and in 1995 it is already above the target set for the year 2000 by the Chinese Academy of Agricultural Sciences. The Academy also assumes that average per capita meat demand will remain fairly stable at about 25kg per year until the year 2020.

Developments elsewhere in the region do not give any unequivocal guidance. Japanese GDP is, even when adjusted for purchasing power parity, more than an order of magnitude above the Chinese mean. However, despite this high level of affluence, average per capita Japanese meat consumption is still below 40kg per year. But it must be also remembered that meat is not the largest source of animal protein in Japan, and that the average Japanese also consumes more than 70kg of aquatic products a year. Taiwanese meat consumption has leveled off at about 50kg per capita a year – but its pork share is now only about half of the total.

The Chinese will not be able to replicate the Japanese eating pattern – and it is most unlikely that they will follow the Taiwanese one. To come closer to Japan's huge ocean fish consumption the Chinese would have to increase massively their marine catches, but given the fact that as of the year 1996 the world ocean is being fully fished, and that about 60 per cent of some 200 major marine fish resources have been either overexploited or are at the peak level of their sustainable harvest (FAO 1997), that is not an option anymore. In contrast, further expansion of freshwater aquaculture is possible, but new gains will require substantially higher inputs of mixed feeds for the intensive production of various pond species. Since cold-blooded carp convert feed better than warm-blooded pigs or chicken, their production is the most efficient route to the higher supply of animal protein – except, of course, for the higher output of milk and dairy products.

Unfortunately, the Chinese, like all East Asian people, have a high incidence of lactose intolerance because their synthesis of lactase, the enzyme responsible for digesting milk sugar, declines sharply after early childhood. This means that a large share of the affected population has difficulty digesting large quantities of milk. Fortunately, for most people this biochemical peculiarity is no obstacle to drinking moderate amounts of fresh milk, and none whatsoever for eating fermented dairy products with lower amount of lactose (yogurt, soft cheeses) or with no lactose at all (fully ripened hard cheeses). And while traditional food preferences and biases make for interesting anthropological studies, such cultural prejudices do not seem to pose insurmountable barriers to major dietary changes. As far as dairy products are concerned, Japan is a perfect example of an impressively rapid shift. In 1945, Japanese consumption of milk, yogurt and cheese was almost zero; today their average annual per capita intake is well over 50kg, compared with less than 2kg in China.

The composition of average diets should further change by including more animal protein produced with high conversion efficiency (freshwater fish, chicken, dairy products), and by the provision of higher-quality non-staple foods (legumes, fruits, vegetables, nuts). And a sustained effort must also be made to eliminate serious regional disparities in average food supply; most coastal provinces now have a surplus of food, but in poor-weather years supply averages in Guangxi or Gansu are still barely above the basic sufficiency level.

The magnitude of the current shortcomings permeating China's food chain has been stunningly illustrated by a five-year survey of grain losses. According to the survey, about 15 per cent of total cereal yield is lost every year during harvesting, threshing, drying, storage, transport and processing. In addition, the waste of staple grain in factory, office and school messhalls, by excessive and inefficient production of spirits and beer, and by poor feeding practices, nearly doubles that total. As a result, China's food and feed loss has recently amounted to the equivalent of at least 60–70Mt of staple grain annually. Reducing it by just one third would increase annual grain availability by about 20–25Mt, enough to feed an additional 100 million people, or eliminate all grain imports – and still be left with several megatons of wheat, rice and corn.

Raising feeding efficiency is imperative, and highly realistic. Before the beginning of Deng's reforms only about one sixth of China's grain harvest was fed to animals, mostly to ubiquitous pigs. In the mid-1980s the share surpassed 20 per cent; it reached 25 per cent in the early 1990s, and plans are for feeding 30 per cent of all grain to animals by the end of the century. Yet Chinese pigs are still mainly fed assorted mixtures of diverse plant matter, including weeds, straw, stalks, bran, oilseed residues, kitchen wastes, tubers, and inferior unmilled grain. Such rations are obviously deficient in protein, and result in slow weight gain and hence in low slaughter rates. While in North America a weaned pig is ready for the market in just six months, the Chinese average is slightly more than twice as long. At 80kg, the mean weight of a dressed carcass is about 40 per cent higher in the USA than in China.

Finally, I should point out the declining need for average food intakes in all urbanized societies. While available food supply in Western countries averages around 3,500kcal a day per capita, the best surveys of actual food consumption show daily means (weighted for age and sex structure of the studied population) of just 2,000–2,100kcal. China's average supply of more than 2,700kcal a day per capita is thus clearly sufficient. Indeed, Chinese publications have recently carried a number of articles pointing out the growing incidence of obesity among children. Increasing average nationwide food availability would make little sense. Instead, three modifications are necessary. China's food must be produced more rationally through a combination of increased yields, improving field efficiencies of major farming inputs, and reduced post-harvest waste.

Further changes and a long-term outlook

With the actual daily food requirements of modern urban societies averaging no more than 2,000–2,200kcal/capita it does not make any sense to supply more than about 2,700–2,800kcal/day: wasting 20–30 per cent of all available food is surely enough. However, among the affluent countries only Japan has conformed to this pattern. Since the mid-1950s, once they recovered from its postwar lows, Japan's average daily intakes have fluctuated very narrowly, between 2,100 and 2,200kcal/capita, while the food supply, highly dependent on imports and hence relatively expensive, has been sensibly stable at between 2,700 and 2,800kcal/capita since the early 1970s. Average US intakes have been similarly stable during the past thirty years, at around 2,500kcal/day for adult males and about 1,600kcal/day for adult females, with the mean for all individuals of all ages at just above 2,000kcal/day (US Department of Agriculture 1997). But, in contrast, to Japan, the US supply averages around 3,700kcal/day, and similarly high rates (3,400–3,700kcal/capita) prevail in most of the countries of the EU (FAO 2002).

China's average food supply has also stabilized during the late 1990s, and a simple comparison of FAO's food balance sheets indicates, as already noted, that it has done so at a level less than 10 per cent higher than the Japanese mean. After reaching virtual parity with Japan in terms of average per capita food energy supply, China's mean rate, according to FAO's balances, increased by nearly 4 per cent during the second half of the 1980s; between 1990 and 1995 it rose by almost 6 per cent; and during the late 1990s by a further 5 per cent (FAO 2002). This means that starting in 1997 the nationwide per capita mean has been, for the first time in the country's modern history, above 3,000kcal/day, and per capita rates of 3,010–3,040kcal/day put China about 8 per cent ahead of Japan. The real rates are not that high, and the main reason is not that FAO's food balance sheets for China include Taiwan. The ROC's higher food supply (in excess of 3,300kcal/capita) makes little difference: given the large disparity of the two populations (1.3 billion vs. 20 million) its exclusion would lower the PRC's mean by less than 0.5 per cent.

The main difference is due to the fact that China's official output statistics have been greatly overstating meat, egg and aquatic production, and that the differences between these output figures and actual consumption have expanded rapidly since the 1980s. Lu's (1998) careful appraisal shows that in 1995 official output figures overstated the actual consumption of red meat and poultry 1.9 times, and that of aquatic products about 1.75 times. Similarly, after a global comparison of expected and reported marine catches, Watson and Pauly (2001) concluded that the catch along the Chinese coast in 1999 was predicted at 5.5Mt compared to officially claimed 10.1Mt, implying a roughly 1.8-fold overstatement.

Using these shares to correct FAO's food balance sheet (based on official output figures) gives China about 2,700 rather than 2,874kcal/capita in 1995 and, assuming the overestimates have not grown larger, about 2,800 rather than 3,030kcal/capita in 2000. Obviously this correction also requires lowering the contributions of animal proteins and lipids by similarly large margins. Comparing the composition of this supply with the optimum dietary guidelines and desirable consumption goals for the year 2000 that were formulated during the 1980s (Chen 1991), shows that the average availability has surpassed these targets in every category except for pulses, with the largest differences for fruits and vegetables.

In overall energy terms, China's per capita food availability remains almost the same as in Japan. If demand were to be the only driving factor of food consumption, two countervailing trends would largely determine its future level: rising food energy intake among lower-income families and decreased food energy consumption of high-income households (Ma and Popkin 1995). The first factor is obviously still more powerful, but given China's already relatively high per capita supply level it is not going to be translated into any major absolute increases. Changes in the composition of China's diet, above all the increased demand for animal foodstuffs, will be thus much more important drivers of the future demand. In spite of the recent large consumption increases, China remains a modest consumer of animal foods even when the comparison is limited to Japan, which has access to nearly three times as much animal protein.

Contrary to some simplistic extrapolations based on erroneous data, Chinese meat intakes will come nowhere near the Western level of consumption – with fats supplying well over 30 per cent, and even more than 40 per cent, of all food energy, and with the annual meat consumption in excess of 70kg, or even 100kg/capita – during the coming generation. According to the exaggerated official figures, China's output of red meat and poultry rose from almost 29Mt in 1990 to 61Mt in 2000, implying average per capita rates of, respectively, 25 and 48kg/capita in 2000 (NBS 2000). But the Chinese consumption surveys show that urban meat purchases have basically stabilized during the 1990s – they averaged 25.2kg/capita in 1990, 23.7kg/capita in 1995 and 25.0kg/capita in 1999 – and that rural consumption had risen modestly from 12.6kg/capita in 1990 to 16.4kg/capita in 1999 (NBS 2000).

In contrast to exaggerated output data, these consumption surveys underestimate the actual intakes as they leave out food obtained by employees from their work units, as well as previously rare, but now increasingly common, dining out, which almost invariably includes a disproportionately large consumption of meat and fish. According to Lu (1998) these intakes would add annually at least 2kg/capita to the nationwide average. Even when taking into account at least the 15 per cent weight difference between reported output (carcass weight) and actual meat intake and post-retail losses, there is still the already noted gap of nearly 50 per cent between consumption and official production claims.

Rising per capita intakes of animal foodstuffs, and continuation of rapid urbanization, are the two factors favoring further increases in meat consumption. But, as in other countries, China's meat demand is also highly income-dependent. Nationwide surveys show urban income elasticities as high as 3.1 for poultry and 1.7 for pork, compared to just 0.7 for both foodstuffs in rural (and relatively rich) Jiangsu (Hsu *et al.* 2002). Consequently, relatively low income in most of China's rural areas will restrain the future meat demand. Moreover, nationwide surveys also show that China's urban consumers are especially sensitive to prices of pork, poultry, and eggs (price elasticities of -1.6, -1.3 and -1.8 respectively), which means that future price increases (resulting, for example, from China's accession to the WTO) might slow the growth in meat demand that is stimulated by higher incomes (Hsu *et al.* 2002). A rapidly ageing population that is more concerned about healthy eating is yet another factor that will moderate the future meat demand.

At the same time, because China's regional, provincial and rural/urban income inequalities had actually risen during the 1990s, it means that overconsumption of food in general, and high intakes of meat in particular, have become common among the more affluent segments of the population in the best-off large cities and in the coastal regions of the country, where tens of millions of people now have more food at their disposal than does the average Japanese. Chinese nutritionists were puzzled when the food consumption surveys of the late 1980s showed an average daily adult food intake of 2,160kcal/capita, lower than the recommended daily level of 2,400kcal/capita (Ge *et al.* 1991). They realized, as did their Western counterparts a generation earlier (Smil 2000a), that they were setting their recommendations too high.

Even when assuming that hard-working rural adults average 2,600kcal/capita, the current age–sex composition of China's population (about 25 per cent of all people younger than fourteen years, 8 per cent older than sixty-five years) means that the weighted nationwide average of daily food requirements is just around 2,200kcal/day, and that the gap between the food availability and the need has widened to about 800kcal/day, or to roughly a quarter of the total supply. This widening gap translates into more food waste, a reality readily evident in China's restaurants. This waste is encouraged by an unfortunate Chinese habit of ordering more than can be eaten by hosts desiring to gain face, and by widespread, and often astonishingly ostentatious, dining at public expense (Wu 1996). In China's largest city, problems with this waste are made worse by a new regulation forbidding farmers to collect restaurant waste for their pigs. Rising bills for waste disposal led a Shanghai branch of Beijing's roast duck restaurant *Quanjude*, where many people ate less than half of what they ordered, to offer 10 per cent discount vouchers to the customers who finish their food (Hu 2001).

And combined with the increasingly sedentary life of many *nouveaux-riches* urbanites, this widening gap between the supply and the need induces excessive eating and translates into an unprecedented extent of obesity, whose higher incidence is eventually associated with the rise of such widespread civilizational diseases as cardiovascular illnesses and diabetes (Ge *et al.* 1996). The deleterious effects of even relatively small shifts toward the Western diet were demonstrated by the two rounds of a large-scale survey done by the Cornell–Oxford–China Project (Chen *et al.* 1990; CTSU 2002). Even small additions of animal foods have resulted in significant elevations of blood cholesterol levels and the increased risk of chronic degenerative diseases (cancers, cardiovascular complaints, diabetes). This trend is almost certain to continue. The globalization of tastes has already brought many fast-food empires into China, and, as in other rapidly modernizing and urbanizing countries, the breakdown of traditional families, high rates of female employment and reduced willingness to cook are fueling the purchases of fast foods full of saturated fat and refined sugar.

And before leaving the subject of China's dietary changes, I must note the spreading impact that China's omnivorous foodways (and medicinal habits) are making on the world's diminishing biodiversity. The country's traditionally indiscriminate omnivory makes for an efficient way of food consumption, as nothing, from a pig's skin to chicken feet, and from silk moth pupae to carp eyes (both considered a delicacy!), gets wasted. But it also entails an appetite for anything that moves, from monkeys to dogs to snakes, and much that does not (abalones, sea cucumbers). Rising incomes lead to rising demand for these unusual foodstuffs, which are consumed not only by China's suddenly rich entrepreneurs and their cronies, but also during banquets eaten daily by legions of corrupt officials. A rare Chinese estimate put the annual value spent on eating, drinking and traveling at public expense at more than 100 billion *yuan* in 1992, a total thought to be highly conservative (Wu 1996).

Many of these dietary predilections, however offensive they may be to Westerners who do not hesitate to eat lambs and calves, are merely a cultural concern. But a seemingly insatiable demand for snakes, turtles and frogs is a major reason for local extinction of many of their species, particularly throughout South China, and illegal imports of these animals, as well as rare coral reef fish, from Vietnam, the Philippines and Indonesia are now extending the reach of China's destructive eating habits all across Southeast Asia. According to a 1999 survey, 26 per cent of all wild animal dishes served in restaurants contained species which are on China's endangered list. The ecosystemic consequences of this perverse gluttony, augmented by the search for such destructive and medically medieval therapies as bear galls and tiger bones, are serious. Perhaps the most noticeable is an increase in the density of mouse and rat populations that were previously held in check by snakes.

As a result, in January 2002 the China Wildlife Conservation Association launched an unusual campaign to save disappearing animals by asking professional chefs to sign a declaration stating that they will refuse to prepare any meals containing endangered species (BBC News 2002). The Association's hope was to collect at least 3 million signatures (the estimated total of China's chefs is at least 8 million), but its campaign faces no small challenge, given reports of 10t of snakes consumed daily in Shenzhen, and 1,000t of snake meat served annually in Shanghai.

Nitrogen in China's agriculture: an unorthodox history

China's modern history has been probed from many perspectives but, as far as I am aware, it has never been looked at through the prism of agricultural nitrogen. Abstruse as this point of view may be to historians preoccupied with kinships, ruling elites, commodity prices or intra-party discords, it is a perfectly natural choice when looking at what is surely one of China's most distinguishing characteristics: its quest to feed the world's largest population from a limited amount of land. But before I plunge into the Chinese specifics, a few introductory remarks on nitrogen, and on its agricultural and nutritional importance and its biospheric cycling, are in order.

Nitrogen in human nutrition and in cropping

Photosynthesis uses carbon, oxygen and hydrogen to construct a variety of simple sugars, and their subsequent polymerization (combination into larger units) produces the two most abundant macromolecules making up the plant mass: cellulose and hemi-cellulose; lignin in woody tissues is also a polymer, but one made up of alcohols rather than of sugars (Smil 2002a). None of these macromolecules dominating the composition of the Earth's plant mass contains any other elements than C, O and H. If humans were able to metabolize cellulose and lignin there would be no need for agriculture. Agriculture is primarily after digestible nitrogen, not after polymerized sugars. Justus von Liebig (1840: 85) – one of the most famous, controversial and highly perceptive founders of modern chemistry – was the first scientist who explicitly recognized this reality more than 150 years ago:

> Agriculture differs essentially from the cultivation of forests, inasmuch as its principal object consists in the production of nitrogen under any form capable of assimilation; whilst the object of forest culture is confined to the production of carbon.

Nitrogen assimilated by plants is eventually transferred into amino acids, which form a variety of plant proteins. Humans cannot synthesize the amino acids essential for their nutrition – but they need them to form their body proteins (Smil 2002a). Consequently, people must ingest all essential amino acids ready-made in proteins present in their food. The adequate supply of dietary nitrogen is an irreplaceable condition of human existence – and, in turn, crops must assimilate adequate amounts of nitrogen from their environment. This is why an inquiry into the natural supply of the nutrient, and into the changing means of the agricultural quest for nitrogen, addresses the very survival of our species. Of course, nitrogen is just one of the three macronutrients, elements needed in relatively large quantities by crops. Phosphorus and potassium are the other two, but nitrogen is truly *primus inter pares*, as it is needed in much larger amounts than any other nutrient. For example, a tonne of wheat will contain 20kg of nitrogen, but only 4kg of phosphorus and 6kg of potassium. And nitrogen is also most often the nutrient that is in the shortest supply in soils from which it could be drawn by growing plants.

This seems counterintuitive, given the relatively low concentrations of the element in crops (by weight, most staple grains are less than 2 per cent N) and its abundance in the biosphere: 78 per cent of the atmosphere is made up of nitrogen, which means that there are some 75,000 tonnes of the element in the air above every hectare of farmland. But atmospheric nitrogen cannot be used by plants because it exists as a tightly bound molecule, N_2 (dinitrogen), which does not participate in any reactions (Smil 1997a). Only two natural processes can perform the difficult task of splitting the dinitrogen molecule: lightning, and enzymatic metabolism limited to a relatively small number of bacterial genera. These two processes sever the strong N_2 bond – lightning with its enormous heat and pressure; bacteria with the help of a unique enzyme (nitrogenase) – and release nitrogen atoms that are free to bind with other elements and create fixed nitrogen in reactive nitrogen compounds. In the case of bacterial fixation, the compound is ammonia (NH_3), while lightning produces nitrogen oxide (NO) and nitrogen dioxide (NO_2).

Subsequently, bacteria convert ammonia to nitrates that are much more soluble in water and hence preferred by plants. Highly soluble nitrates are lost from soils by leaching, and both ammonia and nitrates are carried away by erosion and surface runoff. Eventually, different bacteria convert nitrates first to nitrites and then to N_2 which rejoins the huge atmospheric pool of the element. Nitrogen taken up by crops is either removed from fields in harvested plant parts or it is directly recycled by decomposition of dead biomass. The complexity of the element's biospheric flows opens up many opportunities for moving the nutrient beyond the reach of plant roots, and hence losing the fixed nitrogen for crop production (Smil 1997a). These losses, and the rarity of natural processes that fix nitrogen, meant that the yields in traditional agricultures were nearly always limited by the supply of nitrogen. That is why traditional agricultures devised many ways to maintain adequate supplies of the nutrient – and Chinese farming was certainly one of the classical paragons of this inventive quest.

Traditional nitrogen supplies and their limits

Traditional agricultures had two basic choices when trying to expand food production: they could either convert more land to fields and gather relatively poor harvests from a larger area, or they could raise the yields and get higher harvests from the same, or even a smaller, amount of farmland. Both practices soon ran into nitrogen limits. Gradual release of often rich stores of organic nitrogen present in grassland and forest soils supplied relatively large amounts of the nutrients for several decades after the conversion of these natural ecosystems to fields. But once this reservoir is significantly depleted, annual cropping depends largely on the modest nitrogen inputs in precipitation, from non-symbiotic nitrogen-fixing bacteria, and from recycled crop roots and stubble. The combination of these inputs supplies commonly less than 30kg N/ha, an amount sufficient to produce only low harvests that can feed no more than 2–2.5 people/ha on meager vegetarian diets.

This situation describes very well the early periods of grain farming in the ancient semi-arid core of Chinese civilization in the valley of the Huanghe and its tributaries, where the managed inputs of nitrogen (recycling of stubble and roots left after poor harvests) amounted to less than 5 per cent of the total supply of the nutrient. Later, when the recycling of animal manures and human wastes added up to 30–35kg N/ha, the share of managed inputs rose to around 30 per cent of the total. But recurrent droughts kept depressing the average multi-year yield, and North China's carrying capacity remained below two people/ha until the Tang dynasty (Smil 1993).

More extensive farming in the form of slow increases in the total area of cultivated land continued during the Song, Yuan and Ming dynasties, but this trend was also accompanied by gradual intensification of cropping throughout the Jiangnan. Conversion of natural ecosystems to crop fields reached its highest rate during the late Qing era, but even this relatively rapid extension of cultivated land (roughly its doubling in a century) could not keep up with the country's unprecedented population growth, from about 225 million people in 1750 to 475 million 150 years later (McEvedy and Jones 1978). Intensification of cropping had to become the decisive means of increasing food production in most of the country.

More intensive Chinese cultivation relied on crop rotations, multicropping and intercropping. The first practice means growing a variety of crops in a sequence, often as simple as two alternating crops and as elaborate as multi-year schedules involving half a dozen, or more, different food, feed, fiber or medicinal species. The second practice entails cultivating more than one crop per year in the same field, and the third growing two or more crops simultaneously. The nitrogen needed for these intensive ways of cropping was supplied by extensive recycling of organic wastes – and the only means by which peasants could provide additional nutrient was by cultivating leguminous crops which are symbiotic with nitrogen-fixing bacteria.

Animal manures produced in confinement were collected and applied to fields after composting. The initial nitrogen content of these wastes, largely dependent on the quality of the feed and health of the animals, was low, rarely above 2–3 per cent N, and because of the volatilization of ammonia and leaching of nitrates these wastes tended to lose large shares of the nutrient even before they could be applied to fields. Volatilization of ammonia was also the main reason for substantial nitrogen losses from human wastes that were traditionally collected throughout the country and fermented before application. Animal and human wastes that eventually reached the fields contained usually less than 1 per cent nitrogen, hence the peasants had to store, move and apply huge volumes of these materials in order to supply crops with sufficient nitrogen.

In contrast to Europe, distribution and application of organic wastes in China was done largely without the help of draft animals. Consequently, moving and spreading an average of 10t of wastes per hectare (and sometimes more than 30t/ha on small farms) was one of the most laborious, time- and energy-consuming tasks in China's traditional farming. Detailed labor accounts show that at least 10 per cent of all work in China's traditional farming was connected with fertilizers, and in parts of North China fertilization of grain crops was the single most time-consuming agricultural task, claiming close to one fifth of all human, and about one third of all animal, labor (Buck 1930). Still, the net energy return on this investment was very high: the ratio between labor (food energy) invested in manuring and additional food energy harvested in higher yields was more than fiftyfold (Smil 1994).

Only a small part of crop residues – straws, stalks and vines usually containing no more than 0.5–0.6 per cent N – was left in fields, as most of them were usually removed to be used for feed and bedding as well as for fuel and construction. Rural surveys showed that in China of the early 1930s between 59 and 74 per cent of all major cereal straws and 90 per cent of all cotton stalks were used for fuel (Buck 1937). Most of the residues were burned by rural households, but appreciable amounts were sold by farmers in towns and cities. Some residues were returned to fields later in composts. A huge variety of other recycled organic wastes contained materials with both very high and very low nitrogen content. Cakes remaining after pressing oil from various seeds could have up to 7.5 per cent nitrogen, but this made them also an excellent animal feed. Canal, pond and river mud traditionally spread on fields throughout South China had no more than 0.2–0.3 per cent of the nutrient.

Cultivation of leguminous crops symbiotic with nitrogen-fixing *Rhizobium* bacteria included above all soybeans and peanuts, then a variety of beans (broad, red and black) and field peas. Roots of these crops, with the attached nodules containing *Rhizobium* bacteria, and their partially recycled residues would leave behind appreciable amounts of fixed nitrogen (anywhere between 10 and 60kg N/ha) to be used by subsequent non-leguminous crops. Several leguminous species were also planted as green manures. This practice incorporates plants of various legume species into soil by hoeing or plowing, or, less commonly, by harvesting the plants and burying them in other fields. The incorporation can take place after just forty, but usually after 60–120 days after their planting. In a mild climate, green manures grown during several months added enough nitrogen to the soil to produce a good summer cereal crop. The first written record of Chinese use of leguminous green manures dates to the fifth century BCE, but the practice was almost certainly more ancient (Pieters 1927;

Bray 1984). *Astragalus sinicus* (Chinese vetch, *genge*) was by far the leading choice; other commonly used species included broad beans, clovers and field peas.

Thanks to John L. Buck's (1930; 1937) exceptionally comprehensive surveys conducted during the 1920s and 1930s, we have an incomparable quantitative record of traditional farming practices in China. After combining this unique information with modern understanding of nitrogen flows, it is possible to reconstruct nitrogen inputs in Chinese traditional farming with a relatively high degree of accuracy. I have used this information to prepare nitrogen balances for a number of agroecosystems, ranging from single-cropping with extensive fallowing in the Huanghe valley to intensive cultivation of irrigated farmlands which had supported higher population densities than any other purely organic agriculture.

My detailed reconstructions of nitrogen flows on several Sichuanese and Hunanese farms show that the highest nitrogen inputs in traditional Chinese farming amounted to between 120 and 150kg N/ha. Managed inputs of nitrogen – that is organic recycling and planting of leguminous species – accounted for anywhere between 50 and 80 per cent of the total supply of the nutrient. For example, double-cropping in a complex Sichuanese six-year rota-tion consisting of summer rice followed by broad beans in the first years, and rapeseed, field peas, wheat, barley and tobacco in subsequent winters, received about 150kg N/ha, with 120kg originating in managed inputs. With the effi-ciency of nitrogen utilization ranging between 50 and 60 per cent, total inputs in excess of 120kg N/ha could produce 200–250kg of food protein per hectare, enough to feed 10–14 people from a hectare of arable land – providing they were subsisting on an overwhelmingly vegetarian diet enriched only occasionally by some animal foods.

Yet another traditional Chinese agroecosystem was managed with even higher nitrogen inputs, but as it involved a major component of aquaculture its perfor-mance is not directly comparable with crop-based schemes. The dike-and-pond region in the Zhujiang Delta in South China's Guangdong province evolved over many centuries into the world's most productive traditional food production systems: carp polyculture in ponds and continuous cropping of a wide variety of species on dikes (sugar cane, rice, vegetables, mulberries, fruit) were nourished by annual inputs of 50–270t/ha of organic wastes (Ruddle and Zhong 1988; Korn 1996).

But carrying capacities in excess of ten people per hectare of arable land could not prevail over large areas. The mean was lowered even in the most productive farming regions by the necessity to grow non-food crops (above all fibers), and on regional and national scales it was greatly reduced by climate, above all by the limits on multicropping and by inadequate water supply. A stunning comparison illustrates this depressing effect. Calculations based on the *History of the Han Dynasty* records show that during the fourth century BCE in the state of Wei, a typical peasant was expected to provide each of his five family members with nearly half a kilogram of grain a day – a total identical to the mean per capita supply of grain in North China during the early 1950s (Yates 1990).

Consequently, the early twentieth century mean of agricultural carrying capacity for South China was no more than 7 people/ha, and Buck's surveys indicate that the national average, depressed by northern dryland farming, was about 5.5 people/ha during the early 1930s (Buck 1937). Still, this rate was higher than the contemporary mean for Java, Indonesia's most densely populated island; it was at least 40 per cent above the Indian mean; and it came very close to the Egyptian average (Smil 1994). The last comparison is not entirely appropriate as at that time virtually all of Egypt's farmland was irrigated and a part of it was already receiving inorganic fertilizers.

The traditional pattern of China's cultivation persevered largely intact into the 1950s. A detailed reconstruction of nitrogen flow to China's fields (Smil 2001b) shows that in 1952 all managed inputs accounted for about half of the nutrient reaching the country's cropland, and that the traditional practices were able to feed, much like during the early 1930s, no more than 5.5 people/ha. Because little change had occurred in China's nitrogen supply by 1957, the cultivated area had to increase to accommodate the growing population – but by that time, after centuries of converting natural ecosystems to farmland, there was little cultivable land of good quality left (Crook 1988).

Only marginal gains were possible with even more assiduous recycling of organic wastes. Planting more pulses would have made the average diet even less palatable, and while more green manuring would have produced more fixed nitrogen, it would have also pre-empted cultivation of additional food crops. Both the extensive and the intensive mode of China's traditional farming had reached the limits of their performance. The only way to break through the nitrogen barrier was to turn to inorganic fertilizers based on synthetic ammonia. After nearly a century of unsuccessful experiments by several generations of inorganic chemists, ammonia synthesis from its elements was finally demonstrated by Fritz Haber in 1908. Haber's brilliant invention was rapidly translated into a commercial process by Badische Anilin- und Soda-Fabrik (BASF), at that time the world's largest chemical company, under the leadership of Carl Bosch.

The first commercial ammonia plant began synthesizing in 1913, but the Haber–Bosch process diffused slowly after World War I, and large-scale fertilization took off only after 1950 (Smil 2001b). A number of countries with traditionally intensive cropping preceded China in taking the inevitable step of augmenting organic nitrogen supplies by increasing applications of inorganic fertilizers: Dutch, British, German, Japanese or Egyptian staple crops were already receiving appreciable amounts of ammonia-based nitrogen before World War II. Unfortunately, this fundamental shift did not come in China as a result of deliberate, far-sighted policies – but largely as a response to the greatest famine of the twentieth century.

Modern China: famine and its consequences

When it came to power in 1949, the Communist regime inherited just two small fertilizer plants producing annually about 27,000t of ammonium sulfate (CIA

1975; Chang 1977). Intensive recycling of a large variety of organic wastes and cultivation of green manures remained the mainstays of the country's nitrogen supplies during the first two decades after the establishment of the Communist regime. Historical reconstructions of nitrogen inputs into China's agriculture show that synthetic fertilizers provided only about 5 per cent of the nutrient during the late 1950s and that the share was still less than a third of the total by 1970. Construction of small, coal-based ammonia plants producing ammonium bicarbonate began in 1958, the year Mao Zedong launched the Great Leap Forward. Ignorant of economic and technical complexities, but obsessed with the idea of making China a great power, the Chairman of the Chinese Communist Party followed a primitive Stalinist model of development that equated economic modernization with the large output of steel produced in small plants by mass mobilization of the country's huge population.

The catastrophic consequences of this decision, combined with other fateful blunders in agricultural policy, have been described in the opening section of this chapter: in the three years between 1959 and 1961 some 30 million Chinese died in the greatest famine in human history. More pragmatic policies favored by Liu Shaoqi and Deng Xiaoping finally put the end to that tragedy. One of their measures was the purchase of five medium-sized ammonia-urea plants from the UK and the Netherlands between 1963 and 1965. By 1965 synthetic fertilizers supplied about 20 per cent of all nitrogen reaching China's fields. Then this more normal development was cut short, once again, in 1966 with the launching of Mao's destructive spell of ideological frenzy, political vendettas and localized civil war that became known, most incongruously, as the Cultural Revolution.

In a state of anarchy, China's population grew without any controls from 660 million people in 1961 to 870 million by 1972. The addition of more than 200 million people in a single decade represented the fastest population growth in China's long history, and the highest absolute decadal increment ever recorded by any nation (and not to be surpassed by India's growth during the coming decades). At the same time, industrial and urban expansion and Maoist policies of agricultural mismanagement were shrinking the extent of China's arable land, and the traditional organic agriculture had reached its production limits set by the availability of recyclable nutrients.

In just two to three years after the end of the great famine average yields of staple crops recovered to the pre-1959 level – but then they began to stagnate. By the end of the 1960s China's harvests could not keep up even with the basic food needs of the country's growing population. By 1972 China's average per capita food supply was below the levels of the early 1950s, the time when the country was emerging from decades of instability and war. As described earlier in this chapter, all food in cities was strictly rationed, and peasants subsisted on a monotonous and barely adequate vegetarian diet. Moreover, it was obvious that even an unprecedented degree of population controls – at that time contemplated by the ruling gerontocracy, and soon put into effect in the world's most drastic and personally intrusive program – would not prevent the population total rising to at least 1 billion by the year 1980 and to 1.2 billion during the

1990s. The doubling of China's population between 1960 and 2000 would then result (after taking into account land losses to urbanization and industrialization) in more than halving the per capita arable land in just two generations. But there was no way to double that land's productivity with traditional ways of farming.

The only effective way out of this existential predicament was to intensify the performance of China's agriculture, that is to boost its average staple crop yields. In a country where already nearly half of all farmland was irrigated, this meant one change above all: the rapid increase in applications of nitrogen, the nutrient critical for raising yields. China's fertilizer-production capacity had to increase as rapidly as possible, and the best way to achieve this was to get access to the world's most advanced process of ammonia synthesis. And so the very first commercial deal, immediately following Richard Nixon's February 1972 visit that reopened China to the Western world, was Beijing's order for thirteen of the world's largest and most modern ammonia-urea complexes, the biggest ever purchase of its kind.

Such an order was best filled by turning to M.W. Kellogg of Texas, the world's leading designer and builder of such plants: eight of the thirteen ammonia plants came from this company – and their product is fed directly to urea plants built by Kellogg's Dutch subsidiary (CIA 1975; Chang 1977). Output from these newly completed plants soon surpassed the country's pre-1972 fertilizer nitrogen production. More purchases of ammonia-urea complexes followed during the 1970s, as did more fertilizer imports (mostly urea from Japan).

From the US perspective, Kissinger and Nixon's opening of China to the world was a matter of grand *Realpolitik*, of forging a new strategic alliance. Undoubtedly this was so – but, no less assuredly, from Beijing's perspective it was also a matter of basic survival, a shift dictated by the need to secure a key to the nation's very existence. Without higher yields the country would have to face the very real prospect of yet another famine by the late 1970s or the early 1980s. Conversely, because it acquired the means to break through the nitrogen barrier, China's population is now better fed than at any time during its long history, in spite of the fact that it now stands at more than 1.3 billion. This reality has, inevitably, broader implications: without the synthesis of nitrogen fertilizers, humanity's total count would not currently be surpassing 6 billion (Smil 2001b).

China's dependence on the Haber–Bosch process

In 1979 – the year in which Deng Xiaoping finally consolidated his control of the central government and began turning into reality his bold plans for national modernization – China surpassed the USA to become the world's largest consumer of nitrogen fertilizers; ten years later it surpassed the USSR to become also the world's largest producer of these compounds (FAO 2002). In 1976, the year of Mao's death, Chinese farming derived about 40 per cent of all nitrogen inputs from synthetic fertilizers; a decade later, after the country's peasants set new harvest records and after all food rationing was abolished, synthetic fertilizers supplied 60 per cent of nitrogen reaching China's crops (Figure 3.6). And the importance of nitrogen fertilizers has continued to rise: by 1990 they supplied 65 per cent of the nutrient reaching China's crop fields, and by the year 2000 the share was close to 75 per cent (Figure 3.6).

This means that the mean nationwide application of inorganic compounds is now almost 175kg N/ha of arable land, a rate about 75 per cent higher than the declining Japanese applications, whose mean fell from about 160kg N/ha in 1985 to about 100kg N/ha by 2000 (FAO 2002). And as no less than 90 per cent of the country's dietary protein supply is derived from domestically grown crops (the rest comes from aquatic food, meat and dairy products derived from grasslands, and from grain imports) this also means that roughly two thirds (0.9 × 0.75) of all nitrogen in China's current diet originated in the Haber–Bosch synthesis of ammonia.

Or, to make the point even more impressively, in the year 2000 about 850 million Chinese were consuming food whose proteins were synthesized by crops from inorganic nitrogen applied in synthetic fertilizer. A historical comparison confirms this estimate. During the early 1950s traditional organic farming produced, on the average, no more than 90kg of plant protein per hectare of farmland (including the protein in animal feed); in 2000 China's plant protein output averaged about 250kg/ha, or about 2.8 times above the early 1950s rate. As virtually all of the 1950–2000 increase in protein output (160kg/ha) came from inorganic fertilizers, this implies that nitrogen fixed by ammonia synthesis is now indispensable for producing about two thirds (160/250) of all dietary protein.

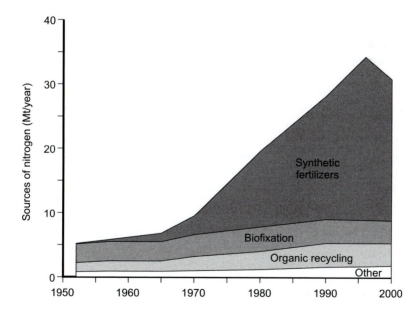

Figure 3.6 Rising shares of synthetic fertilizers in China's supply of agricultural nitrogen
Source: Plotted from data in Smil (2001b).

Predictably, the importance of inorganic nitrogen varies among crops and among provinces. Where the Hunanese rice is still grown in rotations including green manures, the non-fertilizer inputs remain relatively high. The three-year cropping sequence of rice, wheat, rice, green manure, rice, and rapeseed would receive annually 300–320kg N/ha as urea and another 150kg N/ha from biofixation, organic recycling and atmospheric deposition: synthetic nitrogen would thus supply at least 67 per cent of the total input. But China's cultivation of green manures has been in retreat: it peaked at 9.9Mha in 1975, and subsequent steady decline brought their total plantings to less than 4Mha. In contrast, in Jiangsu – where green manuring is virtually absent, biofixation may supply just 25kg N/ha, and organic recycling, irrigation and atmospheric deposition will add no more than 80kg N/ha compared to 380kg N/ha applied to rotations of rice and wheat – inorganic nitrogen will supply almost 80 per cent of the total input.

This high dependence could be lowered a bit, but no fundamental changes are possible. Even if the Chinese were willing to forgo their recent, and much welcome, dietary improvements, and reduce their protein intake to the barely adequate level of the mid-1950s, they would still have to rely on synthetic nitrogen fertilizer to produce at least half of their food protein! These reductions would entail not only large (more than 50–80 per cent) cuts in average consumption of meat and fish, but also much lower intakes of plant oils and fruits. And in the long run the dependence on inorganic nitrogen will have to increase. Even with its greatly reduced fertility, China will add another 300 million people by the middle of the twenty-first century before its total population may level off at somewhere between 1.5 and 1.6 billion people.

Moreover, this much larger population will expect continuing improvements in the quality of its diet. Opportunities for expanding cultivated area are very limited, and higher food imports can never play such a large role in China's case as they did in the development of its smaller Asian neighbors. South Korea has been recently importing 65 per cent of its cereal consumption, and nearly 90 per cent of its oil crop consumption; Japanese imports have supplied nearly 75 per cent of all cereals, all but a few per cent of oil crops, as well as 40 per cent of all fish. If China were to buy two thirds of its recent annual grain consumption (averaging about 450Mt during the late 1990s) abroad, all of the grain recently traded on the world market (250–270Mt/year during the same period) would not suffice. Consequently, all but a relatively small fraction of China's greatly increased demand for food will have to come from further intensification of cropping. As it is most unlikely that other sources of nitrogen (mainly organic recycling and atmospheric deposition) will rise above the recent level of less than 9Mt N/year, there will have to be further substantial increases of average nitrogen applications to China's crop fields during the coming generations.

Their magnitude will depend above all on the future share of animal foods in China's average diet, and on the typical efficiency of fertilizer use. Animal feeding always entails considerable protein losses, with typical feed protein to meat protein conversion efficiencies ranging from 25 per cent for chicken to 10–15 per cent for pork and a mere 5–8 per cent for beef (Smil 2000a). A China that consumes twice or three times as much meat as today, eating it mostly as hamburgers or steaks, and losing 50–60 per cent of all applied nitrogen, can exist only in wishful thinking. A China that consumes twice as much meat per capita as it does now, and does so as a mixture of carp (herbivorous fish is the best converter of feed to meat protein), chicken and pork, and with substantially reduced fertilizer losses, is a practical proposition achievable in a matter of a generation or two.

As higher applications of nitrogen fertilizers bring declining yield response, China is rapidly approaching, and in coastal provinces almost reaching, the economic limits of more intensive fertilization. And with such massive applications, even a fairly efficient use of the nutrient will lead to some unwelcome environmental consequences. Indeed, no other region in the world uses as much nitrogen as the four coastal provinces in East and South China: Jiangsu, Zhejiang, Fujian and Guangdong. Using the official statistics of nitrogen consumption and farmland areas derived from MEDEA's satellite study, their 1995 application rates ranged from about 275kg N/ha in Jiangsu to 350kg N/ha in Zhejiang, and the region's mean was almost exactly 300kg N/ha.

The experiences of other regions that have been receiving high nitrogen fertilizer applications for many decades – particularly northwestern Europe – give us good previews of what to expect. Increased leaching of nitrates into drinking water is already widespread, and we can expect large areas of the Jiangnan to have nitrate concentrations in drinking water well above the WHO limit of 50mg/L. While the health consequences of elevated nitrate levels in drinking water are disputed (l'Hirondel and l'Hirondel 2001), we are much more certain about the effects of excess nitrogen on aquatic life. Because nitrogen commonly limits the growth of phytoplankton and algae, increased escapes of nitrogen fertilizers to China's lakes, ponds and rivers, as well as into shallow coastal waters (the process called eutrophication), will support more abundant growth of these aquatic plants, whose eventual decay consumes oxygen and creates hypoxic or anoxic waters, kills bottom-dwelling molluscs and crustaceans and drives away fish (Rabalais 2002). Algal blooms can also produce dangerous toxins.

Further afield, higher rates of fertilization mean inevitably more denitrification and hence more nitrous oxide. China is already the world's largest emitter of this gas, whose atmospheric concentrations are low (at 310ppb they are equal to only about 0.08 per cent of the current CO_2 level) but which is a much more potent absorber of the outgoing infrared radiation: compared on a 100-year basis, each molecule of N_2O will absorb 310 times more outgoing infrared radiation than a molecule of CO_2 (Houghton *et al.* 2001). Given the gradual decarbonization of the world's primary energy supply, the future importance of the anthropogenic output of N_2O will only increase (Smil 2002b).

Because China does not have the option of following its much smaller East Asian neighbors and to import most of its staple foodstuffs, its continuous intensification of crop production, predicated on higher inputs of nitrogen derived from the Haber–Bosch process of ammonia synthesis, will have to pay much more attention to the overall efficiency of the country's agricultural nitrogen cycle. There is no shortage of effective means that can be widely used to increase the uptake of nitrogen by crops (Fragoso 1993; Prasad and Power 1997; Smil 2001b) – but post-harvest actions are no less necessary: cutting grain losses in transport and storage (excessively high in today's China), reducing food waste at retail and household level (this is surprisingly large for such a poor country), and rationalizing food consumption by promoting healthy diets (obesity is becoming a problem in Chinese cities) would help to moderate the undesirable environmental effects of high nitrogen applications. China's increasing dependence on the Haber Bosch synthesis of ammonia is inevitable – but its economic, environmental and nutritional consequences are not preordained. They could be all impressively improved – or they could become a source of rising concern.

Can China feed itself? Concerns and solutions

China's burgeoning economy and improving food supply were perhaps the best news coming out from the post-Tian'anmen China of the early 1990s. But in 1994 Lester Brown, at that time the president of Washington's Worldwatch Institute, wrote an article arguing that China was rapidly losing its capacity to feed itself, that its grain output had already reached its peak and would fall by at least 20 per cent by the year 2030, and that only massive grain imports could make up for the anticipated deficit (Brown 1994). The following year he published an expanded version of this paper as a short book entitled *Who Will Feed China?* and subtitled, melodramatically, *Wake-up Call for a Small Planet* (Brown 1995). The following passages, from my review of the book in the *New York Review of Books* (Smil 1996a), summarize my basic reactions and set Brown's claims into a wider context of unreconstructed catastrophism.

A catastrophic vision

Brown's analysis of China's food prospects rests on a series of assumptions about what, to him, appear to be irrevocable trends: China's consumers are "moving up the food chain", the country is losing arable land, running out of water, and exhausting its opportunities for further major increases in yields. Because Brown considers all these trends to be virtually unstoppable, his conclusion is that China is heading toward catastrophe. As incomes rise, China's demand for feed grain to produce meat and fish will keep growing. Since there will be no conceivable way to satisfy this demand through domestic grain production (which will be actually declining), the only recourse will be vast, and increasing, imports of grain. This will lead not only to a global increase in food prices but – because Brown does not see any possibility for a major expansion of export supplies – also to world shortages of staple cereals.

How valid is the reasoning behind these apocalyptic predictions? Lester Brown is, of course, a professional catastrophist, a persistent doomsayer who has been turning out forecasts of dire food shortages, crippling energy crises, and planetary environmental collapse since the early 1970s. Only Stanford's Paul Ehrlich can rival him in his long record of prophesying doom. Brown notes with satisfaction in the foreword to *Who Will Feed China?* that his latest doomsday scenario has brought him more attention than anything he has published. No small achievement.

To Lester Brown, problems, setbacks and complications are not merely normal facts of managing – or often just muddling through – an unruly and ever-changing reality. Rather, they tend to be harbingers of an immense global trauma. In the short run this gets him attention – but in the long run he has, much like his confrère Paul Ehrlich, repeatedly been shown to be wrong.

A single example will illustrate this point. In 1974, when OPEC's oil price increases were for a while dramatically misrepresented by energy "experts" as unmistakable signs of the world's running out of fossil fuels, *The Futurist* magazine noted that Brown "refuses to own an automobile and uses public transportation, so that more energy can go into food production". Brown's fear of oil "running out" was so great that he urged us to conserve precious energy for only the most essential of all uses, growing food. Even readers completely uninterested in energy matters know what in fact happened. A generation after Brown's sacrifice, the world's crude oil ratio of reserves to production is at a record high and, adjusted for inflation, oil prices are barely higher than they were before OPEC's first extortionate hike.

But it would be a mistake to dismiss Brown's China predictions as just another scare. Concerns about China's long-term food production capacity are valid. What is so exasperating about Brown's treatment of this topic is his masterful use of highly selective evidence. Brown's book, to use Chinese imagery, badly needs an infusion of yang, light and possibility, to contrast with his unmitigated yin of darkness and decline, especially since he ignores or hardly mentions factors that undermine his view.

I expanded my critique of Brown's claims, and explained a number of realistic solutions and adjustments, in the fourth annual Hopper Lecture (Smil 1996b). The final, and the most extensive, elaboration of these arguments became the last chapter of *Feeding the World* (Smil 2000a), the book I wrote to assess the achievements and prospects of the global food supply. The rest of this chapter's closing section represents a slightly abridged version of that chapter.

If China could do it...

China is a near perfect embodiment of the concatenation of worrisome changes that complicate and undermine the quest for higher food production. The combination of realities that weaken its food-production capacity – its (in absolute terms) still very high population growth, limited (and declining) availability of farmland, widespread and intensifying shortages of water, serious air and water pollution and extensive ecosystemic degradation, reduced growth rates of staple grain yields, and rapid dietary changes – is behind the recent questioning of the country's ability to feed itself (Crook 1994; Brown 1995; Smil 1995a).

At the same time, China's entire food system offers some of the world's most convincing examples of widespread inefficiency and waste. Even a relatively modest effort to eliminate these failures would go a long way toward securing adequate food for coming generations. If a conservative assessment can show that China should be able to meet the challenge, then we may feel much more confident about most of the rest of the world.

China's predicament

The same factors that have made the task of feeding China an uncommon challenge in the past will remain influential during the coming fifty years. First is the necessity to feed the world's largest population (China's 1.25 billion people in 2000 represented just over one fifth of the global total). Second is the limited availability of farmland exacerbated by losses of cultivated land to urban and industrial expansion. The third decisive factor is the deteriorating state of China's agroecosystems, including growing shortages of water and spreading environmental pollution. Two new concerns also matter: dietary transition driven by much higher disposable incomes, a trend particularly pronounced in China's richest coastal provinces; and the declining productivity of farming inputs, above all the falling response of staple cereal yields to intensifying applications of synthetic fertilizers.

The rising demand for food

The country's relative population growth, averaging just 1.1 per cent during the first half of the 1990s, is quite low in comparison with the mean for all modernizing nations (1.77 per cent during the same period), and considerably below the rates for either Southeast Asia or South America, which stood, respectively, at about 1.7 and 1.6 per cent. But the huge absolute increase of China's population during the past generation means that this relatively low growth still translates into a historically high level of nearly 25 million births a year and to net additions of more than 13 million people. These totals will not decline appreciably at least for another decade, and some 200 million people will be added during the next two generations, about as many as Indonesia's total population of the late 1990s.

Obviously, merely maintaining the existing food consumption rates would call for a miniumum 1.1 per cent increase in annual grain harvests; during the last years of the 1990s this would mean adding about 5Mt every year. But if the food supply were to keep up with rising expectations, the actual rates would have to be much higher. Since the beginning of economic modernization in the early 1980s, China's average intakes have moved very rapidly up the food chain, as major per capita consumption increases have brought the typical dietary pattern much closer to those of Japan and Taiwan.

By 1985 – just five years after the beginning of farming privatization – China's average per capita food availability rose to 2,700kcal/day, a rate less than 5 per cent behind the Japanese mean food supply, and it has remained just slightly above that clearly adequate rate ever since (Smil 1985, 1995a). This quantitative rise has been accompanied by major qualitative gains. Consumption of coarse grains and tubers declined as intakes of more finely milled wheat and rice increased. Milling rates for rice returned to 70 per cent or less, compared to the 85 per cent typical of pre-1980 years.

Per capita intakes of traditional non-staple favorites have multiplied several-fold. Between 1980 and 2000, average annual consumption of plant oils nearly quadrupled, while the consumption of eggs and fruits rose sixfold (Figure 3.7). Pork purchases tripled nationwide – with per capita consumption of pork among the highest-income groups in coastal cities surpassing the Japanese national mean – and drinking of alcoholic beverages rose more than fourfold (SSB 1978–1999). Future rates of consumption increases will slow down, but given the still low rate of China's urbanization (about one third of the country's popula-tion was urban in 1999) and great urban/rural disparities of food intakes, the pattern will not stabilize soon. Consumption surveys show that the expenditure elasticities for rice and coarse grains are declining, but those for wheat, meat, alcohol and vegetables are increasing.

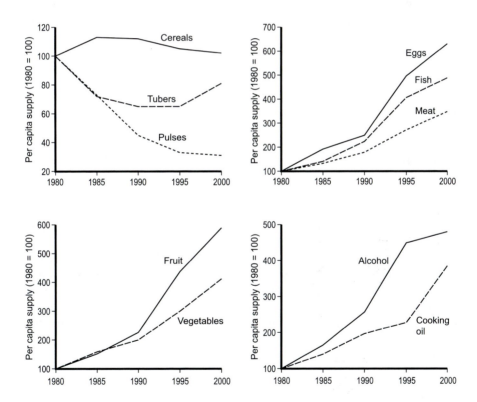

Figure 3.7   Between 1980 and 2000 China's dietary transition followed a universal pattern of declining tuber and pulse consumption, and increasing intakes of animal foods, fruits, plant oils and alcoholic beverages

Source: Per capita rates calculated from data in *China Statistical Yearbook*.

The rising demand for meat and alcohols allows us to foresee easily a doubling of grain demand during the next generation. The advancing Westernization of urban diets will push up the demand for wheat, sugar and oils. At the same time, increased grain harvests will have to come from the shrinking amount of farmland, and to cope with a precarious availability of irrigation water as well as with a more widespread environmental pollution.

Environmental constraints

According to official claims, the country lost about 15 per cent of its farmland between 1957 and 1990 (Smil 1993). Given the country's intervening population increase, the average farmland availability was thus more than halved, from about 0.18 to just 0.08ha/person. Rapid post-1980 modernization brought a spate of new rural and urban housing construction and unprecedented expansion of export-oriented manufactures and transportation links. New peasant houses are rarely built on the sites of old structures, new factories usually take over highly productive alluvial land, and government policies promote multilane freeways instead of rapid trains. Not surprisingly, annual farmland losses have been averaging at least 0.5Mha since 1980, and they have been mostly concentrated in the rapidly developing coastal provinces where intensity of farmland use is highest.

During the past decade water shortages have become seasonally acute throughout most of the North China Plain. Large-scale irrigation of the plain began only in the 1960s with the introduction of the first shallow tube wells, and by the late 1980s the plain had more than two million tube wells irrigating over 11Mha of farmland (O'Mara 1988). Initially, pumping helped to lower the formerly high water table and hence to reduce the extent of soil salinization, but soon it began causing excessive exploitation of aquifers accompanied by spreading ground subsidence (Smil 1993).

During the early 1980s roughly a third of irrigation water on the plain came from the Huanghe, but the combination of recurrent droughts and higher agricultural, urban and industrial demand began exhausting the stream long before it reached the sea. The river's total runoff has recently fallen to as low as two fifths of the long-term mean, as the normally very low summer flow has repeatedly ceased altogether for hundreds of kilometers from its mouth for a period lasting between one and four months. Diversion of Huanghe water, amounting to more than a quarter of its total flow during dry years, also reduces the silt transport to the ocean; a heavy sediment load is thus deposited on the river's bed, particularly in Henan and Shandong provinces. Irrigation thus aggravates the elevation of the river's bed above the surrounding countryside.

Water shortages in the North now affect an area extending over some 600,000km^2, an area about 10 per cent larger than France. But water shortages are not limited to the plain: they have become a near-chronic reality in every northern and northwestern province. At a basin level the Hai–Luan basin has the highest water stress, followed by the Huai River basin (Nickum 1998). On a provincial basis Shanxi (particularly its southern part) and peninsular Shandong face the greatest water shortage; in Shanxi even drinking water is often scarce, and about 10 per cent of the province's peasants suffer chronic shortages of its supply. The planned expansion of surface coal mining and the construction of large coal-fired power plants will further strain this inadequate supply. And although expanding cities are now claiming substantial volumes of water used previously in agriculture, urban water shortages have become the norm in the capital and 200 other municipalities in the region.

Environmental pollution accompanying China's industrial and urban expansion is both widespread and severe (Smil 1993). With about 1.2 billion tonnes extracted annually, China is now the world's largest consumer of coal, producing more SO_2 and particulate matter than all of Europe outside Russia; more than 80 per cent of its waste water is discharged without treatment; and irrigation waters in the most intensively cultivated periurban areas have been polluted by industrial wastes. An even greater water pollution threat comes from hundreds of thousands of new village and township enterprises that have been absorbing rural surplus labor. China's Environmental Protection Agency can only guess at the total amount of untreated waste leaving those factories.

Degradation of ecosystems has an even greater impact, with worsening shortages of water, extensive soil erosion (causing silting of reservoirs and irrigation canals, and aggravating annual flooding), salinization and waterlogging of farmland, overgrazing and pest infestation of grasslands, and disappearance of the remaining mature forests. Huang and Rozelle (1995) estimated that erosion, salinization and losses of farmland may have cost China recently 6Mt of grain a year, more than the additional output needed to keep up with the country's population growth. My more comprehensive, but still incomplete, survey of the economic costs of China's environmental pollution and ecosystemic degradation shows that these are equivalent to at least 10 per cent of the country's annual GDP, and that roughly one fifth of that cost is attributable to losses of agricultural production (Smil 1997b).

While some problems have been eased by higher investment in environmental protection – above all through waste water treatment in large cities, installation of effective particulate-matter controls at large stationary combustion sources, and private afforestation of slopelands – others are worsening. The two most notable examples of the latter category are the rapid expansion of the area affected by acid deposition in Southwestern China (caused by burning high-sulfur coals in the region's rainy climate), and rising concentrations of tropospheric ozone from more frequent, and more concentrated, episodes of photochemical smog (resulting from the rising intensity of automobile traffic in rich coastal provinces). And, as anywhere else, rising rates of fertilization bring lower yield responses, and a higher demand for urban and industrial water uses is now competing with limited supplies for irrigation.

To some observers, the combined effects of these changes were already demonstrated by the post-1984 stagnation of China's grain output (Brown 1995). That year's record grain harvest of 407Mt was followed by five years of stagnation, and although a new record, 446Mt, was set in 1990, it was followed, again, by two years of lower harvests (Figure 3.8). A continuation and intensification of these trends could result in annual grain supply deficits amounting to tens of millions of tonnes during the coming decade, and surpassing 100Mt, possibly even 200Mt, before the year 2025.

Climate change could make China's quest for higher yields even more difficult, and its dependence on imports even greater. There are indications that the twentieth century has already brought greater aridity to eastern and north-

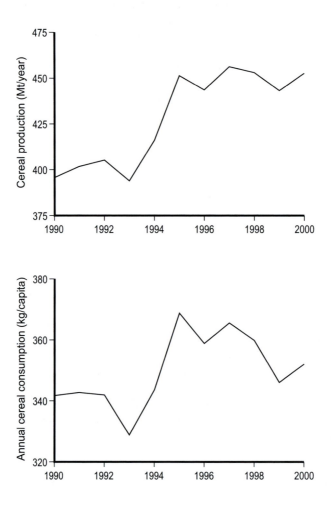

Figure 3.8 China's fluctuating grain harvests and average per capita grain supply, 1990–2000

Source: Plotted from data in *China Statistical Yearbook*.

western parts of the country, and higher temperatures in the North. Chinese studies of the long-term effect of global warming suggest possibilities of lower rice yields in the South, lower corn yields in the East, and lower soybean harvests everywhere except in the Northeast (Smit and Cai 1996).

The implications of China's inability to feed itself would be global. Even if a relatively rich China could afford to buy increasing quantities of cereals on the world market, such purchases would not just lead to price rises in a handful of remaining countries exporting food, they would also gravely reduce, or virtually remove, the access of many poorer nations in Africa and Asia to grain deliveries from the four producers with virtually assured long-term export potential: the USA, Canada, Australia and Argentina (the contribution of Russia's and the Ukraine's exports, potentially quite large, remains highly uncertain).

Pressure on international grain prices would rise as the country's unmet demand moved substantially above the level of recent Japanese purchases (at almost 30Mt a year, now the largest in the world). Annual imports of 100Mt would be equivalent to one half of the recent global grain shipments, and given the fact that future import demand in other populous Asian, African and Latin American countries will almost certainly grow, it is difficult to see that the country could actually secure such a large share. And if its shortfall were to amount to more than 200Mt a year, China could not hope to make this up by imports at any price: a doubling of global grain sales during the next generation is extremely unlikely.

Available resources

Realistic appraisals of agricultural possibilities must rest on reliable information. Unfortunately, not a few analyses of China's agricultural prospects have relied on inaccurate figures or interpreted undeniable realities in misleading ways. To begin with, China's population may stay well below the 1.6 billion people assumed by Brown for the year 2030. In fact, the medium variant of the latest UN revision of long-term forecasts foresees stabilization around 1.5 billion after the year 2030, and the low variant does not even reach 1.4 billion before the total levels off (UNO 2002). In addition to a further significant slow-down of China's population growth, overall demand for food might be appreciably lowered by a combination of ageing (with low fertilities in place since the early 1980s, China will experience one of the world's fastest demographic transitions), more sedentary lifestyles, and concern about healthy diets (traditionally strong in China).

As in many countries around the world, China's official figures have been substantially underestimating the country's arable land, which means that the official yields must be adjusted downwards, and that there are greater unrealized possibilities of increasing future harvests. China's farmland scarcity is thus nowhere near the level observed in South Korea, Taiwan and Japan, the country's neighbors that have increasingly relied on imports of grain, edible oil and meat. During much of the 1990s, China's *Statistical Yearbook* has contained a note warning that "figures for the cultivated land are under-estimated and must be further verified". This is not news: many students of Chinese affairs have known since the early 1980s that the official total of China's farmland – 95Mha listed by the State Statistical Bureau, putting China's per capita mean of arable land below the Bangladeshi average – is wrong.

Even the earliest remote sensing studies based on imagery with inadequate resolution (the LANDSAT Multiple Spectral Scanner with resolution of 80m) indicated that figures used by the State Statistical Bureau, and hence by virtually all misinformed foreigners, were too low. They came up with a total as high as 150Mha, and detailed sample surveys of the late 1980s came up with the range of 133–140Mha (Smil 1993). More recently, Wu and Guo (1994) put the total at 136.4Mha plus an additional 7.4Mha devoted to horticulture. Heilig's (1997) application of land survey data for 1985 to correct the official claims of total cultivated area ended up with 137.1Mha for the year 1995.

The most extensive, and the most accurate, remote sensing evaluation used a stratified, multi-stage area estimation approach: samples of the higher-resolution classified imagery from the Keyhole (KH) series of intelligence satellites (whose latest models return images with resolution of 15cm or better) were used as surrogates for *in situ* data to correct estimates derived from much coarser commercially available images, including Advanced Very High Resolution Radiometer and LANDSAT. This analysis yielded the total of 143.3Mha for the year 1992; with a variation of 5.6 per cent at the 0.95 confidence interval, the actual area could have been as low as 135.4Mha and as high as 151.4Mha (Figure 3.9) (MEDEA 1997). This estimate was subsequently revised to the range of 133–147Mha for the year 1997: failure of the initial appraisal to account properly for fallowed land and intervening conversions of farmland to nonagricultural uses were the main reasons for the reduction.

I believe that even MEDEA's total may be too low, as it does not include aquacultural ponds and orchards, the two intensive land uses which make very significant contributions to the country's balanced diet. Moreover, a large share of today's orchards and ponds has been converted from crop fields since 1980: land use has changed but the land has not only remained devoted to food production as it keeps supplying high-quality protein and desirable micronutrients, but its new uses also provide a variety of environmental benefits. Even when assuming an annual yield of no more than four tonnes of fish, a hectare of carp pond will yield about 800kg of protein, twice as much as the average grain harvest (including the 1.5 multicropping rate) from the same area – and, unlike cereals, carp has adequate amounts of all amino acids. And a hectare of citrus orchard will produce 50 per cent more vitamin C and twice as much food energy as the same area planted to cabbages.

With the inclusion of ponds and orchards, China's farmland is thus anywhere between 140 and 160Mha, and the country's 1998 per capita mean is at least 1,100m^2, compared to 490m^2 in South Korea, 430m^2 in Taiwan, and 420m^2 in

Japan. China's per capita farmland availability is thus at least two and almost three times larger than that of its East Asian neighbors. And unlike in those three countries, there are still appreciable opportunities for reclamation of farmland in China. According to official estimates, the country has at least 33Mha of uncultivated but reclaimable land categorized as wasteland, whose eventual development (perhaps a third of that land could be converted to fairly productive fields, the rest is suitable mostly for planting trees) would result in appreciable food production gains and environmental benefits.

Conversions to appropriate food production uses could be speeded up by large-scale auctioning of rights to long-term (50–100 years) private use of such land. Hanstad and Li (1997) describe the keen interest shown by peasants bidding for the rights to wasteland, and the relatively high investment of labor and cash they subsequently undertake to use the land for planting trees for fruits, nuts, fuelwood and timber. The fruit and nut production potential of large-scale wasteland cultivation is obviously substantial, but environmental benefits – above all reduced soil erosion on previously barren slope lands – may be of equal, or even greater, benefit for the country's agroecosystems.

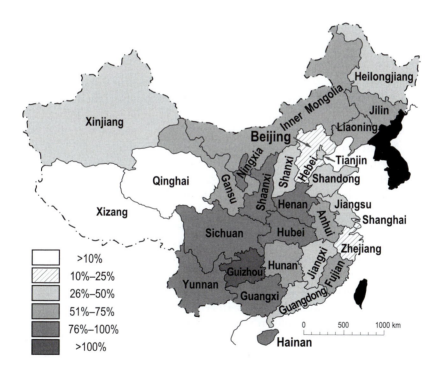

Figure 3.9 Provincial differences between the availability of agricultural land according to the official statistics and to the MEDEA study

In addition, much of the farmland in South China can be cropped continuously, yielding three harvests of staple crops, or up to five harvests of vegetables a year. The cold climate in northeastern China allows for only a single crop, while in northern provinces winter wheat commonly follows a summer crop. China's overall multicropping ratio (sown/cultivated area) in the mid-1990s was 1.56, compared to Japan's 1.03 and Korea's 1.14. With proper rotations, further intensification of China's crop cultivation, raising the multicropping ratio to 1.6–1.65, is possible without damaging the affected agroecosystems.

Underreporting of farmland means that the official figures on China's average grain yields are exaggerated. The difference is smallest for rice (less than 10 per cent) and largest for corn (in some provinces more than 40 per cent). Contrary to Brown's assertion, Chinese yields are not exceptionally high by advanced world standards, and could be increased substantially by higher inputs and better agronomic management. Corn, the principal feed grain, averaged officially 4.9t/ha in 1995, but the actual mean is just below 4t/ha, or no more than half of the average US yield in a good year. Even the average official rice yield of about 6t/ha is more than 10 per cent behind the Japanese mean. This means that the country has more room to improve crop yields by using additional inputs, better agronomic practices and price incentives.

Another important consideration is that China's undoubtedly substantial farmland losses have been exaggerated. Since 1980 the net farmland loss in China has fluctuated between less than 100,000ha (in 1989–1991) and 1Mha (in 1985), with the period of fastest decline between 1992 and 1994. Mean annual loss has been nearly 500,000ha a year since 1980, but this does not mean that the land devoted to food production simply shrank by that much every year. A large part of the reported loss, over 50 per cent in some years, has been due to the restoration of land converted to fields during the years of extremist policies of the Maoist era back to their original, and environmentally much more appropriate, use as orchards, grasslands and fish ponds (Smil 1999c). This change has clearly helped China's nutritional balance, and it has enhanced agroecosystemic diversity. Consequently, it is misleading to treat this changed land use as a loss of food production capacity.

The Chinese authorities recognize the necessity to protect the country's farmland. New rules to control illegal land use changes came into effect on 1 March 1996, designed to improve the enforcement of stricter regulations. Although it would be naive to expect easy compliance in many regions, it is not unrealistic to foresee an appreciable moderation of annual losses. Ke (1996) put the net reduction of farmland between 1978 and 1994 at 4.5Mha, and he projects a similar loss (4–5Mha) during the fifteen years between 1995 and 2010. Even if China were to lose 0.5Mha a year for the next twenty-five years, it would still have more than 800m^2 of farmland per capita in the year 2020 (when its population will be about 1.45 billion people), or twice as much as Japan has today.

A realistic appraisal of China's water availability is also more complex than conveyed by basic, and in this case quite reliable, precipitation and runoff statistics, and less certain data about water stored in aquifers. To begin with, all nationwide means concerning water are not very meaningful, as the country's monsoonal regime results in pronounced annual and seasonal precipitation and evapotranspiration differences progressing along the southeast/northwest gradient. The 500-mm isohyet (running from the central Heilongjiang in the northeast to the Sino-Bhutanese border in the southwest) forms an approximate divide between the dry northern and western interior and wet coastal east and inland south (Domrös and Peng 1988).

China's water supply is thus determined by a strong seasonality of monsoonal precipitation, by a high frequency of droughts north of the great divide, and by large fluctuations in the distribution of annual and seasonal moisture. Densely inhabited parts of northern China, covering about one third of the country's territory, have about two fifths of the total population and grow the same share of staple grains – but they receive only about one quarter of the country's precipitation, and because of high summer evapotranspiration they can access less than 10 per cent of the nationwide stream runoff. Not surprisingly, these northern provinces rely heavily on underground water reserves, yet they possess no more than 30 per cent of all water in China's aquifers (Smil 1993).

A higher frequency of dry years since the mid-1980s has undoubtedly contributed to northern China's water shortages. At the same time, the extent of this natural precipitation shortfall is not unprecedented. Official statistics on areas affected by drought (where yields are reduced by at least 30 per cent in comparison with years of normal precipitation) show large fluctuations of between 1–18Mha a year (see Figure 3.2) (SSB 1978–1999). Risks of flooding are also considerable inasmuch as about a tenth of China's territory, inhabited by nearly two thirds of the population and producing roughly 70 per cent of all agricultural output, is below the flood level of major rivers. Flooding serious enough to reduce crop yields by at least 30 per cent has recently been affecting 4–9Mha of farmland annually (Figure 3.2).

Any serious cutbacks in China's irrigation would have major repercussions for the country's food production. In 1950 China irrigated no more than 16 per cent of its farmland, but now the officially quoted share is 46 per cent (SSB 1997). Assuming that the figures on irrigated land are fairly accurate, the actual share (with 140Mha rather than just 95Mha of arable land) would be just above 30 per cent. This would make China no more dependent on irrigation than India, which irrigates nearly 30 per cent of its farmland. In spite of so many obvious signs of water shortages, existing Chinese practices do not reflect the growing scarcity of the resource. Inexpensive water is primarily responsible for unsustainable and wasteful irrigation, which would be greatly curtailed with the introduction of realistic water fees. (For more on water prices and savings, see the second and the third sections of Chapter 4.) The high potential for water savings is the main reason why Nickum (1998) concluded that China's "water crisis" is localized, and is economic and institutional rather than a matter of a disappearing resource.

China is now the world's largest producer and user of nitrogen fertilizers – but it still has a large potential to increase its fertilizer inputs. Assuming the country has at least 140Mha of farmland, its mid-1990s nitrogen applications were around 170kg N/ha, a rate higher than the declining Japanese average (about 120kg N/ha in 1997). But with an average multicropping ratio of 1.5 this prorates to about 110kg N/ha per crop, a rate lower than the mean applications to single high-yielding crops of US corn or European winter wheat. And while average nitrogen applications in China's coastal rice-growing provinces are just about the highest in the world, large parts of the interior receive considerably less of the nutrient than is the nationwide mean. Clearly, China still has considerable room to increase its average nitrogen applications – and even greater opportunities to combine them with appropriate quantities of phosphorus and potassium.

Post-harvest losses

A key argument of this book – that nearly all assessments of long-term food prospects have been preoccupied with exploring the possibilities of increased supply instead of reducing waste along the whole food chain – is persuasively illustrated by China's enormous post-harvest losses resulting from improper storage of crops, low efficiency of animal feeding and very high waste of cooked food. China's antiquated storage methods cost the country roughly one seventh of its cereal harvest every year (Liang *et al.* 1993). Better storage could make a huge difference because of China's extraordinarily large amount of grain held in state and private reserves. The total, long considered a state secret, was claimed to be 458Mt in 1994, more than the harvest of all cereals and tubers, and more than five times as large as standard expectations for setting aside slightly less than one fifth of annual grain consumption (Crook 1996).

Inefficient feeding of animals, table waste in hundreds of thousands of labor-unit eateries, and wasteful fermenting to alcohol almost doubles the total grain loss to more than 50Mt of staple grain equivalent a year. Current Chinese feeding rates are anywhere between 10 and 50 per cent above the norms prevailing in Western countries. The overwhelming majority of China's pigs (pork accounts for no less than 90 per cent of the country's meat output) is still not fed well-balanced mixtures but just about any available edible matter, hence it is commonly deficient in protein. Not surprisingly, an average Chinese pig takes at least twice as long to reach slaughter weight than a typical North American animal (12–14 months rather than just six months) – and its carcass is still lighter and more fatty (Simpson *et al.* 1994). And hundreds of millions of chickens roaming the country's farmyards take three times as long to reach their (again lower) slaughter weight than do North American broilers.

Production of alcoholic beverages is a particularly fine example of waste that could be sharply reduced by relatively simple technical improvements. Brewing beer and fermenting a variety of Chinese liquors (usually rice- or sorghum-based) consumed almost 20Mt of grain a year in the early 1990s, and the demand has been rising by about 20 per cent a year. But drinking more is only a partial explanation for this huge total: most of China's 40,000 distilleries and breweries are small, inefficient enterprises whose grain consumption is typically

40 per cent higher than in the state-of-the-art factories (Liang *et al.* 1993). And losses during consumption – particularly in labor unit eating halls and the now-ubiquitous banqueting at public expense – are staggering. On 13 December 1994 an official China News Agency report put the annual total of wasted grain at almost 83Mt, and attributed about three fifths of this total to losses during consumption. Articles in the Chinese press have repeatedly noted large quantities of leftovers disposed of by restaurants, hotels and canteens every day (Wu 1996).

Finally, a closer look at the causes of the post-1984 stagnation of grain output reveals that a relative neglect of agriculture, rather than a combination of inexorably degradative changes, has been the most important reason for that trend. As the country, and the world, became mesmerized by the high rates of China's industrial growth, the proportion of state investment in agriculture had been declining, falling by a third between 1991 and 1994 (SSB 1992–1996). Rises in procurement prices paid to farmers for grain delivered under the compulsory quota system lagged behind the high rate of inflation, and often the farmers were not even paid, but issued IOUs. Not surprisingly, peasants responded by planting less grain and more cash crops.

One of Brown's main conclusions, that the country faces the prospect of continuously falling grain harvests, was thus quickly disproved. In 1994, when Brown widely publicized his alarming appraisal, China's harvest fell by 2.5 per cent compared to the record output of 1993 – but it set yet another record in 1995 by reaching almost 467Mt. And in 1996 – in spite of the fact that large parts of the Yangzi valley (particularly Hunan province, which normally produces about 13 per cent of China's rice) experienced some of the worst flooding recorded in modern China – the country's grain harvest reached yet another record of 485Mt (4 per cent above the 1995 level), an increase far ahead of the country's rate of population growth.

Realistic solutions

No single efficiency improvement, likewise no single policy change – even if carried to its technical and economic limits, or even if representing a radical departure from old, irrational ways – has the potential to alter fundamentally a country's long-term food production outlook. Only a combination of such changes, and sustained attention to their diffusion and performance, will make an appreciable difference. Fortunately, in China's case, as in every other large agricultural system, there are many opportunities for addressing the key twin inefficiencies of water and fertilizer use, for improving the management of agroecosystems, for using pricing to promote efficiency, and for investing in research. And although the country's rapidly unfolding dietary transition – above all the rising consumption of animal foodstuffs – results in substantially higher demand for natural resources, long-term adjustments of China's dominant nutritional pattern could make a substantial contribution toward reconciling the demand for better eating with the capacity of agroecosystems to provide the requisite environmental goods and services.

Investment in more efficient forms of irrigation, and more realistic prices for delivered water, could yield surprisingly large water savings. Water prices paid by Chinese peasants on the drought-prone North China Plain are about as realistic as those enjoyed by California farmers growing alfalfa and rice in the semi-desert climate of the Central Valley (O'Mara 1988). During the late 1980s, a decade of extensive drought and chronic urban water shortages, the typical price of China's irrigation water was mostly between 5 and 20 per cent of the actual cost. Higher prices should bring better matching of crops with available moisture and introduce more efficient irrigation.

But higher prices alone may not be sufficient: some regions will also need changes in basic water allocation arrangements. Total distribution, seepage and evaporation losses in China's traditional ridge-and-furrow irrigation amount commonly to 50–60 per cent of carried water. Using an appropriate mixture of water-conservation techniques – such as irrigating every other furrow, carefully scheduling water applications, or replacing corn (an increasingly popular crop in arid North China) with sorghum – could result in additional, and nearly cost-free, supply gains. Fertilizer applications offer equally impressive examples of great efficiency opportunities. Two important approaches – popularization of "fertil-izing by prescription", and optimization of applications based on soil analyses and cropping practices – are becoming increasingly popular among China's cost-conscious farmers. Besides the variety of universally applicable approaches aiming at higher fertilizer use efficiency, two measures would greatly improve China's use of nitrogen fertilizers: major efficiency gains would result from a gradual dismantling of small fertilizer factories making ammonium bicarbonate, and from adjusting the nutrient ratio.

Ammonium bicarbonate still accounted for about a third of China's total output of synthetic nitrogenous fertilizers in the mid-1990s, but its high volatility combined with shoddy packaging means that a large share of the nutrient is lost even before it is applied to fields. This, and the underestimated farmland, means that actual applications of nitrogen are much lower than implied by official statistics – hence the potential to raise yields by higher fertilization is commensu-rably higher. Getting the N:P:K ratios right is a long-overdue goal of Chinese fertilizer applications. Whereas the worldwide mean is now about 100:18:22 (and the United States average is roughly 100:16:35), Chinese applications have been chronically deficient in both phosphorus and potassium, with the nationwide ratio of 100:14:8, and with much higher imbalances in many intensively culti-vated regions (FAO 2002). This chronic excess of nitrogen diminishes the efficiency of nitrogen applications and promotes unnecessarily high losses of the nutrient, resulting in a higher nitrate burden in China's waters, and in higher denitrification rates producing more N_2O (China is already the world's largest emitter of N_2O from farming).

Raising efficiencies of meat production is another area of potentially large rewards. Widespread availability of mixed feeds and better breeds could lower today's feed/meat ratios, not only for pigs but also for poultry and for carp and other freshwater fish. This should not mean giving up the traditional feeding of a great variety of waste organic matter. These feeds are more important in China than in any large livestock-producing country. They range from plain and treated cereal straws and root crops to aquatic plants, leucaena leaves and poultry litter, and they may have contributed as much as 35 per cent of all feed energy used in China's animal food production in the early 1990s (Simpson *et al.* 1994). This share is expected to decline, but it may be still around 30 per cent a generation from now, as properly prepared and upgraded (urea-treated straw is already common in China) waste feeds will keep reducing the demand for high-quality concentrates.

By far the most important way in which long-term dietary transitions could contribute to the higher efficiency of the food system would be by producing animal foodstuffs requiring less feed per unit of final product. Animal foods in the average Chinese diet of the late 1990s – dominated by pork (accounting for almost half of energy content), with rising fish, poultry and egg consumption, and negligible intake of dairy products – take about 3.2 units of grain feed per unit of live weight output. If the shares of animal food were split equally among pork, fish, poultry and eggs, while typical feeding rates were lowered by just 10–15 per cent, feeding would require no more than 2.5 units of grain per unit of live weight output, a 20 per cent improvement compared to the current state. A diet consisting of equal parts of pork, poultry, eggs, fish and milk, and produced with feeding efficiencies another 10 per cent higher (this would still leave them well behind the best Western levels of today), would require just 2.0–2.1 units of concentrate feed. As we have already seen, the Japanese example shows that dairy products, traditionally absent in East Asia, could eventually become a relatively large source of food energy and dietary protein.

The level at which China's meat consumption will eventually saturate is yet another critical variable. A mechanical transfer of Taiwan's experience to China is definitely inappropriate. Taiwan's combination of very high average per capita meat intake (more than 70kg) and very low direct cereal consumption (less than 110kg) is exceptional in Asia, and the island's mean per capita cereal intake is even below the OECD's mean of some 130kg! Differences of scale between the two countries (1.3 billion vs. 20 million people) is another obvious matter to consider. Recent high forecasts of China's meat consumption have been also undoubtedly influenced by erroneous official statistics of average meat supply. FAO's food balance sheets, based on China's official output statistics, put the average per capita meat consumption at 38.1kg in 1995. The *China Statistical Yearbook* puts per capita purchases of urban households at 23.7kg in 1995, and a two-year national nutrition survey conducted between 1992 and 1994 found an average daily meat consumption of 58g, or 21.2kg a year (Cui 1995). This means that an eventual doubling of average nationwide per capita meat consumption would result in a rate only marginally higher than the current value claimed by official statistics!

If China's harvest and postharvest grain losses could be lowered to a rate still somewhat higher than is common in Western countries – say to no more than 8–10 per cent – the country would gain more than 30Mt of grain a year, a total

1.5 times higher than its exceptionally high cereal imports in 1995, and enough to provide an adequate diet for 75 million people! Building modern grain stores capable of handling China's fluctuating harvests will be the key to solving this problem: during the years of bumper harvests millions of tonnes of grain are left out in the open.

Encouraging perspectives

The impacts of possibly rapid climate change must be seen in a proper perspective. Given the size of China's territory and the variety of crops grown, global warming would not only bring risks of lower yields but also possibilities for increased harvests. Where adequate moisture could be provided, Chinese studies forecast higher winter wheat yields throughout the North, better corn yields on the North China Plain, better soybean harvests in the Northeast (the crop's main producing area), and benefits for tea and citrus fruits (Smit and Cai 1996). Other benefits might include northward and westward expansion of the wheat-growing districts, and northward expansion of corn growing. In addition, a long-term view of history would lead Chinese researchers to recognize such shifts not only as threatening changes – but also as useful stimuli for adjustments in farming and for spatial shifts in cropping.

While it is unrealistic to expect that the China of the coming generation could appreciably lower the extent and the intensity of its environmental problems, it could substantially reduce the rate of new impacts, and even turn around some degradative trends. Encouragingly, China's investment in environmental protection is now relatively higher than in any rich nation during a comparable stage of its economic development – and by the year 2000 it should rise to at least one per cent of total GDP (Smil 1997b). Government spending on environmental protection in rich countries began to make a difference only after their average per capita GDPs passed US$10,000, about five times as high as the Chinese GDP mean today. Most of these changes will require a greater commitment to agricultural research, whose findings are necessary to sustain a variety of technical and managerial innovations. The importance of these innovations for China's agriculture has been quite large. Research by Huang and Rozelle (1996) showed that these advances were at least as important in raising food output even during the early 1980s, when most observers interpreted the sharply higher production as the result of newly privatized farming – and during the latter half of the 1980s and in the early 1990s they accounted for almost all of the growth in agricultural productivity.

As there is a significant time lag in application of research findings, China should be spending increasing amounts now to enjoy the benefits during the coming decades. Unfortunately, as the country became rapidly richer the real annual expenditures on agricultural research fell between 1985 and 1990, and they surpassed the peak 1985 level only by 1994 (Fan and Pardy 1992; Huang and Rozelle 1996). Currently they amount to less than 0.2 per cent of the total gross output value of Chinese agriculture; in contrast, US federal funding alone has been equal to about 1 per cent of the value contributed by agriculture to the country's GDP. Finally, the purchasing power of Chinese consumers is still limited. The International Monetary Fund's exaggerated estimates of the purchasing power parity (PPP) of average annual per capita GDP at nearly US$3,000 in the early 1990s were recently scaled down by the World Bank to about US$(1992)1,800, or a mere three fifths of the Indonesian mean (World Bank 1996). Consequently, the rate of dietary transition will not be as rapid in the poor counties of China's interior as it has been in the country's large coastal cities.

Considering this evidence of potential capacity for improving harvests, reducing losses and managing demand, it is not surprising that virtually all researchers who have spent a long time studying China's agriculture agree that the country can do it: that it can feed itself during the coming generations, and that its grain, oil, sugar and meat imports will not destabilize the global food market. The tenor of these conclusions is remarkably similar. Alexandratos (1996) uses a wide range of revealing international production and consumption comparisons to make the persuasive case that China's growing grain imports will remain only a fraction of those depicted in the panicky scenarios offered by Brown. He also notes that East Asia's decline of cereal food consumption reflected above all drastic falls in rice consumption – but as a smaller share of China's population consumes a mainly rice-based diet (rice dominates grain output only in fourteen of China's thirty provinces) this trend cannot be duplicated in China (Alexandratos 1997). China is also still much poorer than its smaller neighbors, and populations living in poverty will increase their grain intake in early stages of their modernization. And so it is much more likely that a generation from now China's direct annual grain consumption will be still closer to 200kg rather than 100kg per capita.

Frederick Crook (1994) expects "Chinese farmers to feed their own population, supplemented by modest quantities of imported grain". Scott Rozelle and his colleagues believe that "China will neither starve the world nor become a major grain exporter. It does seem likely, however, that China will become a much bigger importer in the coming decades" (Rozelle *et al.* 1996). The president of China's new Agricultural University has an unequivocal answer buttressed by detailed technical explanations: "China should and can feed itself today and in the future" (Ke 1996). Hence I conclude this appraisal in the same fashion that I summed up my previous assessments of China's ability to feed itself (Smil 1995a, 1996b). There do not seem to be any insurmountable biophysical reasons why China should not continue feeding itself during the next two generations. Were this not to happen it will not be because meeting this challenge requires reliance on as yet unproven bioengineering advances or on unprecedented social adjustments. A combination of well-proven economic and technical fixes, environmental protection measures, and dietary adjustments, can extract enough additional food from China's agroecosystems to provide decent nutrition during the coming generations without a further weakening of the country's environmental foundations.

New realities

China's post-1994 grain production has certainly not conformed to Brown's catastrophist forecasts, but nobody could have predicted its rapid swings. As the total 1994 grain harvest fell below 400Mt the government decided to stimulate grain production through increased procurement prices and mandated minimum production and reserve levels. These decisions brought a succession of record harvests, with the peak in 1998 (456Mt) more than 12 per cent above the 1993 level, and with the 1999 harvest only a few megatons lower. These huge outputs combined with a falling demand for grain – between 1990 and 2000 intakes of rice and wheat fell by 13 per cent – to fill China's storages beyond capacity, to push grain prices down, and to bring a sharp retrenchment in 2000. The total area sown to cereals declined by 7 per cent, and a widespread drought further reduced the harvest to just over 400Mt; and the 2001 harvest, after further reduction of the planted area, was even a few megatons lower.

In spite of a production level equal to the early 1990s, when China's population was 11 per cent smaller, there have been no grain shortages. Lower demand accounts for only a small part of this discrepancy: China's enormous grain stocks explain most of it. The size of these stocks has been always a state secret, but a variety of new fragmentary information led USDA to re-evaluate drastically its previous estimates of these stocks: instead of about 66Mt of stocks at the end of the 2000/2001 crop year, USDA now believes that the total was about 230Mt, and other estimates are as high as 360–500Mt (Hsu and Gale 2001). This is why, at the time of its lowest harvests in a decade, China was selling large amounts of corn while it was reducing its grain imports to a few megatons. Brown (1995) made a great deal of the fact that China's net grain exports of 8Mt in 1993/1994 turned into net imports of 16Mt a year later, and he saw it as an indisputable fact that the country had emerged as a major permanent importer of grain. What would he make of the fact that during the three crop years between 1998–1999 and 2000–2001 China's corn, wheat and rice imports totaled 2.8Mt while exports of these cereals reached nearly 30Mt (FAO 2002)?

And Brown's dire predictions could not accommodate the fact that China's food balance sheets have shown no decline in average per capita food availability. FAO's (2002) calculations show that between 1997 and 2000 China's average food availability remained almost perfectly steady, with year-to-year fluctuations being less than 0.5 per cent, and that shifts in diet composition continued within this stable overall supply. Following the trend established at the very beginning of the post-1978 agricultural reforms, the average per capita food supply now contains less cereals but more sugar, plant oils, vegetables, fruits, poultry, milk and aquacultured fish than it did in the mid-1990s. I would expect both of these trends – stable per capita food availability and continuing slow shifts of average dietary make-up – to continue during the first decade of the twenty-first century. Urbanization in general, and higher incomes of many city residents in particular, will be the primary drivers of these shifts. The latest urban household survey shows that high-income urban households purchased

18 per cent less wheat and 4 per cent less rice than did the low-income families – but that their purchases of poultry, fruit and milk were, respectively, 1.9, 2.2 and 3.4 times higher (NBS 2000).

Obviously, the dramatic reduction of post-1999 grain harvests has not signified any loss of China's productive capacity, and in no way does it confirm Brown's forecasts of permanently declining cereal production: it merely reflects adjustments resulting from changing demand and grain prices, and China's entry into the WTO. Direct per capita grain consumption is falling, but demand for higher-quality wheat (suitable for baked goods and noodles) and rice is rising (Gale *et al.* 2001). At the same time, the need for feed grains is not increasing as rapidly as anticipated because of the stabilized demand for meat and eggs. Barring any protracted nationwide natural catastrophes, grain production levels during the coming years will thus be determined by government policies regarding grain stocks, WTO obligations and prices of flour, milled rice and animal foodstuffs – and not by any agronomic or environmental limits on China's harvests.

As for the more distant future, I agree with Huang *et al.* (1999) that China will neither empty the world grain markets nor will it become a major grain exporter. Depending on meat prices, perhaps as much as 40 per cent of China's grain demand by the year 2020 may be for feed, but a combination of improved productivity and imports no higher than 25Mt a year should be able to cover even that eventuality. Such a mundane conclusion is the most welcome reality about the future of China's food supply: it clearly signifies the country's maturity and unprecedented security.

Notes

1 Rhodes, R., "Man-made death: a neglected mortality", *JAMA* 260 (1988): 686–687.
2 Yang, D., *Catastrophe and reform in China* (Stanford: Stanford University Press, 1996).
3 Smil, V., "China's food: availability, requirements, composition, prospects", *Food Policy* 6 (1981): 67–77.
4 Chang, G.H. and Wen, G.J., "Communal dining and the Chinese famine of 1958–1961", *Economic Development and Cultural Change* 46 (1997): 1–34.
5 Macrae, J. and Zwi, A., "Famine, complex emergencies and international policy in Africa: an overview", in *War and hunger* (London: Zed Books, 1994) 6–36.
6 Sen, A., "Nobody need starve", *Granta* 52 (1995): 217.
7 State Statistical Bureau, *China Statistical Yearbook* (Beijing: State Statistical Bureau, 1978–1998).
8 Smil, V., "China's food", *Scientific American* 253(6) (1985): 116–124.
9 Aird, J., "Population studies and population policy in China", *Population and Development Review* 8 (1982): 85–97.
10 Ashton, B., Hill, K., Piazza, A. and Zeitz, R., "Famine in China, 1958–61", *Population and Development Review* 10 (1984): 613–645.
11 Peng, X., "Demographic consequences of the Great Leap Forward in China's provinces", *Population and Development Review* 13 (1987): 639–670.
12 Banister, J., *China's changing population* (Stanford: Stanford University Press, 1987).
13 Boss, L.P., Toole, M.J. and Yip, R., "Assessments of mortality, morbidity, and nutritional status in Somalia during the 1991–1992 famine", *Journal of American Medical Association* 272 (1994): 371–376.

14 Lopez, G.A. and Cortright, D., "Pain and promises", *Bulletin of the Atomic Scientists* 54 (1998): 39–43.
15 Pollitt, E. (ed.), "The relationship between undernutrition and behavioral development in children", *Journal of Nutrition* 125(suppl. 8) (1995): 2211–284S.
16 Becker, J., *Hungry ghosts* (New York: Free Press, 1996).
17 Encyclopedia Britannica, *New Encyclopedia Britannica Micropedia*, vol. 4 (Chicago: Encyclopedia Britannica, 1997) 674–675.

4 Environment

The veneration of nature is an ancient ingredient of China's admirably long-lived civilization – but the presence of this attitude has not provided a sufficient counterweight to all those much less admirable forces of environmental destruction whose cumulative effects bequeathed modern China with extensively degraded landscapes. To these old problems were added insults committed in the name of a superior ideology during Mao's years, as well as all the new environmental assaults that have taken place during the post-1980 era of economic modernization guided by a peculiar mixture of state (party) control and no-holds-barred private enterprise. And all of these developments have been unfolding against China's complex geologic, geomorphologic and climatic conditions, which include a vulnerability to major earthquakes, extreme droughts and no less extreme monsoon downpours. I will outline some of these attitudes and constraints in the opening section of this chapter.

Any list of major manifestations of China's environmental degradation that could be chosen for a more detailed appraisal should include widespread deforestation, recurrently intolerable air pollution, ubiquitous water contamination, excessive losses of arable land, and a drastic decline of biodiversity. Space limitations make it impossible to survey all of them, and when a more detailed examination must be limited to a single item, then I have no doubt that what the ancient Chinese called "the first of the five elements" – China's water – is the most appropriate choice. Problems with water are far from being the only difficulties complicating China's quest for modernization. As the consequences of environmental change were added to a longer, well-established list of other factors that might contribute to the political destabilization of a country, or even help trigger violent conflicts, China's worsening ecosystemic degradation and spreading environmental pollution came to be seen as prime candidates for such unwelcome roles. I will assess the possibilities of such developments in the third section of this chapter, "China's environment and security".

The qualitative appraisal of environmental degradation that has been presented in many publications over the past two decades is not enough to assess the impact of these changes. Difficult as it may be, there is a need to establish the cost of China's environmental change. I will present some fairly detailed estimates of its magnitude and impacts, based on a variety of Chinese evidence published during the late 1980s and the first half of the 1990s. Finally, the chapter closes with a recounting and an appraisal of what has been perhaps the most contentious Chinese approach to developing its economy: the pursuit of extraordinarily sized schemes, ranging from the new Great Green Wall of trees to the world's largest hydro dam. I will review the history and perils of these choices in "Megaprojects and China's environment".

Attitudes and constraints: constancy and change

Human transformation of the Earth's environment is obviously the most remarkable, and perhaps the most disturbing, sign of the accelerating evolution of our species. Natural ecosystems are replaced by human constructs, releases of greenhouse gases are now changing even the long-term composition of the atmosphere, and biodiversity is in decline everywhere. The consequences of human actions reached a surprisingly large scale long before the advent of high civilizations with their intensifying agricultures and expanding cities. For example, Alroy's (2001) ecologically realistic simulation of the end-Pleistocene megafaunal extinction in North America demonstrates that even low population growth rate and low hunting intensity would have made the anthropogenic extinction of large herbivores, including woolly mammoths, inevitable, and his model correctly predicts the terminal fate of thirty-two out of forty-one megafaunal Ice Age species.

And as soon as we reach the historical period, that is the time of about 5,000 years ago, we cannot find any better examples of human impacts on the environment than those provided by China's long quest to accommodate its growing population. The manifestations of these impacts, some of them of remarkable antiquity, range from sweeping deforestation to bold hydroengineering projects (irrigation systems, navigable canals), and from painstaking terracing of sloping land to many technical inventions and innovations (including the humble wheelbarrow and ingenious percussion drills), whose deployment made it much easier to harness resources and to transform natural environments into new landscapes whose physical features were so obviously dominated by human design. At the same time, these powerful forces of transformation and subjugation coexisted with feelings of awe and admiration of nature, and with the advocacy of nature's supremacy.

Perhaps most notably, Laozi's *Dao de jing*, the cornerstone of the Taoist belief, advocates taking no action contrary to nature as the best way to have everything properly regulated: *weiwuwei, zewubuzhi*. Or, to express the same sentiment in the words of the book's very next segment, in Raymond Blakney's (1955: 117) translation,

> Doing spoils it, grabbing misses it;
> So the Wise Man refrains from doing
> And doesn't spoil anything.

But this view was never shared by more than a tiny, and reclusive, minority lost in the sea of generations bent on refashioning everything natural around them.

Inevitably, these transforming patterns that marked the country's long history remained recognizable in its post-1949 developments, as many new designs, and delusions, began to guide China's treatment of its (by that time considerably degraded) environment. I sketched these old and new attitudes in the four paragraphs with which I closed the opening chapter of *The Bad Earth*, and in half a dozen paragraphs with which I closed the book. Although twenty years have passed since these lines were published, their sentiment and their verdict stand. Perhaps the only, and not unimportant difference, is that the Party's heavy hand, albeit still very much in evidence, is now felt less intrusively in a number of ways. Unfortunately, this change, so welcomed by hundreds of millions of ordinary Chinese as it eases their lives, has not been necessarily good news for the environment: new destructive forces of blind consumerism have filled the void left by the old destructive forces of the retreating rigid ideology.

At the same time, it must be realized that China's environment would present extraordinary challenges even to a state organized on the most rational principles and pursuing the best-laid plans. Modern history does not lack for great examples debunking the myth of a simplistic geographic determinism – but, at the same time, it would be naive to dismiss many constraints imposed by specific climate regimes, by a country's endowment with arable and forested land, with water and mineral, particularly energy, resources and, obviously, by the size and growth rates of its population. That is why, before taking a closer look at some specific challenges, I will outline these constraints in a "crowded stage" analogy.

Environmental attitudes: constancy and change

A reverence for nature runs unmistakably through the long span of Chinese history (Smil 1984). The poet, always ready to pour full goblets of wine and "drink three hundred cups in a round", found the mountains his most faithful companion; emperors, between wars and court intrigues, painted finches in bamboo groves and ascended sacred mountains; Buddhist monks sought their *dhyana* "midst fir and beech"; craftsmen located their buildings to "harmonize with the local currents of the cosmic breath"; painters were put through the rigors of mastering smooth, natural, tapering bamboo leaves and plum branches; and who wouldn't admire the symphony of plants, rocks, and water in countless gardens?

Attitudes, poetry, paintings, habits, common sayings, and regulations abound with images of nature and a view of man as a part of a greater order of things. Old trees are prized for their antiquity and dignity: ancient pines, frost-defying plum blossoms, elegant bamboo. Flowers are loved and admired: magnolias, lotus, chrysanthemums, peonies. There are birds of exquisite plumage – mountain pheasants, finches, ducks, magpies; animals ordinary – horses and oxen – and extraordinary – dragons and unicorns. There is a universe of peaks and clouds, snow and wind, waterfalls and ponds, reeds and shores, hills and dense forests. The titles of old paintings envelop the mind in the magnificence of nature and induce reverence: *Light Snow on the Mountain Pass*; *Brocaded Sea of Peach-Blossom Waves*; *Summer Retreat in the Eastern Grove*; *Ode on the Red Cliff*; *Listening to the Sounds of Spring Under Bamboo*; *Peaks Emerging from Spring Clouds*.

To stop here, however, as many an uncritical admirer might, would be telling only the more appealing part of the story. There has also been a clearly discernible current of destruction and subjugation: the burning of forests just to drive away dangerous animals; massive, total, and truly ruthless deforestation to create new fields, to get fuel and charcoal, and to obtain timber for fabulous palaces and ordinary houses, wood for cremation of the dead, and (to no small effect) for making ink from the soot of burned pines (one of history's many ironies: glorious accounts of civilization underwritten by the destruction of its natural foundations); the erection of sprawling rectilinear cities (fires would rage for days to consume the vast areas of wooden buildings) eliminating any trace of nature, save for some artificial gardens.

This traditional discrepancy between the environmental ideal and reality could not cease on that October day in 1949 when Mao Zedong spoke from the Tian'anmen to proclaim the founding of a new China. The environmental record of this new China thus carries clear parallels with the past as well as, inevitably, marks of the ruling ideology and advancing modernization. To describe it unequivocally is impossible: what a mixture of some excellent intentions and notable achievements with much casual neglect, astonishing irresponsibility, and staggering and outright destruction! If a simplifying verdict were still sought, I would summarize the record, without being alarmist, as genuinely disquieting.

In general, the attitudes of people who have just emerged from long years of privation to the threshold of life promising a bit more freedom and little more prosperity are not conducive to conservation, savings, and the eschewing of immediate consumption; just the opposite is likely to be true, putting further accelerated pressure on the environment. Indeed, here is a perfect illustration of a key ecological concept well known as the tragedy of the commons, or killing the goose that lays the golden egg.

And as always, in a country where to pass a qualifying examination for the imperial civil service was the dream of millions for millennia, there are complex and uncoordinated bureaucracies always good at promulgating new laws and regulations and holding grand conferences (disguised banqueting, mostly) but much less adept at getting things done. Nor are the provincial interests unimportant, or the considerations of the still heavily militarized economy.

And finally, there is the pervasive state ideology, that political worship, that unpredictable ever-twisting party line that one day makes a capitalist criminal out of a man planting a handful of trees in his backyard while rewarding a county secretary who orders the massive destruction of trees, lakes, garlic patches, and pond ducks – only to turn around the next day and instruct that self-same secretary that he should gain the enthusiasm of the masses for back-yard garlic growing, tree planting, and duck feeding; the party line that encourages a "hundred flowers to bloom" so that the "poisonous weeds" of intellectual independence, courage, and honesty can be more easily identified; the party line that has turned everything into politics and left only the single arbiter to determine merit.

Only a naive mind could not be overwhelmed by this state of affairs. The best outlook is for some gradual localized improvements, and for the prevention of further major degradation in key sectors and areas. That, I maintain, would be a grand success. On the implications of the failure to do so I will not speculate: that they are grim is all too clear and, unfortunately, this outcome is at least as likely as the other.

To believe otherwise would be to perpetuate the fatuous naivety of Western admirers of the Central Kingdom in Communist clothes, at a time when some responsible Chinese are themselves all too acutely aware that many of the devel-opmental policies of the past three decades have led to unprecedented destruction and degradation of the country's environment, and that this poses a real threat to the nation's physical well-being, and hence to its social stability. And all of these informed Chinese who have exposed the country's environ-mental debacle are also aware of, but don't write about, another critical issue – the cloud of political uncertainty that hangs over the future.

In a recent paper, the Policy Research Office of the Ministry of Forestry (1980: 31) concluded starkly but forthrightly: "If we do not take firm and deci-sive action now…the dire consequences are unimaginable". Such is the state of the Chinese environment as viewed by knowledgeable Chinese, and it provokes an unorthodox conclusion: it is not the large population *per se*, nor the relative poverty of the nation, nor its notorious modern political instability, but rather its staggering mistreatment of the environment that may well be the most funda-mental check on China's reach toward prosperity, a hindrance also the most intractable and difficult to deal with.

The record of the past two decades would seem to indicate that my concerns were misplaced, as nothing seems to be able to slow down the country's remark-able economic expansion. But this would be an unacceptably hasty judgment. China has been undoubtedly successful in dealing with some of its daunting environmental challenges and, as a result, many important indicators have either shown encouraging improvements or at least no signs of further deterio-ration. Perhaps the most welcome example is that, although many of the new plantings are in thinly spaced, fast-growing species, the country's total area covered by trees (159Mha in 1999) is now about 30 per cent larger than it was at the very beginning of Deng's reforms a quarter-century ago (NBS 2001). And the most obvious improvement benefiting the largest number of people has been the decline in urban concentrations of fly ash and sulfur dioxide, as many cities have been aggressively substituting clean-burning natural gas for ash- and sulfur-laden coal.

At the same time, many indicators of environmental quality have been getting worse, and a significant share of economic advances has been bought with further impoverishment of China's already strained resource base: water tables on the North China Plain have been sinking ever faster, longer stretches of many rivers have been converted to open waste conduits, the biodiversity of the extraordinarily species-rich southern ecosystems is disappearing. China's many natural constraints do not make a better management of these challenges impossible, but they surely make it much more difficult. Countries in less constraining circumstances have the benefit of larger gaps between the immovable natural supply and rising demand; in China the two aggregates are already uncomfortably close in some instances, and will get inevitably closer in the future. Being aware of these realities, which are surveyed briefly in the following subsection, is not a reason for despair, but merely an essential antidote to the hubris of omnipotent technical fixes.

China's environment: a disquieting analogy

Analogies concentrate our thoughts, and thus trouble our minds. Imagine China as a crowded stage, and Westerners as fascinated spectators. Some onlookers can be seen running across the proscenium, and paying rather large sums for the packaged experience. A few outsiders can be seen well inside the podium, lingering a bit, asking questions, even leaving behind some brand-new props before descending back to the auditorium where they interpret some details of a largely incomprehensible script either to those spectators with a craving for exotica or to some ambitious impresarios present in the audience who think that they could provide a better direction to the whole confusing piece.

Even though some of these outsiders get to play bit parts or get invited to temporarily direct some marginal scenes, none of them truly partakes in the existential happenings on stage. Not only do these walk-on participants read from a different script, but their real interests are either in the decor, make-up, phrasing and the gestures of the actors, or in getting the local production managers to buy as many new and expensive props as possible. They do not really understand how hard life is for most of the actors, and most of them do not want to discover the extent to which the boards and pillars hidden by newly colorful facades are rotten. But what is it we all are watching? The longevity of the stage, its strange adornments and its extraordinary crowding have always cast their spells on the spectators – but to assume that the play can go on as an endless series of repertory reruns is to delude ourselves.

A tragedy, then? The relentless progression toward a feared outcome would seem to make it so. Shortly after 1949, when Westerners lost their access to the stage for about two decades, and could observe the unfolding drama only from a distance, it packed in about 550 million people. That number had doubled by 1989, and demographic imperatives make it virtually certain that, after passing the 1.3 billion mark in 2003, at least another 200 million will be added before the population peaks during the fourth decade of the twenty-first century

(UNO 2002) (see Figure 4.1). Is not the stage getting ever closer to collapsing? Even from afar, many of its boards look shaky. But this is not a classical tragedy. There will be no sudden resolution with a plaintive chorus in the background, no cataclysmic collapse. The simple reality is that some parts of that large stage have caved in already: farming has had to be abandoned on deeply eroded slopelands, on cropland claimed by deserts, and in areas where the water table has sunk below the acceptable cost of pumping. People have had to move elsewhere, adding to the crowding. Other boards are so worn-out that treading on them is exceedingly risky – but where else can the actors go? That question becomes even more acute as millions have been already displaced, and more will follow, by the construction of reservoirs, canals and transportation links. Only a privileged or lucky few can leave the stage, most must stay and move around as best as they can.

But are not parts of the stage much brighter than a generation ago, do not many actors look more prosperous? True, but this is only a superficial decor, and beneath its dazzle the boards are rotting faster than ever, and too many shabby figures can be seen in the background. And the stage gets shakier not only because the crowding increases, but precisely because the actors' lots are getting better. But there will be no classical crisis in this peculiar tragedy, no turning point of the drama – and hence no liberating catharsis. Greater crowding, spreading decay and intensifying pollution will keep on combining into more prominent scenes of degradation, hardship and pain. This process has been unfolding for a long time: the numbers of the suffering actors are already counted in many millions, and they are bound to increase. Can the spectators remain unaffected?

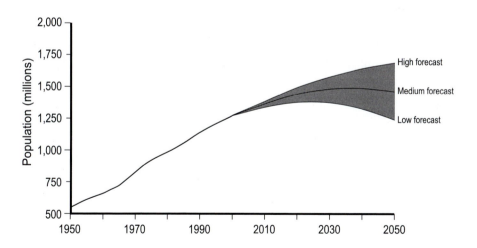

Figure 4.1 Past and future growth of China's population, 1950–2050

Source: Past totals from various issues of *China Statistical Yearbook*; the three variants of long-range forecast from UNO (2002).

La longue durée

Some forms of environmental degradation are noticeable almost instantly, but the consequences of other changes can be fully appreciated only when using very long-term perspectives. As so many events in human history, they are perfect examples of what Fernand Braudel (1972) classed in his *la longue durée* category: complex processes unfolding gradually over very long periods of time, changing reality almost imperceptibly in their early stages and only later at a worrisome pace, and finally resulting in a profoundly different world. The appro priate model is a protracted, multifocal, multicausal decline, rather than acute and generalized collapse brought about by a single decisive factor: China's environmental realities fit this model in every respect.

Impressive improvements of human existence have been paid for by worldwide environmental degradation. The concurrent increase of population and individual well-being does not represent, as Julian Simon (1996) would have us to believe, the triumph of human intellect and organization over the raw forces of nature. The very phrasing betrays a profound ignorance of the biophysical fundamentals of civilizational progress. In order to be more than an ephemeral phenomenon, the process cannot be a contest of forces. Human ingenuity can succeed over a very long run only when it preserves irreplaceable environmental services – from the stratospheric ozone layer shielding the Earth from UV radiation, to the soil bacteria driving the nitrogen cycle – which make life possible. The biosphere's finite resources, and even more so its life-sustaining services, cannot be taxed indefinitely beyond their self-renewing limits (Smil 2002b).

This means that long-term civilizational development is incompatible with what modern economists love to call a "healthy growth", a 3, 4 or 5 per cent annual addition to the gross economic product. To act on this understanding in a civilization whose *modus operandi*, if not its very *raison d'être*, is the fastest possible economic growth, will require an unprecedented transformation of human affairs. Western nations, owing to their combination of very slow population growth, high affluence and technical prowess, have, if they choose to use it, an excellent chance to effect this grand transition during the next two generations. The margins for maneuver are wide: conservation and innovation have the potential of cutting our resource needs by half without lowering our quality of life; adopting more modest – but still fairly affluent – lifestyles could cut resource use even further. In contrast, China's expanding population and its huge developmental needs will put enormous additional claims on all kinds of natural resources. Even when undertaken with unprecedented care, such an expansion will further degrade the country's environment.

Contrasting realities

Only four key parameters need to be quantified in order to appreciate the country's precarious position and to understand the reasons for its prospective decline: the population, and its food, water and energy consumption. During the first quarter of the twenty-first century, the affluent Western nations will add only about 25 million people to their current total of less than 700 million. China will add – using the medium variant of the latest UN forecast (UNO 2002) – nearly 200 million to its 2000 total of about 1,275 million. Western nations, with some 12 per cent of the global population in the year 2000, had nearly a quarter of the world's farmland, or an average of about 0.5ha/person. But this is really an irrelevant figure, because about three quarters of our staple grain harvests are fed to animals in order to provide diets high in animal food-stuffs. The West could easily give up the cultivation of a large share of its farmland merely by moderating its high intakes of meat and dairy products.

In contrast, China, with 21 per cent of the world's population in the year 2000, had only nine per cent of the world's farmland, or just a little over 0.1ha/capita, an equivalent of one third of the Mexican rate and one seventh of the US rate. The only two poor populous countries with less farmland per capita are Egypt and Bangladesh: Egypt, where two out of three loaves of bread are baked from imported US flour; Bangladesh, whose continuing existence as a nation is so patently questionable. Moreover, nearly 300 million Chinese live in provinces where the per capita availability of arable land is already lower than in Bangladesh. And although China's average food supply is now, as demonstrated in some detail in the previous chapter, above the typical need, regional disparities perpetuate the relatively large-scale extent of malnutrition. In order to erase the deficits for at least 80 million people who still do not have enough food to meet FAO's primary nutritional objective of a healthy and vigorous life, and to produce adequate food for its additional 200 million people, China will have to expand its food output by at least 20 per cent during the next two generations.

China's annually renewable water resources represent less than 7 per cent of the global total, and, moreover, they are disproportionately concentrated in the South, and are scarce north of the Changjiang, the area containing about two fifths of China's population and producing a commensurate share of the grain harvest. Even if it were possible to use every drop of the northern stream runoff, per capita water supply would be less than a quarter of America's actual per capita water consumption. Actual per capita northern supply for all uses – agriculture, industry, services and households – amounts to little more than the Americans use just to flush their toilets and wash their clothes, dishes and cars.

The combination of prolonged drought spells and heavy water demand has repeatedly dried out the Huanghe, northern China's principal river, before it reached the sea. This happened for the first time in recorded history in 1972, and starting in 1985 the river dried up in some sections every year until 2000 (*People's Daily* 2000a). In 1997 the river did not reach Bohai Bay for a record 226 days, and the dry bed extended for more than 700km from the river's mouth (Liu 1998). In 2000 and 2001 the river kept flowing even during the dry season (November to late June), in spite of the fact that a severe drought reduced the volume to just 16.4Gm^3 along the river's middle course, the second lowest rate on record (*People's Daily* 2001). Yet the necessity of feeding an additional (approximate) 8 million people every year, to satisfy the rising urban demand and to secure water for growing industries, means that the North's already much overused resources will be under even more pressure during the next two decades.

Western nations also consume over 40 per cent of the world's fuels and primary electricity. This is more than three times their share of the global population, giving them an annual average of more than four tonnes of crude oil per capita. Again, we could give up a large share of this so often wasteful use – SUVs, extravagantly sized overheated and overcooled houses, long-distance flights to gambling casinos, and the amassing of material possessions far beyond anybody's conceivable need – without compromising the real quality of life (i.e. good health care, longevity, access to education, a clean environment). Obviously, our reduced energy use would dramatically lower the pressure on the global environment.

In contrast, in the year 2000 China's consumption of primary commercial energy amounted to about 9 per cent of the global total, again much less than the country's population share. And less than 15 per cent of the low per capita rate, equivalent to about half a tonne of crude oil a year, is used by households, compared to about 40 per cent in the West. I have shown in great detail that a purposeful society can guarantee the combination of decent physical well-being, good nutrition and fair education opportunities only when per capita energy consumption reaches about one tonne of oil equivalent a year (Smil 2003). In order to join the ranks of developed nations, China's per capita energy consumption would have to be at least twice the current mean. But real national modernization is impossible without near-universal literacy and greater access to higher education. Nations with literacy in excess of 90 per cent and with at least 20 per cent of young people enrolled at post-secondary institutions use at least 1.5t of oil equivalent per capita, three times China's current mean.

Looking ahead

China's development during the next two generations will thus require massive increases of food and energy output merely to maintain the existing per capita rates, and unprecedented increments if the country is to approach incipient affluence. Consequently, even if the requisite inputs of resources – be it fertilizer and irrigation water or timber and coal – were used with greatly improved efficiencies, there would be a net increase in their total extraction and hence in environmental degradation and in the generation of pollutants. Feeding nearly 200 million additional people by the year 2025 will require an incremental food supply roughly equivalent to the total current food consumption of Brazil – yet the food production will have to come from a smaller area of farmland. The combination of a larger population and land claims resulting from environmental degradation (erosion, desertification, salinization), and urban, industrial and transportation construction, may reduce the per capita availability of farmland to just 0.08ha/person by the year 2025.

The only way to produce substantially higher harvests from a declining area of deteriorating land, is further intensification of China's already highly intensive crop farming. Yet the country is already relatively more dependent on fossil fuels to grow its food than the USA. This is because it uses on the average four times as much nitrogenous fertilizer per hectare (whose synthesis needs natural gas, coal and electricity), and irrigates a third of its fields (three fifths with pumps). But the crop response to high applications of nitrogen has been declining, while their leaching contaminates waters, and more frequent multicropping and sharply lower recycling of organic wastes contribute to a steady decline of soil quality. As already explained in Chapter 2, a very large share of crop residues is burned by fuel-short rural households rather than being composted and returned to fields. Urban wastes, increasingly polluted with chemicals and heavy metals, are unfit for recycling. And unsustainable rates of erosion (in excess of 15t/ha annually) prevail over at least a third of China's fields.

These natural constraints can be partially negated by bioengineering advances. Genetically modified crops may accelerate the growth of average yields and hence be able to support higher population densities. But more productive crop varieties could not eliminate further farmland losses, halt the erosion and degradation of arable soils, or actually reduce the rates of fossil-fuel-dependent inputs. Indeed, all of these problems have been exacerbated as China's successful adoption of high-yielding rices and wheats has boosted the country's food supply since the 1970s. And only the eventual development and diffusion of nitrogen-fixing grain crops could eliminate further increases in China's dependence on synthetic nitrogen. Such a breakthrough is no nearer to field applications today than it was a generation ago.

Given the absence of readily deployable alternatives, and the need for greatly increased energy use, the dominance of coal in China's energy consumption will continue. Although the fuel's share will gradually decline, as will particulate emissions from large sources equipped with better controls, numerous small sources (now burning more than half of all China's coal) will remain largely uncontrolled, as will nearly all sulfur dioxide emissions, a principal cause of dismal air quality and high respiratory morbidity in China's cities. Accelerated development of hydrogeneration would reduce the environmental effects of coal combustion – but it would magnify other problems which have accompanied the development of China's water power, above all extensive flooding of high-yielding farmland, mass population resettlements, and rapid reservoir silting caused by deforestation and slopeland cultivation.

To believe that alternative energy sources will cover a large share of China's fuel and electricity needs within the next 10–20 years is to ignore the gradual and costly realities of energy transitions (Smil 2003). Recall that after two decades of vigorous and expensive technical innovation the West has increased the efficiency of its energy converters – but its reliance on fossil fuels has remained remarkably stable. A major international complication will be introduced by China's rising share of carbon dioxide generation. The late 1990s reduction of these emissions was an exceptional departure from a long-term trend of rising contributions. Even if China does not surpass the US level during the coming generation, it will be a close second, and as such it will have a critical, but very likely also a contentious, role in any effort to stabilize and reduce the global generation of greenhouse gases. Moreover, emissions of methane from paddy fields and nitrous oxide from intensified fertilization will also rise.

The combination of demographic imperatives and rapid economic growth means that China's already much degraded environment will suffer even more during the next generation. The best outlook for the next generation is that the rate of this environmental decay can be slowed down. Such an achievement would be an essential precondition for first stabilizing, and eventually reversing, the degradative trends, so that China's great stage survives in a tolerable state. And yet, with all of these worrisome trends in mind, there is no preordained progression here, no automatic reason for advocating what most people think of as the classic Malthusian outcome.

That is because human futures, while not infinitely alterable, are amazingly malleable. Malthus (1803: 543–544) himself reflected on this reality in the second, and so inexplicably neglected and unquoted, edition of his famous book when he concluded that

> On the whole, therefore, though our future prospects respecting the mitiga-
> tion of the evils arising from the principle of population may not be so
> bright as we could wish, yet they are far from being entirely disheartening,
> and by no means preclude that gradual and progressive improvement in
> human society....And although we cannot expect that the virtue and happi-
> ness of mankind will keep pace with the brilliant career of physical
> discovery; yet, if we are not wanting to ourselves, we may confidently
> indulge the hope that, to no unimportant extent, they will be influenced by
> its progress and will partake in its success.

The first of the five elements: China's water

There are, naturally, other specific segments of China's changing environment deserving of closer examination – but water makes the most compelling choice, both because of its deep historical links to the rise of Chinese civilization, and because of its critical role in the far-from-accomplished modernization of the country's society. The combination of irreplaceable demand for at least the minimum volume of this resource, of its widespread, and in some regions worsening, shortages, and its indis-pensability for securing more affluent lives for the still growing as well as rapidly urbanizing population, make water management both the most urgent and the most enduring environmental challenge for China's leadership.

Fortunately, concerns about the strained and diminishing northern supply have brighter counterweights, not just in the southern water surplus but in large water conservation opportunities everywhere: China is not only the world's most water-stressed largest economy, it is also the most water-wasting one. Fortunately, there are clear signs of this understanding: easing the current crisis will require not only new supplies, namely inevitable long-distance water transfers, but also the maximum practicable reduction of existing waste. An encouraging shift has already taken place during the 1990s: in 1990 the total volume of waste water discharged by China's industries was nearly $25Gm^3$; by 1999 this rate was reduced to about $20Gm^2$ (NBS 2001). Given the huge intervening increase in China's industrial output, this means that average water intensity ($m^3/yuan$ of production) fell by at least 60 per cent. But first let us take a more systematic look at China's water resources and uses (Smil 1984, 1993).

Water: resources, uses, waste

Art mirrors, succinctly and admirably, the human perception of the environment. When European painters of the seventeenth, eighteenth and nineteenth centuries looked at a landscape, various elements would prevail: light from the high clouds in Jacob van Ruisdael, majestic trees in John Constable, shimmering colors in Claude Monet. In contrast, Chinese painters have always seen their landscapes as *shan shui* – mountain-water – the term containing all the tension and harmony of *yang* and *yin*, evoking whole sets of analogies, lending to landscape painting "a worshipful attitude, making it a ritual act of reverence in praise of the harmony of Heaven and Earth" (Sze 1959). Water, the first of the ancient five elements, the Black Tortoise of the Five Regions of the Heavens, has thus always had a pivotal place in the Chinese culture – and in everyday Chinese life (Smil 1979d). One does not have to agree with Karl Wittfogel's (1957) historical thesis about the emergence and institutionalization of hydraulic despotism in China, to appreciate the close relationship between water and the country's civilization, a link both beneficial and destructive, and a link very much enduring.

Vagaries of precipitation, drought and flood still determine the size of harvests; the arid north still has to endure month after rainless month, while typhoons may be smashing southern dikes. And new dimensions have been added with rapidly progressing industrializaton and urbanization and with expanded irrigation and chemicalization of agriculture: much higher uses of water in general, frequently straining the available resources and leading to shortages of even drinking water; drastically increased extraction of ground waters followed by sinking water tables and surface subsidence; and widespread water pollution of all major rivers, lakes and coastlines. All of these problems are often related to those critical Chinese environmental constraints – the relatively small volume and irregular distribution of the country's water flows.

Yin–yang of waters

> When drinking water think of the spring.
>
> Chinese proverb

The real springs for most of China's waters are thousands of kilometers away from the country's shores, in the Pacific Ocean east of the Philippines and in the equatorial Indian Ocean, where the two mighty cyclonic flows drenching China with seasonal monsoon rains originate every spring (Smil 1993). The dominance of these flows in the precipitation regime of the country imparts the inescapable yin–yang quality to China's water supply. The simile extends not only to the contrast between negatives and positives – destructive floods and droughts have molded the course of Chinese civilization as much as the extensive irrigation and reliance on water transport – but also to the abrupt shifts between the two entities. The sharply divided curvilinear shapes symbolizing egg yolk and white in the yin–yang diagram have recurrent parallels in sudden transitions between lack and surfeit of water.

The spatial distribution of China's precipitation also shows a relatively abrupt decline of annual and seasonal totals along the southeast/northwest gradient. The 500mm isohyet – running from central Heilongjiang in the Northeast to the Sino-Bhutanese border in the Southwest, and roughly coinciding with the direction of several major mountain chains – may be seen as a convenient approximate divide between the dry northern and western interior and the wetter coastal East and inland South (Figure 4.2). Strong seasonality of precipitation, high probability of prolonged droughts, perils of recurrent fluctuations

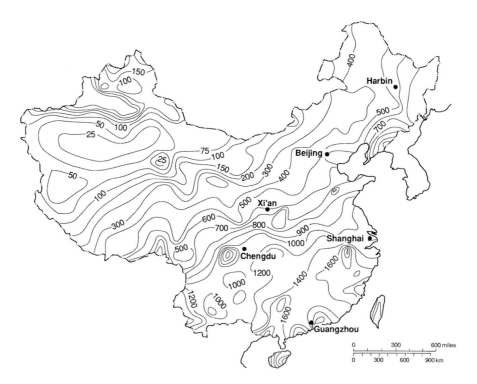

Figure 4.2   The pattern of China's average annual precipitation displays a rather regular southeast/northwest gradient reflecting the dominance of monsoon rains. A more detailed map would show many more singularities of increased or reduced precipitation caused by South China's mountainous terrain

Source: Based on Domrös and Peng (1988: 140).

between droughts and floods, and large spatial disparities in the distribution of annual and seasonal moisture, are the keys to appreciating China's water supply: looking at long-term averages and nationwide totals is highly misleading.

Because all of the densely inhabited area of China is within the domain of the East Asian monsoon, which brings moisture between May and October, it has distinct summer precipitation maxima, strong and early (May and June) in the South, strong and later (July and August) on the North China Plain, and somewhat weaker at the same time in the North. Summer rains bring at least 70 per cent of annual moisture in regions north of Beijing, and 60 per cent on the North China Plain (Figure 4.3). The two wettest months contribute 50–60 per cent of annual moisture, compared to just 25 per cent in Guangzhou. Frequently, much of this rain comes in spectacular downpours. All of China's recorded short-term precipitation maxima come from the North, including the one-hour record of 267mm from Shanxi, and the incredible one-week rain of 2,051mm, amounting to more than three times the mean annual precipitation in the area, between 2 and 8 August 1963 in Hebei (Domrös and Peng 1988).

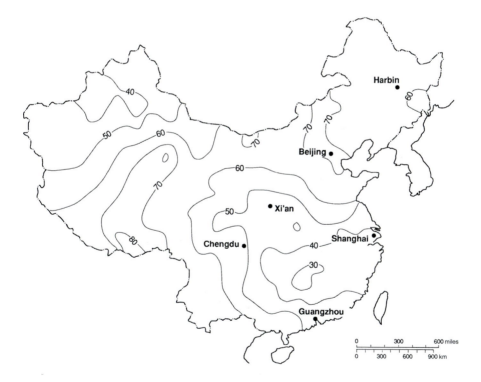

Figure 4.3 The distribution of the annual share of summer (June to August) rains shows their dominance throughout northern China

Source: Based on Domrös and Peng (1988: 169).

Throughout history, China's precipitation records also reveal relatively long and pronounced periods of either abundant or scarce precipitation. Thirty-year running means for Beijing for the years 1724–1980 show annual maxima around 750mm and minima down to about 450mm, a 40 per cent variability. Calculations of dryness/wetness indices for Eastern China between 1470 and 1977 show a long dry spell up to 1691, followed by a wet period until 1890, and a new predominantly dry regime during the twentieth century (Zhang 1988), while a similar study for the North indicates that the region has been relatively dry since 1680 (Zhang and Lin 1985).

Of the 6Tt of precipitation falling on China during an average year (the mean precipitation is 630mm) about 45 per cent, or 2.7Tt, ends up as stream runoff. About 40 per cent of this flow, or 1.1Tt, is potentially usable, and the actual annual withdrawals for agricultural, industrial and household uses during the late 1980s amounted to just over 500Gt, or less than half of the available potential (Smil 1984). Recent actual per capita use has thus been less than 500t/year, a withdrawal equal to less than a quarter of the US value, about 20 per cent below the Indian level, but roughly equal to some European (e.g. Swedish and Polish) rates (WRI 1988).

But China's rate is boosted by the relative southern abundance: the northern values are only a fraction of the national mean. All of China north of the Changjiang, occupying 60 per cent of the country's area, has only 20 per cent of its water resources. A more sensible comparison is to leave out the vast and arid Xinjiang and Qinghai and limit the contrast just to the densely inhabited North: while the region, covering about one third of China's territory, has about two fifths of China's population, grows the same share of staple grains and accounts for nearly 45 per cent of all industrial output, it receives only about one quarter of the country's total precipitation, and its high summer evapotranspiration means that it has access to less than one tenth of stream runoff.

In the basin of the Huanghe, the region's principal river, less than 1,500m^3 of water runoff is available for each hectare of cultivated land, and no more than about 600m^3/person; comparable rates in the Changjiang basin are, respectively, about 6,000m^3/ha and 2,800m^3/person. The Huanghe had its flows drastically reduced during the dry 1980s. In 1981 the river's flow into the Bohai was 48.5Gt, almost exactly its long-term average; by 1986 the runoff dropped to 26.1Gt, and in 1987 it was just below 20Gt, only two fifths of the mean (ZXS 1988a). The river's normally very low early summer flow had repeatedly ceased altogether downstream from Jinan for as long as thirty-seven days, causing reduction of crop yields, disruption of industrial production and enormous difficulties for oil extraction at Shengli, China's second-largest oilfield, near the river's estuary.

This necessitates a high degree of reliance on underground water reserves, but here, too, the northern provinces are disadvantaged. Aggregate underground water resources are now put at 870Gt, of which about 70 per cent is south of the Changjiang. Perhaps as much as 230Gt (an equivalent of less than 9 per cent of stream runoff) can be used annually, but the recent withdrawals are close to 60Gt, with the North accounting for three quarters of the total. As in any semi-arid and arid setting, most of North China's water is used in agriculture, but the growing difficulties with urban supplies became a more acute concern during the 1980s. The situation was particularly tight in the capital Beijing, whose minimum annual industrial and household needs reached 800Mt by the late 1970s, and then kept on increasing by about 7 per cent a year during the 1980s. This would bring the 1990 need to about 1.6Gt, but the city's eight waterworks supplied by large reservoirs could deliver no more than 700Mt (Dong 1990).

Urban consumption is far surpassed by the municipality's vegetable and grain fields, which use about 3Gt, so Beijing and its environs need about 4.6Gt a year. But the recurrent droughts of the 1980s cut the supply capability of the city's two large reservoirs – Miyun and Guanting, which were also serving Tianjin – to as little as 500Mt, or to less than one tenth of their design capacity of over 6Gt. In August 1981 the State Council decided to stop supplying Tianjin (which needs at least 600Mt a year) with water from these two reservoirs, an order necessitating a huge long-distance diversion of water from the Huanghe. Yet this sacrifice made little difference to the capital, whose surface water supply of between 4.22 and 4.49Gt (of which about 3Gt is practically recoverable) during normal precipitation years fell to just 2.5–3.2Gt during the years of prolonged droughts, causing excessive withdrawals from Miyun and Guanting, the complete disappearance of scores of smaller storages, and the intensifying depletion of underground reserves.

Chinese estimates put the maximum annual supply of Beijing's ground water at 2.5Gt. In the 1950s the water table was in places just five meters below the surface, but today the city's more than 40,000 wells draw water from depths of around 50m. During the 1980s the annual drop during the driest years surpassed two meters, and the surface subsidence extended over more than $1,000km^2$. During the early 1990s, annual water shortages during dry years will fluctuate between 600 and 900Mt, and the deficit is forecast to be at least 1.3Gt by the year 2000 (ZXS 1988b). Except for the new Zhangfang reservoir on the Juma He (on the municipality's southwestern border with Hebei) which will supply up to 800Mt a year, there are no nearby exploitable sources of water. Not surprisingly, Beijing's worsening water shortages have become a matter of anxious scientific and public debate, which has even included a questioning of the city's future viability as capital of China (Xinhua 1988).

Beijing and Tianjin are no exceptions: a look at China's northern urban water supplies reveals a repetitive pattern of progressing inadequacy of local or nearby rivers or reservoirs to satisfy the rising demand (aggravated by recurrent droughts), overuse of underground reserves (resulting in sinking water tables, higher pumping costs and extensive surface subsidence), and repeated recourse to long-distance water transfers (often involving the construction of conduits longer than 100km). In 1985, 188 Chinese cities were short of more than 10Mt of water a day, and in forty of these – including Beijing, Tianjin, Taiyuan and Xi'an – these shortages were serious enough to limit economic development. By 1988, frequent news reports claimed that more than half of China's 200 large cities had difficulties with water supply, that the shortages were serious in about fifty of them, and that the average daily deficit had risen to about 12Mt. By 1990 this deficit reached 15Mt, and some of the estimates for the year 2000 went as high as 88Mt (Wang 1985).

Urban water shortages tend to attract a disproportionate share of attention, but, as in any other populous Asian country, China's water use is heavily dominated by irrigation requirements, creating a number of extensive environmental impacts. Among the populous (more than 50 million) countries, only Egypt (where all farmed land is watered), and Pakistan and Japan (each with about 75 per cent watered land), surpass China in their relative dependence on irrigation (Nickum 1990). But this high dependence – according to the official statistics about 46 per cent of all arable land in the late 1980s – is of recent origin. In 1950 the share of China's irrigated farmland was no more than 16 per cent (16Mha); by 1965 this share doubled, mainly thanks to extension of surface irrigation in the rice-growing parts of the country during the 1950s. The second period of expansion came during the late 1960s and early 1970s, with a massive drilling of tubewells on the North China Plain: the total figure peaked at 45.5Mha in 1976 (Figure 4.4). (After a period of decline and stagnation, the irrigated area continued to increase steadily during the 1990s, surpassing 53Mha by the century's end.)

The subsequent decline, amounting to about 3 per cent of the peak area by 1988, has been interpreted as a worrisome sign of weakening crop production

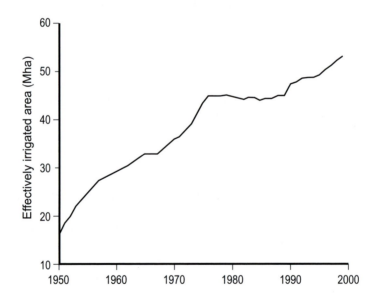

Figure 4.4 The expansion of China's irrigated land, 1950–1990

Source: Plotted from data in *China Statistical Yearbook*.

capacity caused by declining state investment and by *baogan*-induced neglect of irrigation facilities. But Nickum (1990) argues persuasively that the aggregate figures obscure more than they reveal about China's complex and diverse state of irrigation. The basis of China's accounting, the effectively irrigated area, is defined as level land with water resources and irrigation facilities capable of providing an adequate volume of water for crops under normal conditions. During a rainy year, such a plot of land may need no irrigation, while during a prolonged drought it may receive far from adequate moisture. Nor does the aggregate figure tell us about the number of yearly irrigations and their effectiveness.

What matters is the sustainability of irrigation, and its economic effectiveness. Current Chinese practices do not reflect the scarcity value of irrigation water; this leads, on the one hand, to the continuation of unsustainable and wasteful irrigation, which would be greatly curtailed with the introduction of realistic water fees; and on the other hand, to the absence of irrigation in growing crops that bring unrealistically low returns. Nowhere are these problems more apparent than on the North China Plain. This 300,000km^2 in the watersheds of the lower Huanghe, Huaihe and Haihe is a rather recent newcomer to extensive irrigation, but one whose crop yields are now critically dependent on it (O'Mara 1988). The region's almost nonexistent slope (1:10,000), the rivers' unreliable summer flow, and the enormous sediment load carried by the Huanghe and deposited in shallow canals, militated against any expansion of surface gravity irrigation: in 1949 less than 10 per cent of farmland in Hebei, Henan and Shandong was irrigated.

The fundamental change started only in the 1960s with the introduction of the first shallow tubewells. Their drilling peaked between 1971 and 1974, spurred by the increasing availability of fuel from the Daqing oilfield. By the late 1980s the plain had more than 2 million tubewells irrigating over 11Mha of farmland, with slightly more than three quarters relying only on the underground water and the rest irrigated in conjunction with surface water. In the early 1980s the total pumping volume fluctuated between 25 and 35Gm^3 a year, and about 10Gm^3 of the Huanghe was being diverted annually for irrigation in Henan and Shandong. River water irrigated about 17Mha, groundwater about 8Mha. Pumping helped keep down the formerly rather high water table, limiting the spread of salinization and reducing its former extent in Hebei and Shandong by about one quarter between 1960 and 1980.

But it also caused considerable local overexploitation of aquifers during prolonged droughts. Hebei province has been most affected by overpumping, with thirty-one separate depression cones formed over an area of some 1,200km^2, or roughly a fifth of the province's alluvium (Hebei Provincial Service 1986). The scarcity of irrigation water on the plain is best illustrated by the average annual distribution of water per hectare: in 1985 the national mean was about 9,400m^3/ha; the most intensively cropped southern areas received more than 30,000m^3/ha – but Shandong's and Henan's irrigated land averaged less than

4,300m³/ha (Nickum 1990). However, the growing water claims of the plain's large cities and industrial areas will tend to lower even these modest irrigation rates.

Surface irrigation on the North China Plain has another troublesome environmental effect. Diversion of the Huanghe's water, amounting to more than a quarter of the total flow during dry years, reduces the silt transport to the Bohai: up to a quarter of the high sediment load, that is about 400Mt, is now deposited each year on the river's bed in Henan and Shandong. Surface irrigation on the plain thus aggravates the principal long-term threat for its habitation – the inexorable elevation of the riverbed above the surrounding countryside.

There is an important qualitative dimension to China's irrigation prospects: irrigation waters in all of China's intensively cultivated periurban areas, as well as in regions with large numbers of rural and town manufactures, have been increasingly contaminated by industrial waste, in addition to carrying higher concentrations of leached fertilizers and insecticides. The official nationwide total for 1990 waste water discharges was 36.7Gt – the equivalent of the Huanghe's total flow in a moderately dry year – of which less than 20 per cent were treated. Late-1980s estimates of the annual economic loss attributable to water pollution were at least 30 billion *yuan*.

Compared to the huge volumes of water used in irrigation, household water supplies for the rural population are almost negligible, but the extension of an adequate and safe water supply to most of China's population remains a distant goal. Running water is now available to just over 80 per cent of all urban residents in 300 large cities, and in less than a third of small cities and towns. By the end of 1990 about a quarter of the rural population had access to tap water, although only a fraction of this population had the water actually piped into their homes (Xinhua 1989). Even during years of normal precipitation, at least 50 million people in China's rural areas have to live with the extreme scarcity of even drinking water, necessitating long trips to the nearest water source and minuscule per capita availabilities. The droughts of the 1980s worsened this situation: even in the capital, about 90,000 people had difficulty in getting water in 1986.

Chinese planners have been favoring increasingly more voluminous water transfers as the most expedient solution to urban and regional supply shortages: much capital and labor was invested in these schemes during the 1980s. The first major long-distance diversions expressly undertaken to ease critical urban water shortages were the temporary transfers of the Huanghe's water to Tianjin in 1972, 1973 and 1975, when up to 50m³/s was diverted from the river via Henan's Shengli Canal, Weihe and the Grand Canal, for a total length of 850km. In the winter of 1981–1982 this diversion was repeated, with the addition of two more links between the Huanghe and the Grand Canal, necessitating extensive emergency dredging of these conduits and the relocation of some villages (Zhang 1982).

Of the total diversion of 701Mm³ Tianjin actually received 451Mm³. The need for these costly emergency projects ended only with the construction of a permanent 233km-long diversion from Panjiakou reservoir on the Luanhe in Hebei. Luanhe waters were also diverted to Tangshan (a large mining city in Hebei destroyed by the 1976 earthquake) and to Qinhuangdao (the country's largest coal port on the Bohai in northern Hebei). Other notable diversions include water for Dalian (China's third largest port in Liaoning at the tip of Liaodong peninsula) from the Biliuhe, for Qingdao (Shandong's largest port city on the Yellow Sea) from the Huanghe, and for Xi'an (China's ancient capital in Shaanxi) from the Heihe. But all of these diversions will be greatly surpassed, in length as well as in diverted volume, by the transfer of the Changjiang's water through the Grand Canal to northern Jiangsu, Shandong, Hebei and Tianjin.

During most years, water shortages and drought will be the country's most extensive environmental stress, affecting commonly one tenth of the densely inhabited territory: since 1970, areas disastrously affected by drought fluctuated between 1 and 18 million hectares a year (see Figure 3.2). But the obverse threat is still far from negligible: after a period of relatively limited flooding during the 1970s, the 1980s saw between 4 and 9 million hectares affected by floods (Figure 3.2). During that decade the average area disastrously affected by floods rose to about 5.5Mha/year, an almost 2.5-fold increase compared to the 1970s – and the risks of catastrophic flooding have been growing almost everywhere.

About one tenth of China's territory, inhabited by nearly two thirds of the population and producing roughly 70 per cent of all agricultural and industrial output, is below the flood level of major rivers. Throughout history, China's maximum floods have brought enormous water surges (Cheng 1989). The Huanghe at Sanmenxia had a flow of $36,000\text{m}^3/\text{s}$ in 1843, nearly twenty-five times its average; and the Changjiang, the world's third most voluminous river, carried $110,000\text{m}^3/\text{s}$ as it entered the plains of Hubei in 1870, about four times its enormous normal flow. In spite of the absence of flooding for nearly half a century, potentially the most dangerous situation is along the lower course of the Huanghe in Henan and Shandong. Improvement of dikes, construction of the two large flood-retarding basins in Henan and Shandong (storing about 5Gm^3 of water), and progressively lower runoffs have appeared to lower the risk of catastrophic natural flooding. But there has been no extensive dredging along the river's lower course, between Zhengzhou in Henan and the estuary, where it remains confined between about 1,400km of dikes which are at least 3–5m, and up to 11–15m, above the surrounding countryside, protecting roughly $250,000\text{km}^2$ of the North China Plain.

The highest reported elevations are 20m above the surrounding plain near Xinxiang in Henan, 13m near Kaifeng and 5m near Jinan; estimates of the annual rise range between 3 and 10cm a year (Mei and Dregne 2001).

With higher erosion on the Loess Plateau, the river's silt load has increased from about 1.3Gt in the early 1950s to 1.6Gt in the early 1980s, the annual riverbed build-up has amounted to about 400Mt, and the average riverbed rise has been 1m per decade. The latest Chinese estimates are that a breach south of Jinan (in the most vulnerable area) would flood up to $33,000\text{km}^2$, affecting 18 million people and cutting all north/south railways and highways (Xinhua 1987). Counterintuitively, the recent period of northern drought has also contributed to a higher risk of flood damage, as dry riverbeds in many northern cities and villages were used for planting crops, dumping garbage, and even building houses.

Unlike the Huanghe basin, parts of the Changjiang valley experienced several major floods during the 1980s. The principal reason for extensive flooding has been the increasing silting. In the late 1970s it was estimated that serious erosion affected about 20 per cent of the Changjiang basin (Wang and Zhou 1981); a decade later the share was put at 560,000km^2, or just over 30 per cent (Chang 1987). Between 2.2 and 2.4Gt of silt is carried every year through the river's gorges, raising the riverbeds and lake levels in Hubei and Hunan. Four fifths of all lakes in the famed area of thousand lakes in eastern Hubei disappeared owing to the combination of excessive silting and conversion to farmland, reducing the natural flood-storage capacity of this key rice-growing region. Dongtinghu, formerly China's largest freshwater lake in northern Hunan, has fallen to second place beyond Poyanghu: of the annual influx of 160Mm^3 of silt, only a quarter is discharged, and the bottom of the lake is rising by an average of 2.5cm a year (Chang 1987).

The lake's water level during the rainy season is approaching the height of the catastrophic flood of 1954, and exceeding the danger level in sixty-eight different places. Elevation and strengthening of dikes cannot be an effective permanent solution. Moreover, most dikes and spill-over basins along the Changjiang are now able to withstand floods of only a 10–20-year frequency: a repeat of the 1954 flood, assessed by Chinese water-management experts as one of 40-year probability, could lead to the displacement of up to 7 million people, and to unprecedented economic losses (Lampton 1986). And, as always in China's long history, the fear of southern floods continues to be accompanied by concerns about northern water deficits (Smil 2000b).

North China's water shortages

Once again, severe drought is covering a large part of China's north-central heartland, and once again the environmental catastrophists are predicting a massive drop in industrial production, and harvest failures, with global repercussions. Indeed, the overall annual economic loss to industry and agriculture attributable to water shortages has been surpassing $2.4 billion per year. For two thirds of China's 600 largest cities, shortages are a recurrent problem. Is this the beginning of an inevitable environmental crisis? Or is it a matter of natural scarcity made much worse by economic mismanagement?

In absolute terms China is not short of water. It ranks sixth in the world in total water resources. But the country's large population reduces its per capita water resources to just a quarter of the global mean. A highly uneven distribution of precipitation makes China's northern provinces, which lie beyond the zone of vigorous monsoon rains, exceptionally water-poor. Although the region normally receives just enough precipitation to get by, like the prairies of the United States and Canada, dry years come frequently. In fact, large swathes of the region may not see any rain or snow for many months or even for more than a year.

Below-average rainfalls for the period between 1978 and 1986 were followed by a fairly good precipitation, but drought returned in 1997, and this year (2002) it is nearly as bad as at any time during the past generation. Beijing's reservoirs now contain less water than at any time since the early 1980s, when the city had some 3 million fewer people and only a small fraction of its current number of water-gobbling skyscrapers, hotels and restaurants. In early June, Beijing introduced "strict and obligatory" water quotas for industries, restaurants, hotels and universities, and residential and irrigation water was rationed on an experimental basis.

Reservoirs cannot fully compensate for such shortfalls, particularly at a time when China's rapid urbanization multiplies per capita water demand: moving from village to city doubles or triples personal water consumption. Overuse of underground water, accompanied by serious ground subsidence, is thus the norm in all northern cities. Beijing's water table, for example, has dropped by more than nine meters since the early 1980s; as a result, city ground levels are sinking by 1–2cm every year. Even higher subsidence rates are common in parts of the North China Plain, where pumps draw water from increasingly deeper wells for crop irrigation.

Yet even by the mid-1980s many Beijing residents were billed a flat fee (per household) for their water, paying less than 10 per cent of the actual cost of delivered water. That was until April 1996, when the State Council approved increased water prices in Beijing. However, better pricing alone cannot be the solution for complex environmental problems, although in this case it is obviously an essential ingredient of any effective action. More realistic water pricing would certainly prompt greater reuse of inevitably more expensive, treated waste water, while reducing China's appalling water pollution.

Furthermore, water for irrigation, which accounts for about 80 per cent of northern China's use and nearly 50 per cent even in the Beijing municipality, is still largely given away. Prices for irrigation water are rarely more than one US cent per ton, typically no more than 5–10 per cent of the delivered cost. But cheap irrigation water provides no incentives for making its use more efficient. At the March 1997 Forum Engelberg in Switzerland, Song Jian, chairman of China's State Science and Technology Commission, claimed China's agricultural water-use efficiency averaged a mere 10 per cent. The appropriate choice of crops (as well as grain-fed animals) would also help alleviate water-use problems.

None of these proposed changes and adjustments will come easily or inexpensively. Yet all of them are effective; they have been proven to work elsewhere in similar conditions. They can therefore make the difference between recurrent crises and adequate water supplies. It's not fundamentally a matter of economic and technical resources: China has enough of both, but to solve the north-central heartland's water crisis, there must be a determined commitment to allocate them to the challenge.

Searching for solutions

Nihil novum sub sole: certainly not as far as China's grand-scale patterns of water supply are concerned. Parts of the country are repeatedly submerged by flooding waters, while in other provinces peasants drill ever-deeper wells to reach receding aquifers. As I write this, in August 2002, the rising waters of the Dongtinghu,

China's second largest lake, are once again spilling onto surrounding rice fields and into the villages and towns of the lakeside lowland that house more than 10 million people. At the same time, many places on the North China Plain have recently recorded the most rapid decline of water tables in their history. The Ministry of Land and Resources reported that in the year 2000 the average level of Hebei's deep aquifer receded by 2.91m, and that a super-funnel of decreased water tables has formed over some 40,000km^2 by the coalescence of water funnels underneath Beijing, Tianjin, northern Henan and western Shandong (Ma 2001).

Most of the new figures are merely more worrisome versions of the older ones. Official statistics indicate that China's water consumption rose from about 100Gm^3 in 1949 to 557Gm^3 in 1997, and forecasts see the need for 664Gm^3 by 2030 and 750Gm^3 by 2050, bringing the annual requirement uncomfortably close to the total available volume of perhaps as little as 800Gm^3 (and no more than 950Gm^3) (*China Daily* 2002). About 27Mha of farmland now experiences drought each year, the annual deficit of irrigation water has reached 30Gm^3, while the water shortage in urban areas amounts to about 6Gm^3. Looking well ahead, Chinese experts voice concerns about the third and fourth decades of the twenty-first century, when the highest forecast totals of China's population (in excess of 1.6 billion people) could bring down the nationwide average of per capita availability of water to just marginally above 1,700m^3, the volume that is generally recognized as the mark for water shortages on a national scale.

But a closer look also shows a few encouraging signs. As high as the recently claimed water shortage is, the aggregate of 36Gm^3 in the year 2000 is considerably smaller than the forecast made just a decade ago. Although the rate is still below the delivered costs, Beijing saw two more water price rises in 1999, to 1.3 *yuan*/m^3 for domestic, and 1.6 *yuan*/m^3 for industrial use – but as the true cost of water in north Chinese cities averages 5 *yuan*/t, even with that rise the Beijingers get their water at nearly 75 per cent below cost! The central government is definitely paying more attention to the northern water shortages, with the Minister of Water Resources promising to put the conservation and protection of water resources high on the state's investment agenda. The State Environment Protection Administration has been working on large-scale projects to reduce river pollution.

But there is now a fairly broad consensus, although certainly no unanimity, among China's water experts that demand-side management alone – conservation measures (water-saving faucets, showers and toilets), waste water treatment, higher prices and outright limits on water use – will not be sufficient to secure enough water for the provinces north of the Huanghe.

The only viable, albeit still controversial, means of expanding the supply is the long-distance transfer of water. The idea of South/North water transfer (*nan shui bei diao*) goes back to the 1950s (Greer 1979; Biswas *et al.* 1983; Smil 1993; Liu 1998). Possible routes for the transfer were identified and preliminarily surveyed in 1959, and the project was revived in 1978 as a part of the ten-year plan of economic modernization (Figure 4.5). A surprisingly strong public challenge based on environmental considerations, a new force in China's policy-making, and the old problem of the enormous cost of such a project, led to a temporizing decision.

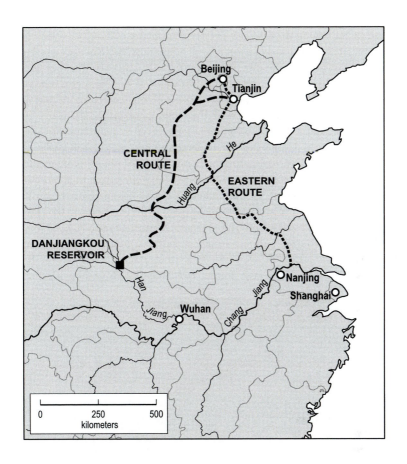

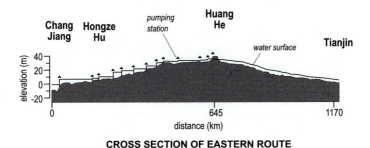

CROSS SECTION OF EASTERN ROUTE

Figure 4.5 The two South/North water-transfer routes under construction. The eastern route, about 1,130km long, follows the ancient Grand Canal, and it will require pumping until it crosses the Huang He. The central route, 1,241km (or 1,267km) long, will carry water by gravity from Danjiangkou reservoir, and eventually from Sanxia

Instead of approving the full-scale project transferring 30Gm³ of water along the eastern route, from Jiangsu via Anhui and Shandong, the State Council chose a greatly scaled-down version to move only about 2Gm³ and even then not all the way, but only to the Donping Hu in Shandong, just south of the Huanghe. The principal economic argument against the full-scale version of the eastern route that takes the advantage of the Grand Canal has been the necessity of raising the water by a total of 40m along the way, a feat necessitating at least 1GW of pumping capacity, as well as major widening and dredging of the ancient, and now also heavily polluted, canal.

Detailed studies of the middle route resumed in 1990, and this alternative came to be seen by many experts as both economically and environmentally more acceptable. Water would be taken from an enlarged Danjiangkou reservoir on the Han River in northern Hubei (Figure 4.6). Its capacity would be boosted by 11.6Gm³ to 29.1Gm³ by raising the dam from the present 157m to 171.6m (Liu 1998; Xinhua 2002). The middle route's main advantage is that no pumping would be required, as the water would be carried by gravity in a canal snaking along the southern and western edges of, respectively, the Funiu and Taihang Mountains all the way to

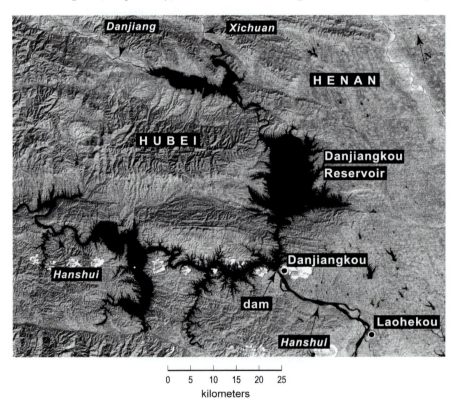

Figure 4.6 LANDSAT image of the doubly bifurcated Danjiangkou reservoir in northern Hubei and southern Henan. The central route of the South/North water-transfer canal will start from the enlarged easternmost bay of the reservoir's largest part just north of the dam

Beijing's Yuyuantan Lake; a spur from Xushui in Hebei would carry water across the Haihe Plain to Tianjin. Moreover, water delivered by the middle route would be much cleaner than the flow traveling through the Grand Canal (Figure 4.5). The main disadvantage is the necessity of displacing large numbers of people. These would total about 50,000 along the canal's route, but 200,000 people would have their houses and fields flooded because of the raised Danjiangkou dam, whose original construction has already displaced some 380,000 people (Liu 1992).

A surprising decision taken in November 2001 calls for both the first and second phases of the eastern route (from the lower Changjiang to Shandong, and then to Tianjin), and the first phase of the middle route from Hanjiang to Beijing and Tianjin – carrying initially $9.5Gm^3$, and 13–$14Gm^3$ by the year 2030 – to be completed by 2010. The total cost of these two segments, shared 60:40 by central government and local authorities, will be more than 180 billion *yuan* (or US$22 billion when converted at the official exchange rate), and Beijing may receive the first deliveries of $1.2Gm^3$ of Changjiang water as early as 2007. Laudably, the project also includes more than 40 billion *yuan* to be invested concurrently into improved irrigation and widespread adoption of water-saving equipment in northern households and industries. Moreover, clear water passages and about 100 new sewage plants are planned to sharply reduce water pollution in the Grand Canal, which is now heavily contaminated in parts.

Water-saving measures should reduce the consumption in the areas that are to receive the diverted water by $4.1Gm^3$ a year. This would be equal to about one tenth of the eventually anticipated annual transfer of 38–$48Gm^3$ (with the middle route carrying about $15Gm^3$), making it clearly the world's most voluminous diversion of water. China's largest previous water transfer was the gravity-driven 286km-long diversion of the Luanhe to the Beijing and Tianjin areas: completed in 1984, the project has an annual capacity of $19.5Gm^3$, while the pumped diversions from the Huanghe to Qingdao and from the Dong River to Shenzhen and Hong Kong have capacities of, respectively, 6.85 and $6.2Gm^3$ (Liu 1998). The only Western water diversions that compare in their scope with the South/North transfer – the nearly 1,100km of canals and pipelines of California's State Water Project, taking water from the northern part of the state, and the diversion of the lower Colorado river to California, Arizona and New Mexico – have the capacity to move, respectively, $5.2Gm^3$ and $9.3Gm^3$ every year (CDWR 2002; Gelt 1997).

Inevitably, there are many technical and environmental concerns with a project of such unprecedented magnitude. These range from the basic questions of supply adequacy to some engineering challenges. Perhaps the most important consideration in the first category is the highly variable rainfall in the basin of the Han River, which results in recurrent low water levels in Danjiangkou reservoir. What will happen if there is an unusually long spell of low precipitation surpassing the dry periods of 1965–1966 and 1991–1995? This problem should be solved by building a connection between the Danjiangkou and Sanxia reservoirs, a relatively short link of about 150km to the Du River, the Han River's southern tributary, but one requiring considerable pumping to cross Daba Shan.

How to cross the Huanghe – just north of the Dongping Lake with the eastern route, and near Zhengzhou in Henan with the middle route – may be the most challenging engineering problem. Siphoning under the river's bed is the favored solution, but it will require some controls of silt deposition. Another major uncertainty is the fate of the aqueduct crossing the flood-prone Henanese plain: will the Sanmenxia and Xiaolangdi dams be able to moderate a catastrophic flood traveling down the Huanghe and threatening the new aqueduct?

China's environment and security: simple myths and complex realities

Growing concerns about China's long-term water supply have also become one of the most prominent examples used by a newly influential school of thought that sees a clear and direct connection between the state of the country's environment and its broadly defined security. Most of the proponents of this view appear to be unaware that their thinking has roots in the classical geographic determinism of the late nineteenth century, and, as I will explain in the following section, its relatively rapid public acceptance owes a great deal to its fortuitous timing as a successor to, and clearly a partial substitute for, the fortunately lessened concerns about the risks of a thermonuclear conflict between two global superpowers.

During the early 1990s I was asked to prepare several China-based contributions to this interesting research genre (Smil 1992a, 1992b, 1995b). But the fact that I diligently searched out some important links between China's deteriorating environment and its long-term security did not mean, to the disappointment of some of my catastrophically-minded colleagues, that I subscribed to a simplistic deterministic notion that saw, to caricature it by hyperbole, an inevitable regime change behind every eroding slopeland. All those new securitarians who were inclined to argue along these lines would not approve of the following analysis (Smil 1997b) – but I feel that it remains a fair appraisal of a concern that does not have to turn inevitably into a catastrophe whose impacts would go far beyond China's extensive borders.

The Chinese language abounds in sayings and proverbs so succinct that they vex even the best translators. They are often so illuminating that they provide perfect encapsulations of countless realities. When asked to contribute again to the currently fashionable literature on environment and security,[1] I found myself once more a reluctant participant in a quest whose main thrust can be most appropriately described by the ancient saying *xin yuan yi ma*. The four characters stand for heart, gibbon, idea and horse. It means you have an idea in mind, but the essence of your thoughts is really somewhere else.

So it is, I feel, with the recent spate of studies on environment and security. After the sudden demise of the superpower confrontation deprived political scientists of their ultimate security concern, apocalyptic nuclear war, they made a nimble readjustment. With no small help from Robert Kaplan, whose none-too-subtle visions of the future world became required reading for Washington bureaucrats, they discovered a worry perhaps almost as impressive.[2] While environmental degradation does not happen in a blinding flash, it does share two important characteristics with nuclear exchange. First, its spatial reach could be truly global; and second, its social and economic effects could be highly devastating. The precipitous loss of a large share of stratospheric ozone would endanger all higher living organisms that have evolved in the biosphere protected from UVB radiation by the oxygenated atmosphere. Rapid climate change with a substantial rise of average temperatures could have effects ranging from new precipitation patterns to northward diffusion of malaria. These are, of course, the best-known, and potentially very worrisome, examples of environmental transformations.

In thinking about the new horse of environmental degradation, it is really the old gibbon's heart of national security that many of the new securitarians want to preserve. They alter, dilute, and extend the meaning of security beyond any classical recognition, but they never give up on its original idea, which embodies conflict and violence. This is because that idea carries them to the heart of existential anguish and mortal peril, fears without which their message would not merit such an anxious hearing by politicians, the military, or the mass media. The new securitarians must be aware that the challenges posed by environmental degradation are not manageable by a well-established national security apparatus geared to preventing and fighting violent conflicts. Yet they wish to have that apparatus to embrace their ideas. They promise not just diffuse, incremental deterioration, but potentially violent conflicts whose "management" should become a matter for the highest levels of national policy-making.

Inevitably, policies guided by the fear of environmental catastrophe would affect the armed forces and intelligence-gathering organizations called on to fight this new global threat. These institutions, no matter what their real belief may be, have nimbly recognized the political value of these new fears – and hence the potential for funding.[3] Many new securitarians have gone much further and redefined security in a totally all-encompassing manner. The United Nations Development Program (UNDP) now maintains that security is concerned "with how people live and breathe".[4] With such a definition, one would expect security studies to be preoccupied with absolutely everything, from nutrition and unemployment to pollution and drug trafficking. The UNDP actually lists all these variables. It seems that the only ingredients it excludes is clinical depression, a feeling that makes millions of people very insecure indeed![5] A very politically incorrect question arises: why should anyone take this methodological farce seriously?

Of course, there is an obvious answer. Individual scholars, granting agencies, policy-makers and politicians all need to see suitably frightening concerns on their horizons; worries that provide a rich substrate for papers, meetings, consultations, commissions and strategic initiatives; and actions that make their participants full of the most satisfying feeling that they are helping to save the world. Consequently, environmental security has become a veritable growth industry, bringing together such unlikely confrères as Defence Intelligence Agency (DIA) analysts and Greenpeace activists. In spite of their considerable differences, they share many unmistakable commonalties, as illustrated in recent alerts on environmental security.

Most of these studies display the simplistic bent common to recent converts to great causes. Many natural scientists must be amused, if not appalled, by the often crass environmental determinism of the securitarians (eroding slopelands = environmental refugees = overcrowded cities = political instability = violence; or water scarcity = civil or interstate war). Any thoughtful historian, and especially those fascinated by the complex relationships between civilizations and their environment, must be astonished by the utter neglect of long-term historical perspectives. The two most obvious weaknesses are, first, an apparent ignorance of the history of environmental pollution and ecosystemic degradation in affluent nations; and second, a lack of appreciation of the quintessential role played by scarcity and crises in stimulating technical and social innovation.[6]

Even the most eager promoters of these new perils find it difficult to make connections between the environment and national security. Moreover, some of the political scientists who refused to board the new security train have been waging a war of ideas, almost to the point of denying any links at all between the two supervariables. Exaggeration, hesitation, meandering, tedious definitional debates and recriminations have been an inevitable result of this state of affairs.[7] As a natural scientist, albeit one keenly interested in the socio-economic implications of environmental change, I will not attempt to add to the suspect canon of theoretical generalizations regarding the peculiar relationship between the environment and security. Unique combinations of environmental settings, economic (mis)fortunes, cultural expectations and social cohesion make any such generalizations highly suspect. Instead, my goal is to examine critically current Chinese realities, as well as the most likely short-term trends, in order to identify any links between China's environment and its security.

What security?

Ullman's expanded definition centers on the presence, over a relatively brief span of time, of drastic military or non-military security threats to the quality of life. In so doing, it captures both individual and policy-making concerns and significantly narrows the range of practical policy choices.[8] But even when working within this broad framework, one must make a distinction between truly drastic new threats and serious, but recurring, old patterns which are better publicized. Appraising the available policy options requires distinguishing what appears alarming, but is in fact ephemeral, from what is truly worrisome and long-lasting. The dynamic nature of both technical and socio-economic fixes continually expands and alters the realm of these choices.

With nearly 1.25 billion people by the end of 1996, China is the world's most populous nation. It possesses nuclear weapons, borders more than a dozen other countries, carries a burden of historical myths, and is prone to radical upheavals. Its security obviously matters. The state of China's environment matters not just to the Chinese but to its neighbors as well. Ecosystems which have been much abused for millennia must now endure an extraordinarily large and rapid quest for modernization.[9] While the concept still finds only a very few supporters among economists, economies are nothing but complex subsystems of the biosphere. Hence, any degradation of a nation's environment inevitably weakens its long-term capacity for sustaining individual well-being and high levels of total output.[10] Given China's size, any major failure on the road to modernization would have wide-ranging international repercussions.

Although these matters are exceedingly difficult to quantify, my detailed and fairly comprehensive economic estimates suggest that environmental degradation costs China about 10 per cent of the country's gross domestic product every year, a conclusion echoed by a recently published, independent Chinese study.[11] Does this indisputably serious burden affect China's security? If so, in what way? Were it to grow further, could it be restricted to merely a marginal aggravation, barely consequential in comparison with the traditionally present forces of disintegration, raging from the centrifugal tendencies of distant provinces to recurrent outbursts of violence, and from touchy nationalism to vicious infighting within the gerontocratic elite? Or could it become China's major contribution to a world disintegrating into Kaplanesque anarchy? These questions are best answered by a closer look at the most important components of environmental change in China.

Environmental pollution

Maintaining that the only effect of more intense environmental pollution over a much greater area is to degrade the quality of life, the new securitarians ignore the process of industrialization and urbanization as a whole. Furthermore, they do so without a proper historical perspective. Deteriorating quality of air, water and soils; increasing background noise; foodstuffs contaminated by long-lasting residues of wastes and synthetic chemicals; and exposure to aesthetic blight have accompanied economic modernization around the world. They are all in abundant, and often revolting, evidence throughout China. However, when viewed in historical perspective, these degradations could be seen as merely regrettable, and often surprisingly temporary by-products of changes that have allowed impressive declines in infant mortality, a steady increase in life expectancy, larger disposable incomes and greater social mobility. China has quickly developed some of the world's worst environmental quality indicators, but it has also experienced unusually impressive improvements in major quality-of-life indicators – a benefit also enjoyed by other late modernizers, notably South Korea and Taiwan. These two major differences – the speed of environmental degradation and the rate of improvement in certain quality-of-life indicators – have been dictated by the extraordinarily rapid pace of the recent modernization effort.

China is now the world's largest producer and consumer of coal, an inherently dirty fuel requiring efficient combustion and advanced emission controls to prevent high levels of air pollution. Even the most efficient form of coal combustion produces a great deal of particulate matter as well as sulfur and nitrogen oxides, and it is a leading source of carbon dioxide (CO_2) emissions, the most important anthropogenic greenhouse gas. Particulate controls using electrostatic precipitators are relatively cheap and highly effective, but desulfurization is expensive and nitrogen oxide removal even more so. Most of China's coal is burned without any controls in tens of millions of small coal stoves and in small and mid-sized boilers providing heat, steam and hot water for millions of small enterprises, offices and public facilities. Coal is also by far the most important fuel for generating China's electricity, but only the largest power plants commissioned during the past decade have satisfactory particulate emission controls, and there is no commercial desulfurization of flue gases.

Not surprisingly, this brings recurrently heavy episodes of classic (London-type) smog to most Chinese cities, and it creates semi-permanent hardship in all northern urban areas during winter. In addition, the recent rapid multiplication of passenger cars and trucks has been responsible for no less objectionable and no less recurrent episodes of heavy photochemical (Los Angeles-type) smog. China's cities and the surrounding countryside are thus blanketed by very high levels of particulate matter, sulfur dioxide (SO_2), nitrogen oxides, volatile organic compounds and ozone, with concentrations of some of these pollutants being commonly of an order of magnitude above the recommended hygienic means. China's SO_2 air quality limit is 60 micrograms per cubic meter ($\mu g/m^3$) an annual mean, while actual average concentrations in Beijing range from 80 $\mu g/m^3$, in the cleanest suburbs, to 160$\mu g/m^3$. In the worst polluted northern cities they commonly surpass 300$\mu g/m^3$.[12] The inevitable consequences of this combination include a higher incidence of respiratory and cardiovascular diseases and premature mortality among the most sensitive individuals.

The news on water pollution is no better. Even according to official – and very likely too optimistic – statistics, less than half of all waste water is treated, mostly in the simplest way, before it is returned to streams, lakes and ponds. More importantly, during the early 1990s, only about a quarter of all treated industrial waste water conformed to acceptable standards after discharge. Chinese environmental journals abound with reports of high waterborne concentrations of heavy metals, phenols and waste oils. Stream monitoring shows rising levels of dissolved nitrates.

These trends are nothing unexpected, as they replicate those the Western world experienced during the earlier – and not so distant – stages of its industrialization. For example, until their substantial reduction, beginning in the late 1970s, US per capita SO_2 emissions were more than ten times as high as the recent Chinese mean. In fact, the absolute level of Chinese SO_2 emissions is still no higher than US totals were during the 1980s. Furthermore, even though total North American and European SO_2 emissions have declined appreciably since the late 1970s, Central European rates are still considerably higher than those in China, both in terms of per capita and per square kilometer (km^2). Atmospheric concentrations of particulate matter and SO_2 were commonly as high in London during the early 1950s as they have been in Beijing during the 1990s.

During London's infamous episode of heavy smog pollution in early December 1952, average levels of SO_2 stayed above $1,000\mu g/m^3$ for four consecutive days: together with extremely high levels of particulates, they were responsible for some 4,000 premature deaths.[13]

Moreover, some environmental degradations remain more intense in the West than in China. For example, the average annual concentration of nitrates, originating from synthetic fertilizers, manures and nitrogen oxides from combustion, has recently been between 15 and 20 milligrams per liter in the lower basin of Germany's Rhine River, roughly twice as high as in the lower Huanghe, and four times as high as in the Yangzi River as it flows through Jiangsu province.[14] At the same time, an important and rarely appreciated difference is that, little as China spends on environmental protection, these outlays are relatively higher than those of Western nations, or of Japan, at a comparable stage in their economic development. Government spending on environmental protection in these countries did not begin to make a difference until after their average per capita gross domestic products (GDP) passed US$5,000, nearly three times as high as the Chinese mean today.[15]

Perhaps the most encouraging indicator of China's environmental progress, of which securitarians of the catastrophic bent appear to be quite unaware, has been a rapid decline of the country's energy-to-GDP intensity. This measure is a powerful marker of two critical trends. Lower energy-to-GDP ratios indicate greater economic efficiency, and also suggest that the economy is putting a relatively lesser burden on the environment. A long-term decline in this indicator has been pronounced in both North America and in Western Europe, but Chinese improvements are occurring at an even faster rate (for details see the last section of Chapter 2). In addition, the average intensity of water use by industry has also declined, reducing the output of waste water. Both of these trends should continue during the coming years, since China's energy and material intensity efficiencies remain far below their potential.

While industrial efficiencies have improved remarkably, major gains are yet to be made at the household level. Hardly any Chinese apartments are built with wall or ceiling insulation or double-glazed windows, and even fewer have individual temperature controls. Fiberglass and thermostats in millions of newly built apartments would bring energy savings and environmental benefits for decades to come.

The state of China's environment has become a focus for both international aid efforts and for extensive transfer of advanced pollution prevention and clean manufacturing techniques. The United States, Japan and the European Union are all eagerly proffering their considerable advisory and technical capacities to deal with China's energy and environmental challenges. Japanese involvement has been by far the most notable. Japan's New Energy Development Organization is introducing better coal cleaning, more efficient combustion, and simplified flue gas desulfurization.[16]

Inevitably, the rapid pace of China's modernization will bring higher investment in environmental protection. The official target is to double the rate of current investment in environmental protection by the year 2000. At present, it is still short of 1 per cent of GDP. Among the most encouraging specific plans for the near future is the project aimed at cleaning up three heavily polluted rivers in the densely populated eastern coastal region (Huai He, Hai He and Liaohe), and three major lakes (Tai Hu, Chao Hu and Dianchi).

What has been gained by the recent environment-degrading dash toward modernization is surely impressive. Quality-of-life gains have been quite substantial, both in terms of improvement rates and absolute levels achieved. The country's infant mortality is now well below 30/1,000, comparable to Argentina. Life expectancy is now very close to seventy-one years, slightly ahead of Russia. Average per capita GDP, expressed in terms of purchasing power parity, was close to US$2,000 in 1995, comparable to Japan in the mid-1950s and to many countries in pre-World War II Europe. And per capita food availability rose to within less than 5 per cent of Japan and is now equivalent to about 112 per cent of the rate needed to satisfy nutritional needs compatible with a healthy and active life. Judged by these principal quality-of-life indicators, China should no longer be bundled with the low-income developing countries.[17]

Clearly, these are not indicators of a country on the brink of a catastrophic collapse. While incomes will continue to rise fairly rapidly, other indicators may rise only slowly or level off. Major changes will take place among environmental indicators. For example, overall life expectancy will increase, but the causes of death will reflect a higher incidence of cardiovascular diseases and malignancies, as opposed to infectious disease. Consequently, I would argue that China's environmental pollution, while undoubtedly objectionable and certainly harmful to millions of individuals, will not lower the overall quality of life for the average Chinese citizen. Many of its worst excesses will almost certainly be reduced. While its impacts will still be widespread, they are likely to be compensated for by other gains, at least in the judgment of the average citizen if not in the feelings of Western visitors working with ahistorical assumptions and unrealistic expectations.

Perhaps the most helpful way to think about the road ahead is to realize that, in terms of income, China will be traversing ground covered by most of today's affluent countries between 1930 and 1970; in terms of pollution control, the country's experience will more likely resemble the rich world's achievements between 1955 and 1975 (albeit with strikingly different ratios of resources/population when compared not just to North America but also to most European countries). Consequently, I do not foresee circumstances in which mounting environmental pollution would threaten the country's (broadly conceived) security interests to such an extent that either an appreciable decline in the quality of life or increase in civil violence might occur. The historical lessons are clear. As a society's standard of living increases, environmental pollution is a major stimulus to higher efficiency of energy and material conversions, and, through stricter regulations, eventually to an improved quality of life. There is no reason why China should not replicate this experience.

Ecosystemic degradation

The problems encompassed within this broad definition of ecosystemic degradation are too intractable to rectify via straightforward technical solutions. Reducing and eliminating ecosystemic degradation requires constant and skilled resource management, ranging from appropriate agronomic techniques to ongoing planting, and nurturing of trees. As with environmental pollution, China's record in this area is clearly worrisome on a number of fronts. Not all aspects of ecosystemic degradation are amenable to monetization. Most notably, we have no satisfactory means of valuing biodiversity, the key outcome of evolution and the guarantor of biospheric viability. As it happens, China's pre-modern biodiversity was exceptionally high.

Excessive erosion now affects about one third of the country's soils. Even when using official criteria, forest coverage remains below 15 per cent. Cumulative losses of arable land during the past forty years have been larger than all of Germany's farmland, and the annual loss rate of around half a million hectares is still unacceptably high. Conversion of wetlands to crop fields has severely damaged one of the major stores of biodiversity and reduced water storage capacity. The deforested and overgrazed regions of northern China are threatened by desertification. Conservative estimates show that these degradations already cost China the equivalent of at least 5 per cent of GDP annually, and none of these trends can be radically reversed in a matter of years. But, as with the pollution effects, these developments have their obverse in encouraging changes. Perhaps most notably, the quality of afforestation efforts has improved significantly. Survival rates are now well over 50 per cent, compared to approximately 10 per cent a generation ago. Since the mid-1980s, the government has been limiting the allowable cut in state forests, and turning to substantial imports of wood. Recently, China has been spending about a billion dollars per year to import logs, pulp and paper from North and South America, Europe and Russia.

Although China is still losing its mature trees, the total forest area has been stabilized, and it may have actually grown a bit during the past few years – the first reversal in modern Chinese history. According to figures issued by the Ministry of Forestry, China's forested areas rose from a low of 115.28 million hectares in 1981 to 124.65Mha by 1988, and reached 128.63Mha by 1992. The annual increment in new timber was 366 million m^3, and annual consumption was 327 million m^3, yielding an annual surplus averaging 39 million m^3 of timber during the period 1989–1991, the first such gain in many generations. In December 1993 it was announced that total annual growth had surpassed 400 million m^3, while consumption had declined further to 320 million m^3. If true, this would mean a fundamental reversal in a single decade, with the 1989–1993 annual surplus being equal to exactly one quarter of all tree felling.[18] Even when heavily discounted, there is little doubt that the precipitous decline of China's forests has stopped, and perhaps even been slightly reversed.

New surveys show that the country has actually at least 30 per cent, and perhaps as much as 45 per cent, more arable land than is listed in official statistics, and tougher new regulations are being put in place to limit losses of the most valuable farmland. For more on China's farmland, see the last section of Chapter 3.

Besides the scare over "Who will feed China?", the other event related to the environment that has attracted a great deal of recent attention has been the record floods during the summer of 1996. Not surprisingly, the flooding in China is already interpreted as the beginning of a worsening trend directly attributable to ecosystemic degradation. This does not appear to be very likely. Saying this is not to claim that excessive rainfalls, or other unpreventable natural extremes, cannot be aggravated by human actions. In China's case, there is no doubt that misguided environmental policies have contributed to the severity of catastrophic flooding by encouraging deforestation and the destruction of lakes and wetlands. Deforestation opens the slopes for direct impact by raindrops which, together with accelerated runoff, strips away most of the protective layer, reduces the water-storage capacity of the watershed, and increases soil erosion. The difference can be dramatic. While a forested terrain in central China will lose no more than a few tonnes of topsoil per hectare annually, a clear-cut slopeland will lose more than 30, or even 50, tonnes per hectare annually, and in north China's highly erodible Loess Plateau, the rate may easily surpass 100 tonnes per hectare per year.

The destruction of wetlands has affected the central part of the Yangzi valley in the province of Hubei, the area formerly known as the land of thousand lakes, particularly hard. I still remember my astonishment when, some twenty years ago, I compared the first cloud-free satellite images of Hubei with the US and Japanese maps prepared during the early 1940s. While the maps showed a score of medium- and large-sized lakes and numerous smaller water surfaces, LANDSAT images in the 1970s revealed that the lake area had been reduced by half. After the beginning of de-Maoization, official sources revealed that of nearly 1,100 lakes larger than 1,000 *mu* (approximately 66.6 hectares) fewer than 400 remained by 1978. The province's lake water surface had fallen by 75 per cent! Needless to say, such a drastic loss of water storage must be reflected in more intensive flooding.

Given ever-higher population densities and the rapidly rising economic product, the damage caused by an identical volume of water in the mid-1990s must be at least two to three times as high as it would have been in the mid-1970s, and a high multiple of the mid-1950s level. However, given China's vastly increased level of economic activity, such damage may be a smaller fraction of annual GDP than in the past, and the overall effects may be surprisingly limited. For example, in 1995 natural disasters affected crops on about 4.5 million hectares, roughly 5 per cent of the officially claimed farmland, and reduced output to as little as one fifth of normal yields. Yet China still proceeded to produce a record harvest of cereals.

Moreover, careful chronicling of areas affected by floods shows no obvious trend. Although there was an increase in the total area affected between 1970 and 1986, annual totals were substantially lower than during the worst flooding of the 1950s and 1960s. The obverse situation to China's recurrent flooding –

the commonly cited warnings about water shortages so severe that they could cripple urban life of drought-prone northern provinces, where some two fifths of China's population live and an equal share of industrial capacity is located – offers a perfect example of the ignoring of economic realities, both by Chinese and Western environmental doomsayers. I will illustrate this by comparing Beijing's pre-1996 water prices with those of the city where I live.

Winnipeg, a city of some 700,000 people with no heavy industrial production, gets its water from Lake of the Woods, one of the large glacial lakes left behind by the last Ice Age. This water requires hardly any cleaning, and no pumping is needed as the water flows to the city by gravity. Yet with sewerage rates included, we are charged about US$1.30/m^3. Until the State Council approved increased prices in April 1996, the inhabitants of Beijing – a city of 11 million people where half of all water comes from expensive underground pumping and where Stalinist planners located many water-guzzling, heavy industrial enterprises – were paying 0.3 *yuan*/m^3, that is a mere $0.035/m^3 at the official exchange rate, and only around $0.15/m^3 when using a liberal purchasing parity rate. Even more remarkably, in comparison to Winnipeg a cubic meter of Beijing water costs less even as a share of average disposable family incomes! The approved rate increase for water will boost the new rate to about $0.25/m^3, still only a fifth of the cost in Winnipeg, a city enjoying one of the most abundant water supplies in the world.

Rather than being an exception, China's urban water prices have followed the world norm in undervaluing limited natural resources. Alarms about imminent and crippling resource scarcities thus appear in a very different light when one recognizes that the commodities in question have been, until recently, largely given away, using enormous government subsidies that have eliminated incentives for efficient use or substitution. There are other factors behind water scarcity in Beijing. Until recently, many households did not have a water meter and were charged a flat monthly fee. While this has been largely remedied, rice, a crop traditionally not grown in the area, is still planted in the Beijing municipality and in the surrounding Hebei province, a choice about as smart, and about as heavily subsidized, as growing rice in the semi-deserts of California.

Once again – without in the least trying to denigrate the extent or intensity of China's environmental degradation or the challenges facing a rapidly modernizing country with relatively limited amounts of key natural resources – I simply do not see why sensible policies, now increasingly in evidence, should not bring incremental improvements and prevent the kind of deterioration that might seriously affect the country's socio-economic security or even push it into external conflicts.

Different future

Undoubtedly, today's China is full of unrealistic expectations. Its large population means that its rich natural endowment translates into relatively modest per capita resource availability, and its huge potential demand for all kinds of resources means that the country will not have the option of relying on imports of basic commodities to the extent Japan or the USA have done.[19] Inevitably, a modernized China will not be a copy of North America. It will have to find a new consumption equilibrium, but so will the affluent nations, as too many of our demands are unsustainable. However, this reality does not have to translate into any objectionable declines in real quality of life. We have come to understand that improvement of health and educational indicators and the realization and maintenance of a comfortable standard of living do not keep pace with rising incomes or material consumption. J-bends, or saturation levels, often form at surprisingly low rates of energy use or disposable income.

Admittedly, it will take some time to get used to this profound lesson and to reorient economies accordingly. Yet the task is eventually unavoidable. We cannot keep increasing energy conversion and material output without serious environmental consequences. Managing this challenge will be a major task for the first half of the twenty-first century. In this sense, China's predicaments are simply more circumscribed and more demanding versions of the tasks that will face every nation. Fortunately, there appear to be no insurmountable biophysical reasons why even China cannot achieve a great deal of incremental advances along this demanding path. Extremist policies that have plagued so much of China's modern development may yet undermine much that has been already achieved. However, if China were to enjoy a generation of political stability, widening personal freedoms, and cooperative relations with the other four fifths of humanity, there is no reason why the state of its environment should not become a catalyst for further socio-economic advances, rather than a factor contributing to instability, conflict or even violence.

The cost of China's environmental change: quantifying the economic impact

Those environmental catastrophists who were disappointed by my criticism of exaggerated claims of new securitarianism as it applies to China, found plenty of material that was more to their liking in my comprehensive evaluation of the economic impacts of China's environmental change. This detailed report, prepared originally for the East–West Center in Hawaii (Smil 1996c), made it clear that those economic costs of China's environmental mismanagement that can be at least partially quantified are not trivial, and that the real toll must be considerably higher.

We have been valuing natural goods for millennia: as categories and intensities of our desire change – fossil fuels instead of furs, silicon instead of copper – so do the outputs and prices. But one underlying reality has helped us make the growing populations more affluent in spite of the obviously limited amount of natural riches: a remarkable substitutability of most of the natural resources made possible by even more remarkable human inventiveness. And so the recurrent worries about running out are repeatedly relegated to forgotten cases of mistaken thinking. Here is just one example among many: in the age of wired communication we worried about running out of copper, but now most our messages run through glass (optical fibers) whose main ingredient is just clean sand – or through the air.

But we rely on nature not just for goods, but also for environmental services that include benefits ranging from pollination of crops by bees to soil formation by earthworms; from insect pest control by birds to decomposition of organic wastes by bacteria and fungi; and from oxygen release by photosynthesizing plants to nitrogen return to the atmosphere by denitrifying microbes (Smil 1997). There are no viable, biosphere-wide substitutes for these services: without them all our civilizing efforts would almost instantly fall apart. Consequently, these natural services are in many ways truly invaluable, and hence any monetization of human environmental impact is bound to be inherently incomplete.

Nevertheless, even the exercises limited to quantifying damages and degradations that are more amenable to monetization are helpful and revealing. The cost of air pollution can be measured indirectly by declining crop yields or by the increasing number of visits made by asthmatics to hospital emergency departments. The cost of soil erosion can be at least partially captured by quantifying the burden of additional cleaning of excessively silted canals, and of the disappearing water storage capacity in reservoirs. Even when they are based on fairly conservative assumptions, these valuations show that much of the vaunted modern economic growth is an illusion, as a substantial part of its undoubted benefits is erased by pollution and ecosystemic degradation, whose costs are never considered by standard economic accounts.

All quantifications of the economic costs of environmental change are inherently uncertain and open to adjustment and argument. But their goal is not – in any case unattainable – exactitude. They call our attention to those impacts of human activities that the traditional economic calculus leaves out: unabashedly, economists call them "externalities", but ecological economists and ecologists are appalled by this treatment. That is why I dared to enter this tricky realm of environmental accounting: to bring a more realistic – though necessarily imperfect and in many ways flawed – assessment of the impact that China's modernization is having on the country's already much damaged environment (Smil 1997b).

As their shared ancient Greek root attests, economics and ecology are just two great branches of the same tree – but today's mainstream protagonists of economical and ecological thought appear to have little in common. A closer look reveals a great deal of intellectual cross-pollination and creative ferment at the disciplinary edges[20] – but, generally, there is still that distinct feeling that ecologists have too few numbers to make irrefutable arguments about the extent and the intensity of appropriate environmental management.

Of course, ecologists can offer a great deal of quantitative evidence concerning degradative processes, ranging from coastal eutrophication to tropical deforestation, and they have come to understand the intricacies of such anthropogenic changes as acid deposition or heavy metal accumulation. But nothing would help to make their argument stronger than the availability of realistic assessments of the economic impacts of environmental pollution and ecosystemic degradation. Persuasive figures on economic losses caused by these changes would make it possible to offer revealing cost-benefit analyses and to reorient public policies, as well as environmental laws and investors' thinking, toward more effective preventive actions.

Converting this need to acceptable results is an extraordinary challenge, even for affluent economies with long traditions of good statistical services and with a deepening interest in environmental matters in general, and in ecological economics in particular. Major difficulties complicate the task. As yet, there are no generally accepted standard procedures for such evaluations.[21] These methodological uncertainties mean that individual researchers have no choice but to use subjective judgments about which variables to include and how to treat those inclusions.

For example, if a researcher is to quantify the health effects of chronically high urban air pollution, the approach may range from a minimalist account, limited to the value of labor time lost due to higher upper-respiratory morbidity, to the all-encompassing valuation monetizing every individual discomfort and including the cost of premature death. In the first case, it is not too difficult to work out the productive time lost to respiratory illness through sample surveys of major employers or health care providers, to compare it with a similar population living in a clean city, and to multiply the excess total by typical wage rates.

When pursuing the second choice, an enterprising researcher will uncover relatively rich, and fascinating, literature on the monetization of personal suffering and the value of life – but no objective criteria for putting monetary value on the respiratory discomfort, physical limitations and anxiety induced by recurrent asthmatic attacks provoked by rising levels of photochemical smog. And as far as the value of life is concerned, actuarial practice, economic considerations and moral imperatives will present choices whose totals may differ by up to an order of magnitude.[22]

But even a standard set of procedures would not make the challenge much easier: specific figures are needed as basic inputs in such calculations are commonly unavailable, even in affluent countries with extensive statistical services.[23] Again, simplifying assumptions and subjective choices becomes unavoidable, weakening the persuasiveness of the eventual bottom line. Although some very ingenuous estimating procedures may have been employed in the process, the cumulative effect of even small departures from reality can easily halve, or double, the final figure![24]

But perhaps the most limiting factor is the impossibility of any meaningful monetization of degraded or lost environmental services. If a peasant on a treeless plain removes straw from the field in order to cook or to heat the house, how can we value that loss? The value of plant nutrients in removed straw can be expressed rather easily by equating it with the cost of synthetic fertilizers needed to replace them. But the recycled straw would have improved the water-retention capacity of the soil, and it would have also provided feed for myriad bacteria and fungi, as well as for numerous soil invertebrates, without which there can be no living, productive soils, and hence no sustainable farming. How does one monetize those irreplaceable ecosystemic services?

But none of these obstacles should prevent us from trying. As long as we understand the limitations – that the valuations provide useful ranges of approximations and never any correct single-figure answers, that all of them are incomplete, and that even the most comprehensive ones will almost certainly undervalue the real impact of human actions on the long-term integrity of the quality of the environment – we can interpret the results.

Still, getting to that point is difficult, and the challenges are particularly great in countries where such evaluations may be needed most: in large, populous and still growing nations engaged in rapid socio-economic modernization which puts enormous demands on the integrity of their environment.

China's recent record is remarkable in every one of these aspects. This nation of more than 1.2 billion people adds at least 13 million people a year, or the equivalent of France in less than five years;[25] during the 1980s its GDP growth was surpassed only by that of South Korea, and during the early 1990s it was the world's highest, with annual rates up to 14 per cent.[26] But this unprecedented growth and modernization goes on in landscapes previously much abused by irrational industrial and agricultural practices, on a territory endowed with absolutely large but relatively limited natural resources, and in environments whose air, water and land are already much polluted.[27]

At the same time, China is a country abounding in dubious statistics and unverifiable claims, and peopled by masses of uncooperative bureaucrats prone to treating any unflattering figure as a deep state secret. If the Dutch or Germans try to express the economic cost of their environmental degradation, that may be one thing[28] – but doing the same for China may seem overly ambitious. Surprisingly, a Chinese study was actually among the earliest attempts of its kind: it was initiated in 1984, and when published in 1990 it put the cost of the country's environmental pollution at about 6.75 per cent of its 1983 annual GDP.[29] Soon after I learned about this study I began to gather materials for a more comprehensive assessment, one that would also quantify at least some major consequences of ecosystemic degradation.

I eventually did most of the work on this project at the East–West Center in Honolulu,[30] but even before this assessment was completed I thought it would be interesting if a small group of Chinese researchers were to make, quite independently, a similarly comprehensive evaluation. I hoped that a comparison of the two studies would show both the usefulness and the limitations of these valuations. When The Project on Environment, Population and Security directed by Thomas Homer-Dixon at the University of Toronto provided the necessary support, I was able to ask Professor Mao Yushi, a noted Chinese economist, a member of the Chinese Academy of Social Sciences (CASS) and now the director of Unirule Institute of Economics in Beijing, to commission studies on the economic costs of China's environmental pollution, deforestation and land degradation.[31]

With both assessments now available,[32] the opportunity to appraise the economic impact of China's environmental change is better than in the case of any other large modernizing nation. Readers interested in detailed assumptions will have to refer to the two studies; here I will just review some of China's most important environmental concerns, highlight the conclusions of both studies, and explain the reasons for some major differences in their results.

Air and water pollution

A small, pioneering opinion survey done in China a few years ago found that the public ranked air and water pollution only behind earthquakes and floods on the list of environmental hazards – but that people with science or engineering degrees put the two pollution risks ahead of natural disasters.[33] China's severe air pollution problems are all too obvious, a result of the country's traditionally high dependence on coal (whose combustion produces the classic smog, made up of suspended particulates and SO_2) and of the recent rapid increases of vehicular traffic (whose emissions of volatile organic compounds, nitrogen oxide and carbon monoxide, take part in complex reactions resulting in photochemical smog).

While Chinese coals are of fairly good quality, only about a fifth of them are cleaned and sorted before combustion, and typical conversion efficiencies in tens of millions of household stoves and in thousands of small industrial and commercial boilers remain very low, resulting in extraordinarily high emission factors per unit of delivered useful energy.[34] High urban densities, common commingling of residential and industrial areas, improperly vented household stoves, and use of smoky biomass fuels in rural areas, are additional factors aggravating the situation.

The combustion of fossil fuels now produces close to 20Mt of SO_2 and about 15Mt of particulates a year, and monitoring shows the long-term averages of both pollutants to be multiples of maxima recommended by the World Health Organization.[35] For example, for SO_2 these limits are no more than $40–60\mu g/m^3$ for the annual mean – but in Beijing even the cleanest suburbs average $80\mu g/m^3$ a year, and the annual mean is double that value in the most polluted locations. Still, these are low levels compared to annual means (in $\mu g/m^3$) of over 400 in Taiyuan and Lanzhou, and over 300 in Linfeng, Chongqing (Sichuan) and Guiyang (Guizhou).

In accordance with European and North American experience, particulate and SO_2 damage to crops is relatively small, with most of the yields losses experienced in suburban vegetable farming. Damage to materials is considerably higher, and it is bound to grow with intensification of acid deposition in the rainy South.[36] But it is the damage to human health that is most worrisome. I have estimated that at least 200 million Chinese are exposed to annual particulate concentrations of above $300\mu g/m^3$, and at least 20 million are exposed to twice that level. In addition, the diffusion of new industries means that 100–200 million rural inhabitants may already breathe air nearly as polluted as in cities.

These very high exposures resemble urban values that prevailed in West European and North American cities two to four generations ago, and they contribute to higher incidence of respiratory diseases, ranging from upper respiratory infections to lung cancer. But assessing the share attributable to outdoor air pollution is particularly difficult in China, because most people are also exposed to very high levels of indoor air pollution from inefficient stoves, and the nation abounds with smoking addicts.[37]

Water pollution is even more ubiquitous in China than air pollution. Several years ago a survey of nearly 900 major rivers found that more than four fifths of them were polluted to some degree, over 20 per cent so badly that it was impossible to use their water for irrigation.[38] As for the drinking water, its quality meets state standards only in six of China's twenty-seven largest cities drawing on surface sources, and in just four out of twenty-seven instances where underground sources are used.

Municipal wastes are commonly released untreated, even in large cities. Half of Shanghai's waste is discharged into the Yangzi and into Hangzhou Bay; and the Songhua River and Ji Canal in Jilin and Heilongjiang still contain tens of tonnes of mercury, the legacy of pre-1977 uncontrolled releases which caused waterborne Hg concentration higher than in Japan's Minamata Bay.[39] And the recent multiplication of small and medium-sized rural and township enterprises outside large cities has brought a variety of water pollutants into China's countryside. In Jiangsu province (the one surrounding Shanghai) there is now about one such enterprise per square kilometer! Unknown volumes of untreated waste from these plants goes into streams and networks of canals, contaminating waters used for drinking (about half of China's population draws its drinking water from surface sources), animals and irrigation.

Besides such common industrial pollutants as industrial oils, phenols and heavy metals, China's waters are now receiving much higher levels of nitrates leached from heavy fertilizer applications. The country is now the world's largest consumer of synthetic nitrogen fertilizers, with annual applications averaging around 200kg N/ha, and surpassing 300kg N/ha in the most intensively cultivated provinces. With the addition of animal and human wastes, such nitrogen loadings will eventually lead to serious nitrate contamination.[40] The economic burdens of water pollution range from declining fish catches in streams and reservoirs, and a growing frequency of red tides affecting China's shrimp aquaculture, to increased mortality and a higher incidence of tumors among livestock, and steadily growing rates of cancers of the liver, stomach and esophagus. Studies in the worst-affected localities found the incidence of cancers of the digestive system to be 3–10 times higher than in unpolluted places; other findings included enlarged liver, anemia, skin diseases, premature hair loss and a higher incidence of congenital deformities. Water pollution also helps to make viral hepatitis and dysentery the two leading infectious diseases in China.

Waterborne pathogens and parasite eggs in organic wastes recycled to cropland continue to be a major problem in China's countryside. The frequency of ascariasis, ancylostomiasis and trichuriasis among China's vegetable farmers has been in excess of 90 per cent in some regions.[41] Substantial economic losses also arise due to the impossibility of using polluted water in industrial and agricultural production, and due to additional costs incurred in tapping new resources.

My conservative calculations put the total cost of China's air and water pollution at roughly 30–45 billion of 1990 *yuan*, while Xia's total came close to 100 billion of 1992 *yuan*. Even when increasing my estimate by about 20 per cent in order to account for China's high rate of inflation during the early 1990s, Xia's estimates are considerably higher. As shown in Table 4.1, most of the difference is explained by the treatment of impacts on human health.

Differing assumptions about population totals exposed to particular pollution levels, and different costs ascribed to typical treatments or lost labor hours, are major factors. For example, while Xia and I do not differ that much as far as the total urban population exposed to excessive air pollution is concerned, his averages for treatment costs of chronic bronchitis and lung cancer are, respectively, 2,100 and 12,700 *yuan*, compared to 800 and 5,000 *yuan* used in my estimates. Such disparities are typical of many previous studies attempting to capture pollution's toll on human health.[42]

Table 4.1 Economic costs attributable to air and water pollution[a]

Category	Estimated costs in billions of yuan[b]	
	Smil (1990 yuan)	Xia (1992 yuan)
Air pollution	11.0–19.2	57.9
Damage to human health	3.8–6.5	20.2
Damage to plants	2.9–6.0	7.2
Damage to materials	2.0–4.0	6.5
Acid rain[c]		14.0
Water pollution	9.7–14.0	35.6
Damage to human health	4.1–6.7	19.3
Losses of food production	2.6–3.4	2.5
Industrial losses	2.5–3.3	13.8
Solid waste disposal	9.0–10.5	5.1
Total	29.7–43.7	98.6

Notes:

[a] As some minor subcategories are not shown, the listed values may not add up to category totals.

[b] To convert 1990 *yuan* to 1992 values, add approximately 20 per cent.

[c] My estimates for acid rain damage are subsumed in other air pollution categories.

Land use changes and soil degradation

This broad category ranges from the desertification of China's extensive interior grasslands to the disappearance of its coastal marshes but – given the combination of China's relatively low per capita availability of agricultural land and continuing population growth that will add at least 300 million people during the next twenty-five years – losses of farmland and qualitative decline of arable soils are the most imminent concerns. China's arable land area is substantially larger than the total of 95 million hectares claimed by the State Statistical Bureau: best values based on sample surveys and remote sensing are in the range of 120–140Mha.[43] This means that in per capita terms the country still has more than twice as much farmland as South Korea and Japan, its truly land-short East Asian neighbors.

At the same time, official totals of China's recent farmland losses may err on the low side. Cumulative losses of arable land during the past forty years have been larger than Germany's total farmland, and the annual loss has averaged about half a million hectares since 1980. In addition, much of the lost area has been of good quality, alluvial soils in coastal provinces experiencing the fastest rate of urban and industrial expansion.

In addition to farmland losses, China's agriculture is also affected by lowered soil quality, a change due mostly to greater soil erosion and to a decline in both the extent and the intensity of traditional recycling of organic wastes; improper irrigation, and more intensive cropping relying on higher applications of agro-chemicals, are the other leading causes.

A nationwide survey conducted on almost half of China's farmland identified various degrees of excessive soil erosion on 31 per cent of the land. Erosion rates are not high only on the naturally highly erosion-prone Loess Plateau. In Sichuan, China's most populous province with more than 110 million people, 44 per cent of fields were eroding during the late 1980s beyond sustainable level (a fourfold increase compared to the early 1950s), and 2Mha of cultivated slopeland (or nearly a third of the province's total) had annual erosion losses averaging 110t/ha.[44] For comparison, recent US water erosion rates averaged just over 9t/ha, and wind erosion amounted to over 7t/ha for a total of about 17t/ha.

I quantified the economic costs of farmland losses and soil quality deterioration by calculating the value of lost harvests, decreased yields (or lower livestock production) and nutrients lost from eroded soils, as well as by estimating the burdens of faster reservoir silting, cleaning of silted canals and urban water supplies, and increased damage due to flooding. I also added approximations of key ecosystemic services provided by lost paddy fields and wetlands and by degraded grasslands. Ning's coverage of detrimental effects arising from land use changes and soil degradation closely resembled my line-up. Given the nature of this accounting exercise, there is an excellent agreement between the two sets of calculations: my median value, adjusted for inflation, differs from Ning's total by less than 10 per cent (Table 4.2).

Table 4.2   Economic costs attributable to land use changes and soil degradation[a]

| Category | Estimated costs in billions of yuan[b] | |
	Smil (1990 yuan)	Ning (1992 yuan)
Farmland loss and degradation	5.8–12.1	12.5
Soil erosion	11.0–26.4	17.2
Reduced crop yields	0.3–0.8	0.4
Loss of nutrients	5.0–15.0	16.2
Reservoir silting	1.3–1.8	0.6
Clearing of canals	1.4–1.8	
Flood damage	1.0–3.0	
Deterioration of grasslands	3.7–5.4	3.3
Total	20.8–44.6	35.8

Notes:

[a]As some minor subcategories are not shown, the listed values may not add up to category totals.

[b]To convert 1990 *yuan* to 1992 values add approximately 20 per cent.

China's deforestation

By far the greatest disparity between the two studies concerns estimates of the economic consequences of deforestation – but the huge difference is not due to irreconcilable assumptions concerning the resulting soil erosion, stream silting, or the loss of water-retention capacity. Indeed, a closer look shows great similarities on all of these accounts. The reason lies in a fundamentally different approach to the scope of the problem. Professor Wang took what I would label a deep ecological perspective. First he estimated that China had lost a total of about 290Mha of forest since the beginning of the country's history. Roughly half of this loss was due to conversion to farmlands, settlements and transport networks, an environmental change unavoidably exacted by the growth of an ancient civilization – while the other half represents excessive deforestation, an area that could have, with proper management, remained forested and been harvested on a sustainable basis. Then he proceeded to calculate the impact of this excessive deforestation on the desiccation of northern and northwestern China, as well as on accelerated erosion that results in stream and reservoir silting, and in increased damage during flooding.

In contrast, my estimates of the environmental cost of deforestation are based on the current extent of the excessive cutting of mature growth. Curiously, that approach could not be followed if China's official statistics were taken at their face value. According to recent claims, China's total wood increment has been surpassing the annual cut during most of the early 1990s: if true, this would mean no net deforestation. Even if we were to accept this obviously exaggerated statement, its impact appears in a different light once we put it together with the changing composition of China's forests.

During the early 1990s no less than three quarters of China's timberlands were young or middle-aged stands, while the growing stock ready for harvesting in mature forests amounted to less than a fifth of all standing timber, a total which could be cut in just seven to eight years. Forests approaching maturity will decline from almost a third of all timber in the late 1980s to less than a seventh by the year 2000.

Ministry of Forestry figures show that of the 131 state forestry bureaus in the most important timber production zones, twenty-five had basically exhausted their reserves by 1990, 40 could harvest up to the year 2000 – and by that time almost 70 per cent of China's state forestry bureaus would basically have no trees to fell.[45] In addition, the official figure for the average growing stock in forest plantings – 28.27m^3/ha – makes it quite clear that the new plantings, whose growing stock may be yielding a statistical wood surplus, offer little hope for replacing the felled mature forests, whose growing stock would be at least 70–80m^3/ha, for many decades. Consequently, even if real, the recent quantitative growth of Chinese forests hides a major qualitative decline.

In any case, estimates of the economic cost of China's deforestation should be based on figures realistically representing long-term trends, rather than capturing short-term aberrations. A careful appraisal of available evidence indicates that the overcutting of China's mature forests – that is harvests above the average annual increment of wood in stands storing the largest volume of phytomass harboring the greatest biodiversity, and able to provide various ecosystemic services incomparably better than recent plantings – has been recently proceeding at a rate of at least 50 and up to 100 million cubic meters a year.

With harvestable wood volume averaging around 90m^3/ha this loss would translate to an annual disappearance of 0.5 to 1 million hectares of mature forest. In terms of lost sustainable supply of timber alone, this overcutting would cost between 13 and 26 billion *yuan* a year. Weakened, or destroyed, ecosystemic services include diminished water-storage capacity, reduced protection against both wind and water erosion (its rates are likely to increase by two orders of magnitude), and – effects which are most difficult to quantify – changes to local and regional climate, contributions to changes in the biospheric carbon cycle and possible planetary warming, and consequences for national and global biodiversity.

Monetization of these effects remains highly uncertain, with multipliers ranging from 1.5 to more than 20 times the value of the cut timber.[46] Chinese foresters have put the combined ecosystemic benefits of mature forests between 8 and 25 times the profit from harvested timber sales. For example, a detailed study done for Changbaishan natural reserve in Jilin concluded that if the forest's water-storage capacity were to be replaced by a reservoir, if the soil-erosion control were to be achieved by terracing of slopes, and if pesticides were used to control insects instead of forest-sheltered birds, the reserve's worth would be equivalent to about 49,000 *yuan* (1990) per hectare, more than twenty times the value of sustainably harvested timber from the same area.[47]

Naturally, that ratio would rise with the inclusion of the forest's contribution to local and regional climatic controls and to its preservation of biodiversity. Considerable value could be also imputed to future recreational worth and, in the long term, to the value of forests as potentially major carbon sinks. But even using 1.5 as the minimum multiplier value would result in between 20 and 39 billion *yuan* for lost ecosystemic services from 0.5–1.0Mha of excessive cutting. The value of timber lost due to unsustainable harvest and to forest fires brings up the grand total of forest mismanagement to roughly 40–70 billion *yuan*.

While I based my calculations on annual losses of 0.5–1.0Mha, Wang's cumulative total of excessive deforestation comes to about 140Mha – but his calculations, amounting to 245 billion *yuan*, did not include any adjustments for lost ecosystemic services, which represented the highest share of my estimates. If such costs were included, Wang's unusual historical approach, calling attention to the true extent of human impact on forests, would have ended up with an even higher total. On the other hand, some costs estimated by Wang were also considered by Ning (above all the effects of soil erosion), so a simple addition of the two sets of estimates would involve some double counting.

Wider perspectives

Although we tried to make our accounts as comprehensive as possible, we had no choice but to leave out a number of critical effects. Major impacts that could not be quantified due to the lack of basic information include such diverse categories as the increasingly important effects of photochemical smog in and near China's large cities; damage attributable to China's nuclear weapons sector; declining fish catches in China's seas; and the foregone recreation value of lost forests, wetlands and beaches. Even more importantly, neither set of calculations tried to attribute any monetary value to human discomfort and suffering, reactions arising not only from excessive morbidity and premature mortality, but also from chronic exposures to high noise levels in China's cities.[48] Finally, neither study could ascribe any definite value to China's loss of biodiversity, and to the country's already huge, and rising, contribution to emissions of greenhouse gases, a highly worrisome source of potential biospheric instability.

Consequently – Wang's estimate of deforestation costs aside – both sets of calculations are based on clearly conservative assumptions. As a result, there can be no doubt that the economic burden of China's environmental pollution and ecosystemic degradation was no less than 5 per cent of the country's GDP in the early 1990s. A range of 6–8 per cent is the most likely conservative estimate, and values around 10 per cent would be in line with a more comprehensive, although still far from all-inclusive, coverage. Eventual monetization of a number of elusive valuations could raise the rate to around 15 per cent of the country's annual GDP.

These burdens greatly surpass China's recent spending on environmental protection: during the 1980s and early 1990s the annual investment in this area was equal to just 0.56–0.81 per cent of the country's GDP. Only in 1996 came an official promise to raise this figure to just over 1 per cent by the year 2000. Even so, that would be an order of magnitude lower than the most likely economic cost.

What these burdens mean in international comparison is much more difficult to say. Unfortunately, it is much easier to note what currency conversions should not be used in order to express these costs in US dollars; to facilitate international comparisons rather than to choose the right value. Conversion using official exchange rates, the method favored until very recently by the World Bank, greatly underestimates real values (it puts China's GDP at less than US$500 per capita), while the purchasing power parity (PPP) method favored by the International Monetary Fund (resulting in a per capita GDP of nearly US$3,000 in 1995) clearly exaggerates.

The latest World Bank study argues that China's actual GDP was about US$2,000 in 1995, a rate implying PPP roughly four times larger than the exchange rate.[49] Using this conversion, the annual burden of China's environmental pollution would be about $50 billion (using Xia's total), that of land degradation around $20 billion, and excessive deforestation would carry an annual price tag of no less than another $20 billion (my lowest estimate), but possibly over $100 billion (Wang's historical appraisal). Even the lowest likely grand total of about $(1992) 90 billion is a huge sum, a total slightly larger than the value of all of China's exports in 1992.

In closing, I must stress the dual nature of these valuations. These were exploratory exercises based on a necessarily limited amount of information, and requiring repeated assumptions; as such, they make no claims of accuracy, they can give no more than basic approximations, and they are open to easily justifiable critique. At the same time, all of their inherent weaknesses and uncertainties cannot negate their undeniable bottom line: the presented evidence is sufficiently robust to allow a number of practical conclusions.

First, there can be no doubt that China's recent environmental changes already carry economic costs of roughly an order of magnitude higher than the country's annual spending on environmental protection: tripling, or quadrupling, these outlays would easily meet even the strictest cost-benefit criteria. Second, given the fact that the economic burden of China's environmental pollution and ecosystemic degradation may already be in excess of one tenth of its annual GDP, the country's recent aggressive quest for modernization must be a matter of serious national, and international, concern.

Perhaps the most obvious cases of contrasting economic benefits and environmental damage arise with the construction of modern megaprojects, engineering structures of uncommonly large size or processing capacity – be they large dams or steel mills, huge surface mines or massive offshore oil-drilling platforms. Cost-benefit appraisals and environmental assessments now routinely consider at least some of the environmental costs of these megaprojects, but unanticipated or underestimated impacts have been common, resulting in often truly tragic or economically burdensome consequences. I will close this chapter by describing just two of China's notable megaprojects: one whose failure is now a matter of indisputable record, the other one still under construction, but perceived to be creating more environmental problems than any other project in China's long history.

Megaprojects and China's environment: a tale of two dams and rapid trains

Large-scale environmental degradation is a ubiquitous reality of the modern world. So is the fact that big events and spectacular effects power modern media and generate widespread public attention. The daily deaths of 125 people in motor vehicle accidents across North America is not news; a bus crash that kills thirty-five people instantly is. This principle is generally applicable. Using an example previously discussed in this book, building of tens of thousands of small dams across China, of which thousands had to be soon abandoned because of rapid silting or shoddy construction, was not worthy of any front-page attention; China's decision to build the world's largest hydroproject, whose reservoir may silt much faster than was anticipated by the original design, is.

Megaprojects are responsible for a small share of overall ecosystemic degra-dation and environmental pollution, but they attract attention to these regrettable phenomena, and they symbolize the frequent failures of our designs to minimize environmental damage, to anticipate risks and to approach the harnessing of natural resources with at least some humility. During the 1990s China's Sanxia (Three Gorges) dam, the world's largest hydroelectric project, came to exemplify these shortcomings as it received enormous media attention around the world. But we will have to see first the project's completion and then years of operation before we will be able to tell which of today's many worries will have materialized, and to what extent. But we already have an example of a spectacular failure of what was at its time China's largest hydroproject: Sanmenxia on the Huanghe.

And so in this section on megaprojects I will deal first with Sanmenxia, whose failure I helped to bring to a wider Western attention during the late 1970s by combining Soviet sources from the 1950s, newly released Chinese materials, and satellite images of the reservoir acquired by LANDSAT, launched in 1972 (Smil 1979b, 1979c). Only then will I take a closer look at some aspects of Sanxia, and I will contrast these two cases of worrisome devel-opments with suggestions for highly desirable megaprojects whose completion would make China a better place.

Sanmenxia

The poetically named Gorge of the Three Gates (Northern Gate of Man, Central Gate of the Soul, and Southern Gate of the Devil), located in Henan approximately 12km downstream from the rectangular river bend near Tongguan, was to be the largest and the most important of the original Huanghe cascade (Berezina 1959). Designs made with Soviet aid were finalized in 1957 for a 110m-high and 839m-long concrete gravity dam with 121m-wide base and 32m-wide top, which was to create a 3,500km^2 reservoir and to retain as much as 36Gm^3 of water, 1.5 times the average annual volume of flow at the site.

The giant project (at the time of its planning second only to the Soviet Kuibyshev storage facility) was to control 98 per cent of the annual runoff of the Huanghe, to cut the heaviest summer flood flow from 37,000 to between 6,000 and 8,000m^3/s, to provide irrigation for 2.6Mha, and to enable the installation of 1.1GW of electricity-generating capacity. The total expenditure was to be a staggering 1.6 billion *yuan*, or approximately US$700 million at 1957 values. The main problem envisioned in building Sanmenxia dam was the flooding of numerous villages and the displacement of a large number of peasants. Originally, the highest reservoir surface was to be at 350m above sea level, a height that would have caused the flooding of 130,000ha and the evacuation of 600,000 people. To lessen the immediate impact, the reservoir was to be filled initially to only 335.3m above sea level so that only 215,000 villagers would be displaced; the remaining impounded area was to be flooded during the next 15–20 years, and the affected peasants gradually resettled.

The planners were, of course, aware of another serious difficulty – the danger of extreme silting. However, they thought that this could be controlled by a variety of measures. The master Huanghe plan of 1955 foresaw the enormous construction of 215,000 works to protect the heads of gullies, 683,000 check dams, and 79,000 silt-precipitation dams, as well as extensive afforestation, grassing and terracing to curtail erosion. The combined effort of these projects was to extend the life of the reservoir to at least 50–70 years. As the experts confidently concluded, any "difficulties that may arise in power generation, irrigation and navigation as a result of silting up the reservoir…will be comparatively easy to deal with" (Teng 1955: 15).

Although Soviet hydroelectrical engineers had at that time considerable experience of large and complex projects, their appraisal of silting at Sanmenxia turned out to be an astonishing and potentially extremely dangerous miscalculation. But the Soviet engineers were withdrawn just before the dam was completed in September 1960, after three and a half years of construction. The Chinese had to face the serious problem alone. Not only had the silting of the reservoir greatly exceeded the original projection – more than 90 per cent of incoming mud and sand was being retained in the lake – but the accumulation became especially worrisome as these deposits started to extend rapidly upstream to the Wei He above Laotongguan, elevating the inlet channel and gravely endangering the densely populated agricultural plain and the city of Xi'an, China's ancient capital and now her eleventh-largest urban area.

The first turbines were already installed, but power production had to be stopped because the lowest water intake for a generation was still higher than the natural river level at Dongguan, allowing rapid silting of the lower Wei He to continue. The removal of turbogenerators and the abandonment of water storage did not solve the problem, because spillway intakes were too high and silt kept accumulating. The only solution was a major reconstruction of the dam to increase the silt-discharging capacity of the reservoir. This difficult and lengthy process started in February 1965. During its first phase, one that lasted four years, two tunnels with a width of 11m and a total length of 900m were cut through a rock cliff on the left bank of the dam, and four of the eight penstocks were turned into discharging outlets in order to double the discharge from 3,080m³/s to 6,000m³/s at 315m above sea level. The second phase raised the discharge to 10,000m³/s at 315m by opening eight outlets at the bottom of the dam and by lowering the remaining steel penstocks and one of the new silt-discharge tubes by 13m.

By the end of 1973 the reconstruction was finished, and the Chinese engineers had installed the first small 50MW turbine, specially coated with two layers of epoxy resin and corundum to withstand the sandy-mud abrasion. Two more 50MW sets were later added, and the total capacity will be eventually only 200MW, less than 20 per cent of the original design. Two other key roles of the reservoir – storage of water for irrigation, and, above all, guarding against floods and prevention of damage to dikes downstream in Henan and Shandong – have been no less compromised by the reconstruction. Minimum discharge had to be raised. Because the floodwaters between July and October carry more than 80 per cent of the annual silt load passing through Sanmenxia (although the volume constitutes only 60 per cent of the average flow), summer flood impoundment had to be cut drastically to minimize silting.

Consequently, water is now stored only between flood seasons when the river carries some 40 per cent of its average annual flow but only 10–20 per cent of its silt load. The Chinese strategy of "storing clear water and discharging muddy water" is well confirmed by satellite monitoring. Winter and spring LANDSAT images show the gorge segment of the reservoir between the dam and the Huanghe's confluence with the Wei He filled with relatively clear water, swelling in the least confined place to a width of more than 6km and covering as much as approximately 250km² (Figure 4.7). On the other hand, at the peak of the flood season the reservoir below Tongguan shrinks to a narrow ribbon of silted water with an area as small as 90km² (Figure 4.7). Conditions upstream from Tongguan are almost the reverse. When the summer floodwaters burst from the confines of Longmen (Dragon Gate), they create a shallow, muddy lake approximately 120km long and 3.5–7km wide. In contrast, the winter flow meanders erratically in numerous channels amid silt deposits.

What has been the effect of Sanmenxia reservoir in Shaanxi, Henan and Shandong? The reservoir has very likely worsened the danger of flood in Shaanxi, and, as the Chinese also admit, the reduced version cannot eliminate the risk of flooding in the lower reaches. However, Sanmen reservoir can at least alleviate the summer flood by moderating the rate and the force of the flow; the Chinese claim that the reservoir did halve the force of the 1977 summer flood, the worst high water in the river's upper and middle course in forty years.

Only a few corrections and additions should be made in 2002, based on the most comprehensive Chinese description of the project and its history published in 2000 as a part of China's review of major dams for the International

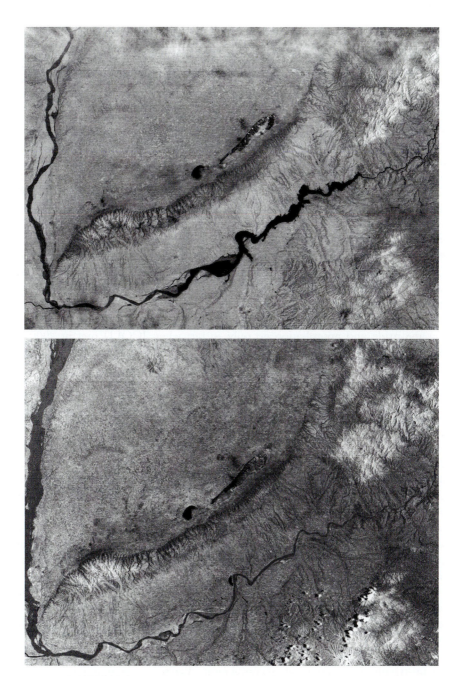

Figure 4.7 LANDSAT images (spectral band seven, in the near infrared) of Sanmenxia
reservoir. The first image (1 May 1978) shows a relatively clear (black), wide
and deep lake below Laotongguan. Only five weeks later just a narrow ribbon
of deeper water remained in the reservoir as a highly silty flow (grey) was
discharged through the dam

Committee on Large Dams (ICOLD 2000). Sanmenxia's second reconstruction was not completed in 1973 as originally claimed. Its first stage lasted from 1969 to 1979, and it included the reopening of eight diversion outlets, the excavation of five penstock intakes, and the installation of five 50MW generators; the second stage (1984–2000) involved the conversion of bottom outlets #1–8, and the reopening and conversion of bottom outlets #9–12. Not surprisingly, there is no information on the cumulative cost of this thirty-five-year-long reconstruction.

Every year Sanmenxia makes $1.4Gm^3$ of water available for spring irrigation downstream, servicing up to 2.67Mha of fields; the reservoir's water is also used by several major cities, including Zhengzhou, Xinxiang and Kaifeng, and by the Zhongyuan oilfield. With additional turbogenerators installed in 1994 and 1997, the total capacity is now 400MW, a third of the original design, but the load factor remains very low. The operation mode of storing clear water and discharging muddy flow (*xu qing pai nun*) limits the hours of generation to a few hundred a year, compared with an average of nearly 2,900 hours for all of China's large hydrostations. The Chinese, making a virtue of the costly necessity, now describe the project as a great learning experience and a training ground for the construction, operation and management of large dams: "Sanmenxia is considered as the cradle of high dam construction in China" (ICOLD 2000: 4). But the pride and approbation go only so far: when ICOLD met in 2000 in Beijing, Sanmenxia was not on the list of more than forty hydrostations that participants could visit after the conference on tours roaming all over China.

And, unfortunately, it appears that the key blunder in Sanmenxia's design – underestimating the future rate of reservoir silting – is to be repeated as the Chinese builders are nearing completion of the Sanxia dam, the world's largest hydrostation, and undoubtedly its environmentally most controversial megaproject. But before I turn to this now-infamous megaproject, I should briefly describe what could be best termed Sanmenxia's bigger twin, the Xiaolangdi dam, built during the 1990s (Power Technology 2002). The dam, 1,667m long and 154m high, is just 130km downstream from Sanmen Gorge and 40km north of Luoyang in Henan. When fully filled its reservoir should create a 130km-long lake of $12.8km^3$. Its hydroelectric capacity of 1.836GW is the largest on the Huanghe (and as of the year 2000 the fourth largest in China, after Ertan, Gezhouba and Lijiaxia), and the project's other long-term purpose is to control, in conjunction with other dams, a once-in-a-thousand-years flood.

Unlike the original Sanmenxia that was to store water and block silt (*xu shui lan sha*), Xiaolangdi was designed with silt-discharge tunnels to store clear water and discharge the muddy flow, but the deposition behind the dam will still be considerable: its is estimated that over the next fifty years the reservoir will reduce the amount of silt deposited downstream of the dam by the equivalent of about twenty years' normal accumulation. Electricity generation began in January 2000, but it had to stop on 20 May as another severe drought forced the central government to order the release of water in the reservoir to relieve downstream shortages (Becker 2000). The likely recurrence of such episodes will make it impossible to reach the planned generation target of 5.1TWh a year that would imply nearly 2,800 hours of operation, almost equal to China's average that includes southern rivers with dependable water flows.

The Three Gorges (Sanxia) project is undoubtedly the greatest *cause célèbre* of the now worldwide anti-dam-building movement that gathered both breadth and intensity during the 1990s. Spectacular gorges in western Hubei and eastern Sichuan – whose plunging cliffs and rushing waters were admired and feared by generations of poets, nature connoisseurs, river boatmen, merchants and travelers – suddenly became a symbol for the destruction and desecration of rivers by megaprojects. And in this case it was to be the largest project of them all. Not the highest or the longest dam – those primacies belong, respectively, to the Rogun dam on the Vakhsh in Tajikistan (325m tall) and to the Yacyreta-Apipe dam on the Parana between Paraguay and Argentina (69.6km) – nor the most voluminous lake (39.3Gm^3 compared to the 170Gm^3 of Bratsk reservoir on the Yenisey). But the dam will house turbogenerators with 18.2GW of installed capacity, making it 44 per cent larger than the next largest hydrostation, Itaipu on the Parana between Brazil and Paraguay, rated at 12.6GW. And the dam's peak flood discharge will be 124,300m^3/s, another world record (ICOLD 2000).

In my first book on China's energy (Smil 1976a) I noted, when reviewing China's plans for hydroelectricity expansion, that the largest of the Changjiang projects, the 15–20GW Sanxia dam, might be built before the year 2000. As plans to start the construction intensified during the mid-1980s, I was asked by my Beijing colleague and friend Mao Yushi, acting in this instance on behalf of the China Energy Research Society, to contribute to a collection of papers that would provide comprehensive reasoning why Sanxia should not be built. I wrote my brief contribution by approaching the problem from a general systems point of view (Smil 1989), and leaving the details to my better-informed Chinese colleagues. The piece was written in 1987, when the project was to have the capacity of "only" 13, rather than 18.2GW, and when the Economic Construction Group of the Chinese People's Political Consultative Committee (1987) surprised everybody by publishing its call against proceeding with the Sanxia project in the short term.

The book came out during the period of relatively free speech just preceding the Tian'anmen killings (Tian and Lin 1989) and these were my principal arguments why Sanxia should not be built (Smil 1989).

After decades of studies and scores of expert appraisals, it is hardly possible to come up with new technical details in order to spare China the unnecessary and multiply unprofitable endeavor of building the world's largest dam. Instead of recapitulating various well-appreciated particulars, I will make just one fundamental argument against the construction.

This overriding argument concerns the very size of the project. Undoubtedly, it is unnecessarily large – and as such it is unforgiving and excessively demanding. Sanxia's 13GW will require an unprecedented level of investment and concentration of skilled labor – but these challenges can be met by a combination of domestic and foreign expertise and funding. The project can be obviously built, but why should it be so huge? If China is to learn from the West it should not copy its outdated strategies. During the 1950s and 1960s, post-World War II reconstruction and the quest for higher individual affluence favored the construction of ever-larger engineering projects, be they power plants, steel mills or car factories. But since then all of the leading Western economies have come to recognize the perils of such projects: their inordinate demand for financial and human resources, their negative environmental side effects, and, above all, their inherent inflexibility.

Clearly, the optimum levels have been overshot on numerous occasions, and adjustments during the past fifteen or so years have been setting new, more manageable standards. Perhaps the best way to generalize this important trend is to say that we have discovered the advantages of being complexifying optimizers rather than simplifying maximizers. A simple assessment may show the purely economic benefits of a very large project – but a complex evaluation of its indirect costs makes these investment gains doubtful, and a consideration of possible long-term risks that cannot be quantified in the project's planning stages definitely sways the optimum toward a smaller, albeit still relatively large, size. In the case of large hydroelectric projects, the greatest long-term concern is certainly about their environmental consequences.

Whatever the eventual negative effects of Sanxia may be – and they could include such sudden dangers as massive rockslides in the reservoir area, and such gradual degradation as the loss of coastal fishing in the East China Sea (China's richest fishing grounds off the coasts of Jiangsu and Zhejiang obviously depend on the influx of nutrients in the Changjiang waters) – these risks would be unnecessarily heightened by the large size of the project. If China had little choice in siting large hydrostations Sanxia would become at least more understandable. But the country abounds in excellent sites suitable for building hydroelectric projects that, while large, could be more manageable than Sanxia.

The construction of six or seven plants of 2GW each, instead of the 13GW Sanxia, would have a much more positive influence on the country's economy, owing to the diffusion of regional economic multiplier benefits in a nation that must encourage decentralization in order to prosper – while minimizing any long-term environmental complications. Multifocal development of large, but not gigantic, energy capacities is thus a sounder strategy than an extreme concentration of resources on one project whose eventual long-term environmental consequences may transform its simplistically seen economic benefits into an overall loss for the society.

Remarkably, one month after the Tian'anmen massacre, a previously scheduled and unusually long article by Sun (1989), detailing his opposition to the Sanxia project, nevertheless appeared in the *Beijing Review*. Afterwards, all domestic publications questioning the merits of the projects were suppressed. Meanwhile, I explained in greater detail in my second book on China's energy (1988) why the project was not a desirable choice from a number of perspectives.

When Probe International was putting together a critique of the Three Gorges Water Control Project Feasibility Study (Ryder 1990), a government-funded Canadian undertaking that basically rubber-stamped the Chinese desire to build the dam, I was asked to contribute a chapter from an energy perspective.

I did so (Smil 1990), but my contribution was overshadowed by a quote from me that the editors chose for the back cover: "This is not engineering and science, merely an expert prostitution paid for by Canadian taxpayers". But by the time that opposition to the dam had become fashionably international, I was not writing about Sanxia any more. By the early 1990s all key arguments against the dam had been identified and appraised, ranging from the human cost of massive forced resettlement to both upstream and downstream environmental impacts and safety concerns. I had been aware of most of these arguments for many years, I had articulated many of them at a time when the project was a matter of concern only for a small group of energy experts – and I was convinced that nothing more could be done.

I believed this, above all, because of Li Peng's key position: China's premier at that time was an electrical engineer trained in Stalinist Russia, and it was clear that he would do anything to ensure that the project was approved and built. If there ever was a battle lost long before it commenced, it was the opposition to Sanxia. So I decided that no more could be done, but recently I agreed to write a short entry on Sanxia for the *International Encyclopedia of Environmental Politics*, whose partial reprint brings the story up to date (Smil 2002c).

The Three Gorges (Sanxia) area of the Changjiang (Yangzi) is a spectacular section of China's largest river in western Hubei province, beginning about 40km west of Yichang where the river leaves the mountains and enters the Hubei plain. The three gorges (Xiling, Xia and Qutang) confine the river to a narrow channel by tall, steep rocky slopes extending more than 100km westward into eastern Sichuan. The gorges appear to be an obvious location for a very large dam, and the first mention of such a project was contained in Sun Yatsen's 1919 plan to develop China's industry. In 1932 the Nationalist government announced its intention to build a dam in the region, and in 1944 the US Bureau of Reclamation prepared a preliminary construction plan.

After the worst ever flood in the river's middle and lower basin in 1954, Soviet hydroengineers helped China to conduct necessary surveys, and silting and design studies, and the Beijing government set up the Changjiang Valley Planning Office which became the project's principal, and steadfast, promoter during the next three decades. The dam was also favored by the ministries of water resources and electric power, which also saw the gargantuan project as an outstanding mark of China's technical maturity. The world's largest electricity-generating capacity, effective flood control in the heavily populated Yangzi basin, and improved navigation as far inland as Sichuan were to be the project's principal benefits.

But the enormous cost of the project was the principal cause for repeated postponement of the final decision to proceed with the construction of the Three Gorges dam. In 1984, after the country's economic situation began improving with the progress of Deng Xiaoping's economic reforms, the State Council approved the construction of a 175m-high dam to start in 1986. But a more relaxed political situation in China of the mid-1980s led to unexpected public debate about the merits of the project – and to its wide-ranging criticism. In 1986 the Economic Construction Group of the Chinese People's Political Consultative Congress recommended to the State Council and to the Communist Party's Central Committee that the project should not go ahead. A year later an edited book published in Hunan gathered a wide range of arguments against the dam, and in February 1989 an unprecedented alliance of journalists, engineers, scientists and public figures organized a press conference to launch a new book vigorously arguing against the dam.

None of these arguments swayed the leadership. Not long after the Tian'anmen massacre of June 1989, any criticism of the project in the Chinese media was strictly forbidden, and Dai Qing, the editor of the 1989 book and the country's best-known female journalist (who trained as an engineer and became an environmental activist), was jailed for ten months (Dai 1994). Although no criticism of the project appeared in the Chinese media until 1999, Dai Qing continued her campaign against it, both in China and abroad, throughout the 1990s.

The final decision to proceed with construction was taken on 3 April 1992, when a motion approving the project was put to the National People's Congress (China's normally docile version of a parliament) and was passed with an unprecedented third of all delegates either abstaining or voting against. At that time the bureaucracies in favor of the project had, as I already noted, the strongest possible ally in Li Peng, the country's Prime Minister, who thought the dam was a most desirable proof of the country's technical prowess.

Some preparatory work at the site had been already done before the final vote; work on the main construction site and on the river's diversion began in 1993. The world's third most voluminous river was diverted from its main channel on 8 November 1997. The completed dam should be 175m tall, its reservoir will inundate about 630km^2 of land and displace at least 1.2 million people. The dam will have about 18GW of generating capacity and produce annually 84TWh of electricity. Sanxia will thus become by far the world's largest hydrostation: the Itaipu project on the Parana between Brazil and Paraguay has 12.6GW, and the largest Russian and American plants generate about 6GW, as does Egypt's Aswan dam across the Nile.

But the project's progress has done little to eliminate the widespread opposition, in China and abroad. A long list of arguments against the dam embraces human, engineering, economic and environmental considerations. The human impact of the project is unprecedented, as the dam's 600km-long reservoir will displace anywhere between 1.2 and 1.5 million people. Because there is very little suitable (i.e. flat and fertile) land available for their resettlement in the dam's immediate vicinity, reclamation has been proceeding on slopes steeper than 25°. In the spring of 1999, Zhu Rongji, Li Peng's successor as China's premier and a man who has not shown any enthusiastic support for the project, urged an end to such dangerous practices.

The lagging pace of resettling hundreds of thousands of people, together with chronic construction problems (including the collapse of a bridge in the resettlement area), led to other official expressions of concern in the spring and summer of 1999. The original plan to resettle most of the displaced people close to their former towns and villages is proving to be quite impractical, and more than half a million peasants will have to be moved far from the site, most of them even into other provinces.

The key engineering argument against the Sanxia dam questions the necessity of such a gargantuan project in a country which has the world's largest hydroelectricity-generating potential and hence no shortages of sites where smaller (although in absolute terms still very large) dams could be built at a lesser financial, environmental and human cost. By concentrating on more manageable projects, China could rely much more on her domestic engineering capability, while most of the electricity-generating equipment needed for the Three Gorges project will have to be imported. And with smaller projects there would be a welcome diffusion of regional economic multiplier effects, an important consideration in a nation which must encourage decentralization in order to prosper.

The official Chinese projection for Sanxia's total cost is 200 billion (1996) *yuan*, or close to US\$ (2000) 25 billion when converted by the official exchange rate. A quarter of this sum is to be spent on the dam itself and a fifth on the resettlement. But, as we have learned from numerous megaprojects inside and outside of China, this total is almost certainly a substantial underestimate, and the final cost may be easily twice as high.

While engineering and economic considerations are undoubtedly important, concerns about the environmental effects of this unprecedented undertaking came eventually to dominate the surprisingly widespread opposition. Environmental risks that have been discussed most frequently include excessively rapid siltation of the reservoir caused by extensive deforestation in the river's upper basin; loss of silt deposition downstream from the dam and possible coastal erosion of the river's delta; flooding of sites containing toxic wastes; fluctuation of water levels at the reservoir's upper end, exposing long stretches of the riverbed loaded with untreated waste from Chongqing, a city of more than 10 million people; risks of reservoir-induced earthquakes in the seismically active area; dangers of massive rock slides causing the overtopping of the dam; and effects on the river's biota, including such rare species as the white river dolphin. Other concerns range from the loss of one of the world's most spectacular landscapes and tourist attractions to the encroachment of salt water into the Yangzi delta during periods of low water flow.

While the environmentalists lost the fight in China, their arguments were critical for shaping Sanxia's perception abroad. Probe International, the International Water Tribunal and the International Rivers Network have been among the dam's most outspoken opponents (Ryder 1990). The governments of the USA and Canada, two of the Western world's most experienced builders of large dams, were initially rather enthusiastic supporters of the project. In 1985 a US consortium made up of government agencies and private companies began laying the ground for a joint project with China to build the dam, and in 1986 a feasibility study undertaken by a consortium of Canadian and Chinese institutions and paid for by the Canadian taxpayers through the Canadian International Development Agency, endorsed the official Chinese design (CIPM 1988). But both governments eventually refused any direct participation in this controversial project, as did the World Bank.

Completion of the project is planned for the year 2009, but delays are almost certain. Disclosures made in 1999 about the use of substandard concrete in the dam's foundations, and the necessity to invite foreign quality-control engineers in order to circumvent widespread corruption at the site, confirm such a conclusion. But abandoning the project at this relatively late stage is very unlikely. Although opponents of the dam still feel that the government may decide to build a lower dam (165m), such a decision, while reducing the flooding and population displacement, would halve the amount of planned electricity generation. Only one thing remains certain: Sanxia dam will continue to be a highly controversial project and a great environmental *cause célèbre* for many years to come.

There seems to be no end of bad news regarding Sanxia. As I close this review of China's most spectacular and most controversial megaproject, I read about the problems facing the massive cleanup of settlements, animal sheds, cemeteries and garbage and toxic waste dumps that will be submerged by the reservoir. The original budget for this cleanup was a mere $1 million compared to $1.4 billion for the resettlement of people. But without an effective cleanup of the reservoir bed the water quality could be compromised for decades to come. Moreover, large numbers of rats not killed during the cleanup would move to higher ground and infest new settlements (TGP 2002). Another greatly underestimated problem is the cleanup of more than 1Gt of industrial and 300Mt of urban waste water discharged into the Changjiang, and shortly into the uppermost part of the Sanxia lake, by the new supermunicipality of Chongqing, now administratively the world's most populous city. While Zhang Guangduo, a Qinghua University expert and a lead examiner of the project's original feasibility study, concluded that $37 billion was needed for this cleanup, only $5.37 billion was committed by early 2001 for a period of ten years (TGP 2001).

Far more intractable is the problem of excessive silting. Recently announced plans for the construction of two more megaprojects in the Changjiang's upper basin – Xiluodu (11.4GW) and Xiangjiaba (5.7GW) on the Jinshajiang in Sichuan, whose combined capacity will be just 6 per cent smaller than that of Sanxia – have been prompted more by the need to trap sediment before it reaches the Sanxia reservoir rather than by any immediate need for more hydrolectric power in the region. Pre-1985 monitoring put the mean annual sediment load in the Three Gorges at 521Mt – but about 710Mt actually passed through the site in 1998 (TGP 2001).

But I should end this megaproject story on a more upbeat note. A few years ago I did actually write an editorial for the *Asian Wall Street Journal* arguing that China needs megaprojects – but only those that will improve the environment even as they are providing great economic and social benefits. What follows is the essence of those suggestions (Smil 1999d)

Environmentally desirable megaprojects

The Three Gorges Dam on the Yangzi River, now in its second phase of construction, is reportedly running into problems. This past week the authorities announced that foreign firms would take over supervision duties because the local overseers couldn't guarantee quality. The dam's other problems are already well documented: it is simply too big, it is taking too long to build, it costs too much and it will cause too many environmental problems. Wobbly foundations are not the dam's only problem – top-level support for the project also appears to be weakening. In a clear contrast to his predecessor Li Peng, who remains the dam's biggest supporter, Premier Zhu Rongji did not even mention it in his annual report on the work of the government. Opponents of the dam hope that this may be the beginning of the project's end. The best solution at this point – after so much money has been spent, the river diverted and hundreds of thousands people already uprooted – would be to fix the structural problems and proceed with a substantially scaled-down version of the project.

But this experience should not dampen China's enthusiasm for more appropriate megaprojects. Their days may be over in affluent countries, but China, like any other modernizing country, needs them. That is, China needs the right kind of megaproject in order to put in place many essential, long-lasting and highly beneficial infrastructures. There is no shortage of excellent examples from elsewhere in the world. Cold War fears were the proximate reason for US President Dwight Eisenhower's decision to construct an interstate highway system, but the resultant web of multilane roads makes the country the safest place to drive. The French decision to build large nuclear power plants has been both an economic and an environmental success. And long before it became a rich country, Japan took a bold step with its bullet trains, which were twice as fast as any scheduled service at that time.

China's greatest challenge during the coming generation will be the movement of tens of millions of people into its rapidly growing cities. Maoist policies basically froze China's urbanization until 1984, the year when food rationing tied to place of residence ended. Since that time China's cities have added about 100 million people, and at least 150 million more will move in during the next quarter-century. Three kinds of megaproject will help the country meet the challenge.

A much more aggressive program of widespread, state-of-the-art subway construction   Huge numbers of people will have to be moved within the cities, and subways are the fastest, most efficient means to do this. In every metropolitan area of more than

2–3 million people, China should be planning or building the first few links of gradually expanding networks. It is counterproductive to wait until the city tops 10 million, as in Shanghai's case. Beijing, too, has lost a great deal of ground – new radial connections augmenting its circular line would have benefited the city much more than the construction of multilane ring roads, now the major source of chronic photochemical smog and generator of clogged-up traffic.

A bold commitment to build the world's most extensive network of high-speed trains, traveling at more than 300 kilometers per hour, throughout the eastern third of the country Official Chinese policy envisages that eventually every family in China will have its own car – and practical steps in that unfortunate direction have included numerous joint ventures with foreign automakers, and the construction of multilane highways. This is a mistake in a country which has relatively modest crude oil resources – but already one of the world's worst problems with smog.

A network of rapid intercity trains would limit the loss of China's precious high-quality periurban and alluvial farmland, and would go far toward reducing the country's rising ozone concentrations, the worst product of photochemical smog. These transport systems should be electricity-driven, helping to maximize the country's energy conversion efficiency.

A massive effort to put in place the world's largest, most advanced and most efficient system of municipal and industrial water-treatment plants Two thirds of China's rivers, the sources of water for daily use, are seriously polluted. Advanced recycling would create new water supplies throughout North China, where more than half a billion people experience recurrent and even chronic water shortages. Appropriate pricing of the recycled water would raise the ridiculously low rates paid for water by China's urban dwellers, farmers and industries, and hence compel more efficient water use. This would obviate the need for a massive south-to-north water transfer from the Yangzi to the Yellow River basin. This interbasin transfer, contemplated since the 1950s, could have even more disastrous environmental effects than the Three Gorges dam.

At his recent Washington press conference, Premier Zhu boasted of his country's more than $100 billion in foreign reserves. It would be a sign of a farsighted policy – of a vision commensurate with his wish to see China among the leading nations of the world – if he committed a share of this wealth to these three "no-regrets" megaprojects.

As this book goes to press, four years after the above comments were written, there has been no wholehearted embrace of the three suggested no-regret priorities, while the Sanxia dam, the paragon of China's questionable megaprojects, is moving toward its completion and work has begun on China's other questionable megaproject, the South/North water transfer. The history of every nation offers many examples of unwise choices and missed opportunities, some only marginally important, others truly fateful. Politicians may use these facts for recrimination or for defining their own agendas; historians may take them as bases of what-if scenarios to construct alternative pasts. I view them with the mixture of regret and frustration. "Better late than never" is a poor consolation when knowing that the right decision could have been making a difference for many years.

Some steps I have advocated for two decades were finally taken during the 1990s. The first link of Shanghai's metro light-rail system (north–south line) opened in April 1995, the first phase of the first Guangzhou subway line began running in summer 1997, and the Ministry of Railways completed initial design work for a Beijing–Shanghai high-speed train in June 1998 (Railway Technology 2002). The Ministry of Construction, and a number of other central institutions, are now engaged in developing and implementing standards for energy-efficient buildings and appliances. All laudable, but all mere beginnings: China has a very long way to go before putting in place modern, energy-efficient and environment-sparing infrastructures.

Notes

1 My previous writings touching, or confronting, matters of environment, conflict, and security have been: "Environmental change as a source of conflict and economic losses in China", occasional paper series of the project on *Environmental Change and Acute Conflict* 2: 5–39 (Cambridge MA: American Academy of Arts and Sciences, 1992); "Some contrarian notes on environmental threats to national security", *Canadian Foreign Policy* 2(2): 85–87, 1994; "L'environnement et la politique internationale", *Etudes internationales* 26(2): 361–371, 1995; "China's environmental refugees: causes, dimensions and risks of an emerging problem", in K.R. Spillmann and G. Bachler (eds) *Environmental Crisis: Regional Conflicts and Ways of Cooperation* (Berne: Swiss Peace Foundation, 1995) 75–91.
2 R. Kaplan (1994) "The coming anarchy", *The Atlantic Monthly* 273(2): 44–76. Kaplan preaches with conviction and with the simplistic zeal of a prophet. His conclusions are based on unqualified generalizations unmindful of enormous environmental and socio-economic peculiarities; he does not hedge his remarks and he sees no detours or surprises on the road ahead. He knows the environment will be "a terrifying threat" to our security, and not satisfied with some local skirmishing, he predicts a frightening array of wars driven by the disappearance of fish and appearance of refugees.
3 See, for example, K. Butts, "National security, the environment and DOD", *Environmental Change and Security Report* 2: 22–27, 1996. And one can have no doubt about a speedy bureaucratic appropriation of the concern when reading that the first conference on "Environmental security and national security" organized by the US Department of Defense in June 1995 called on various governmental agencies "to prioritize international environmental security issues in order to enhance US national security".
4 UNDP, *Human Development Report 1994* (New York: Oxford University Press, 1994). See also UNDP, "Redefining security: the human dimension", *Current History* 592: 229–236, 1994.
5 As a former citizen of the Soviet empire, I draw an obvious analogy with politics in Communist states, where even the most mundane affairs became matters of political import, requiring guidance, vigilance, struggles, and campaigns waged by the ever-alert Party. The how-people-live-and-breathe school of security studies goes even beyond that. Communists had an obsessive interest in my class background, and the ever-present informers in my casual remarks, but with breathing they left me pretty much alone. Obviously, conceiving politics or security in such a fashion robs the terms of any real meaning.

6 Among many relevant recent contributions, see: "The liberation of the environment", *Daedalus* summer 1996; J.L. Simon, *The State of Humanity* (Oxford: Blackwell, 1995); V. Smil, *Energy in World History* (Boulder: Westview, 1994).

7 For a sampling of these arguments, see: D. Deudney, "The case against linking environmental degradation and national security", *Millennium* 19: 461–476, 1990; G. Porter, "Environmental security as a national security issue", *Current History* 592: 218–222, 1994; T. Homer-Dixon, M. Levy, G. Porter and J. Goldstone, "Environmental security and violent conflict: a debate", *Environmental Change and Security Project* 2: 49–71, 1996.

8 R. Ullman, "Redefining security", *International Security* 8. 129–153, 1983.

9 For detailed analyses of the state of China's environment, see: V. Smil,, *The Bad Earth: Environmental Degradation in China* (Armonk: M.E. Sharpe, 1984); Smil, *China's Environmental Crisis: An Inquiry into the Limits of National Development* (Armonk: M.E. Sharpe, 1993); and R.L. Edmonds, *Patterns of China's Lost Harmony* (London: Routledge, 1994).

10 These concepts are discussed, for example, in H. Daly and J.B. Cobb, *For the Common Good* (Boston MA: Beacon Press, 1989); V. Smil, *Global Ecology* (London: Routledge, 1993).

11 V. Smil, *Environmental Problems in China: Estimates of Economic Costs* (Honolulu: East–West Center, 1996); V. Smil and Mao Yushi (coordinators) *The Economic Costs of China's Environmental Degradation* (Boston MA: American Academy of Arts and Sciences, 1998).

12 For details see Smil (1996), note 11 above.

13 P. Brimblecombe, *The Big Smoke* (London: Routledge, 1987).

14 For more on nitrates in the environment see V. Smil, *Cycles of Life* (New York: Scientific American Library, 1997).

15 I am using a conversion based on the most plausible purchasing power parity value, not on the official exchange rate. While the latter calculation puts China's per capita GDP at only some US$500, a misleading underestimate, the former valuation puts China's 1995 GDP at about US$1,800/capita. For the latest reappraisal of China's GDP, see World Bank, *Poverty Reduction and the World Bank: Progress and Challenges in the 1990s* (Washington DC: World Bank, 1996).

16 I.Yamazawa, S. Nakayama and H. Kitamura, *Asia-Pacific Cooperation in Energy and the Environment* (Tokyo: Institute of Developing Economies, 1995).

17 All of these figures are readily available in: World Resources Institute, *World Resources 1996–97* (New York: Oxford University Press, 1996), or at http://www.wri.org/wri.

18 For a critique of these figures see V. Smil, "China's environment: resilient myths and contradictory realities", in K.K. Gaul and J. Hiltz (eds) *Landscapes and Communities on the Pacific Rim* (Armonk: M.E. Sharpe, 2000) 167–181.

19 For example, if China were to import 70 per cent of its total grain demand, the share corresponding to recent Japanese imports, it would absorb more than the total mass of corn, wheat and rice sold annually worldwide.

20 Even when limited to English-language books, the comprehensive list of relevant writings would be too long. The following volumes will give a wide-ranging introduction to recent thinking: F. Archibugi and P. Nijkamp, *Economy and Ecology* (Dordrecht: Kluwer, 1989); R. Costanza (ed.) *Ecological Economics* (New York: Columbia University Press, 1991); H. Daly and K.N. Townsend (eds) *Valuing the Environment* (Cambridge MA: MIT Press, 1993).

21 For a detailed survey of possible valuation techniques see: J.A. Dixon *et al.*, *Economic Analysis of Environmental Impacts* (London: Earthscan, 1994).

22 A.M. Freeman, *The Measurement of Environmental and Resource Values* (Washington DC: Resources for the Future, 1997); S.E. Rhoads (ed.) *Valuing Life: Public Policy Dilemmas* (Boulder: Westview, 1980).

23 This is obvious by looking at the analytical framework recommended for national assessments of environmental impacts by the United Nations: UNO, *Integrated Environmental and Economic Accounting* (New York: UNO, 1993).

24 For example, estimating that 80 per cent of people in a region are exposed to excessive concentration of a pollutant whose effects cause a 40 per cent rise in the incidence of upper respiratory morbidity, and that a typical illness event is associated with a 30 per cent increase in absence from work, there will be roughly a 10 per cent rise in lost labor hours. Changing the fractions marginally to, respectively, 70, 30 and 20 cuts the total by more than half.

25 Thanks to a generation of fairly strict birth controls, China's relative population growth, recently at just around 1.1 per cent a year, is much lower than in any other populous modernizing nation (India's rate has been about 1.9 per cent, Brazil's 1.6 per cent) – but the huge base makes the absolute additions still highly taxing.

26 China's inflation-adjusted GDP averaged 9.4 per cent a year between 1980 and 1991, compared to South Korea's 9.6 and India's 5.4 per cent. Since 1991, China's growth rate of just above 10 per cent has been unmatched worldwide.

27 Two comprehensive surveys of China's current environmental ills are: V. Smil, *China's Environmental Crisis* (Armonk: M.E. Sharpe, 1993); and R.L. Edmonds, *Patterns of China's Lost Harmony* (London: Routledge, 1994).

28 The two country studies – the Dutch one calculating pollution costs in the year 1985 and the West German account for the years 1983–1985 – ended up with very different conclusions. The Dutch study put the annual cost of air and water pollution and noise at just 0.5–0.9 per cent of the country's GDP, while the German total was 6 per cent, an order of magnitude higher: J. Nicolaisen, A. Dean and P. Hoeller, "Economics and the environment: a survey of issues and policy options", *OECD Economic Studies* spring 1991: 7–43. The main reason for the higher German value was in accounting for the disamenity effects of air pollution and for the impact of noise on property values.

29 National Environmental Protection Agency, *Environment Forecast and Countermeasure Research in China in the Year 2000* (Beijing: Qinghua University Publishing House, 1990).

30 V. Smil, *Environmental Problems in China: Estimates of Economic Costs* (Honolulu: East–West Center, 1996).

31 Mao Yushi chose Professor Wang Hongchang of the CASS to prepare a paper on deforestation, Professor Ning Datong of the Beijing Normal University to write about land use changes, and Xia Guang of the National Environmental Protection Agency to evaluate costs of air and water pollution.

32 V. Smil and Mao Yushi (coordinators) *The Economic Costs of China's Environmental Degradation* (Boston MA: American Academy of Arts and Sciences, 1998).

33 Zhang Jianguang, "Environmental hazards in the Chinese public's eyes", *Risk Analysis* 14: 163–167, 1994.

34 Conversion efficiencies range from just around 5 per cent for steam locomotives and 10–15 per cent for poorly designed traditional stoves to 30–40 per cent for better urban stoves and 50 per cent for small boilers. In contrast, the best household natural gas furnaces have efficiencies in excess of 90 per cent, as do the largest industrial boilers.

35 For comparison of recent air pollution levels in the world's largest cities, see: Earthwatch, *Urban Air Pollution in Megacities of the World* (Oxford: WHO/UNEP/Blackwell, 1992).

36 Zhao Dianwu and H.M. Seip, "Assessing effects of acid deposition in southwestern China using the MAGIC model", *Water, Air, and Soil Pollution* 60: 83–97, 1991.

37 On indoor air pollution see: K. Smith and Youcheng Liu, "Indoor air pollution in developing countries", in J.M. Samet (ed.) *Epidemiology of Lung Cancer* (New York: Marcel Dekker, 1994) 151–184.

38 China is now the world's largest producer of cigarettes, and its total of 350 million smokers is growing by 2 per cent a year; the average number of cigarettes smoked rose from 10 per person per day in 1994 to 14 in 1996: *China News* internet files, 25 November 1996.

39 D. Gao *et al.*, "Mercury pollution and control in China", *Journal of Environmental Sciences* 3: 105–11, 1991.

40 For details on nitrogen enrichment of the biosphere see: V. Smil, *Cycles of Life* (New York: Scientific American Library, 1997).

41 Ling Bo *et al.*, "Use of night soil in agriculture and fish farming", *World Health Forum* 14: 67–70, 1993.

42 Recent cost-benefit studies of controlling air pollution in the Los Angeles Basin are a perfect example. Total annual health benefits from reduced morbidity were found to be as low as US$ (1990) 1.2 billion, or as high as US$ (1990) 20 billion: A.J. Krupnick and P.R. Portney, "Controlling urban air pollution. a benefit-cost assessment", *Science* 252: 522–528, 1991; J.V. Hall, A.M. Winer, M.T. Kleinman, F.W. Lurmann, V. Brajer and S.D. Colome, "Valuing the benefits of clean air", *Science* 255 (1992): 812–817. Given the cost of US$ (1990) 13 billion which may be required to clean up the basin's air, morbidity costs alone can either easily justify the effort, or make it economically quite unappealing.

43 For more on China's changing farmland, see: F.W. Crook, "Underreporting of China's cultivated land area: implications for world agricultural trade", *China Agriculture and Trade Report* RS–93: 33–39, 1993; V. Smil, "Who will feed China?", *The China Quarterly* 143: 801–813, 1995.

44 Han Chunru, "Recent changes in the rural environment in China", *Journal of Applied Ecology* 26: 803–812, 1989.

45 Li Yongzeng, "Chinese forestry: crisis and options", *Liaowang (Outlook)* 1989(12): 9–10.

46 See, among many others: D. Heinsdijk, *Forest Assessment*, Wageningen: Center for Agricultural Publishing and Documentation, 1975; R. Repetto, R. Solorzano, R. de Camino, R. Woodward, J. Tosi, V. Watson, A. Vasquez, C. Villalobos and J. Jimenez, *Accounts Overdue: Natural Resource Depletion in Costa Rica* (Washington DC: World Resources Institute, 1991).

47 Qu Geping and Li Jinchang, *Population and the Environment in China* (Boulder: Lynne Rienner, 1994).

48 For more on noise in China's cities, see V. Smil, *Environmental Change as a Source of Conflict and Economic Losses in China* (Cambridge MA: American Academy of Arts and Sciences, 1992).

49 World Bank, *Poverty Reduction and the World Bank: Progress and Challenges in the 1990s* (Washington DC: World Bank, 1996).

5 Looking ahead by looking back

When thinking about the future of large nations – and particularly those burdened by a long and recently highly traumatic history – most prognosticators and judges of national fortunes find it very difficult not to succumb, largely if not completely, to extreme scenarios. Perhaps the most prominent example from the last generation is the judgment of Western "experts" of the USSR/Russia's importance. First the USSR was seen by too many experts as an invincible state whose military might and international influence would only grow; after its demise other experts quickly wrote off Russia – with its alcoholic pandemic, falling life expectancy and shrinking population – as a country largely, if not entirely, irrelevant to the course of modern history. And perhaps the most obvious post-9/11 example is the US attitude to the Saudi royal family: officially still valued, if a reluctant, time-tested ally, but in the eyes of families of 9/11 victims a particularly odious enemy being sued for $1.2 trillion as an accomplice of terror.

Hence it comes as no surprise that we have been told about China as an inevitable superpower whose aggressively pursued interests will soon clash perilously with those of the USA and recreate a new Cold War-like contest – as well as about China beset by a combination of challenges (coping with its ageing population, trying to secure enough food, water and energy, and keeping in check various centrifugal forces) that will make it preoccupied with its internal affairs and amenable to international cooperation. I will not add to these dubiously extreme judgments. Instead, I will close this book by stressing first our dismal record in forecasting, and then outlining some key contending trends.

Failed forecasts

During the second half of the twentieth century, forecasting has grown from a relatively infrequent activity to a ubiquitous enterprise that is eagerly embraced by institutions ranging from universities to governments, and from multinational companies to NGOs. Its topics range from short-term forecasts of business performance to long-term explorations of international security, and its techniques include highly formalized quantitative models as well as a variety of probabilistic approaches. All of these efforts share one outstanding feature: at best a mediocre, and typically a dismal success rate. Here is a simple test of this conclusion. Choose a major national or international event of the last three decades of the twentieth century, go back ten, or even just five years, and try to find out if anybody's forecast fits.

You will immediately start piling up a long list of hugely important events that were entirely unanticipated only five years before they took place. A handful of examples will suffice. Who in 1967 forecast Nixon's *tête-à-tête* with Mao; in 1974, Shah Reza Pahlavi's flight from Iran and Ayatollah Khomeini's ascent; in 1985, the collapse of the USSR; in 1989 the Nikkei index plunging to below 10,000 (when it had peaked at nearly 40,000); or in 1996, US troops in Afghanistan? Indeed, at least three of these five cases were utterly unforeseen just a year before they took place, the last one not until 9/11. And China's modern history contains so many surprising policy reversals that I singled them out (in an editorial I wrote for the *Asian Wall Street Journal* on the occasion of the fiftieth anniversary of the Communist state) as one of the most important characteristics of the post-1949 era (Smil 1999e).

China's unstable past and future

Reviewing Communist China's accomplishments and failures, one important characteristic of the country's eventful history during the latter half of the twentieth century emerges: numerous and abrupt reversals of the most fundamental public policies. This is a sign of China's underlying instability, and a good reason to be wary of future shifts. Some of these dramatic reversals have been welcome, and indeed essential, ingredients of Deng Xiaoping's post-1978 reforms. In less than five years Deng turned the world's most communalized, rigidly planned and badly underperforming agricultural system into tens of millions of small private enterprises. The farmers' enthusiastic response to new market opportunities lifted China's average per capita food availability, after two decades of at best subsistence stagnation. The doors were opened to the arch-villains of Maoist ideology, the despicable and ruthless capitalist exploiters in charge of multinational corporations, who suddenly became valued foreign friends and were given permission to make a profit in China.

But unanticipated abrupt reversals of key policies marked the Maoist years. During the first decade of Mao's reign, China's attitude toward the Soviet Union went from friendly deferral to an "elder brother", to abusive tirades against an overbearing hegemon. And in 1957, not long after he exhorted the country's intellectuals to speak boldly and critically – to let 100 flowers bloom and 100 schools of thought contend – the Great Helmsman used the resulting outpouring of criticism to identify "poisonous weeds" and launched a generation-long persecution of scholars and artists.

Of course, Mao's worst series of reversals came in 1958 when, after the country completed its first Stalinist five-year plan, he abruptly jettisoned what he thought to be a too ponderous economic advance in favor of the grassroots-driven Great Leap Forward, a move of unprecedented economic delusion and disdain for the fate of his subjects. But in the standard Western judgment Mao is now remembered not for the deaths and suffering he brought to his own people – but for his later "good" reversal, for chatting sagely with Henry Kissinger and for giving Richard Nixon the unforgettable experience of seeing a revolutionary ballet.

Shortly before the great opening-up to the USA, the Maoist leadership came up with yet another abrupt reversal, this time in population policy. In 1957, after Ma Yinchu, an eminent economist and the president of Beijing University, cautioned the leadership about the rapid growth of China's population, he was dismissed from his post and became a non-person for the next twenty-two years. The faster the population growth the better, Mao concluded in 1957.

When the Party realized that Mr Ma was right, it responded with the world's most aggressive and highly intrusive program of population control, including birth quotas, reporting of menstrual periods and forced abortions. Today, however, the pendulum is again swinging back. The Party is starting to worry about the prospect of supporting a rapidly ageing population. So the government is officially retreating from its draconian one-child policy.

One recent abrupt reversal with enormous socio-economic impacts has been the total ban on logging in the Yangzi River's upper basin. The logging in those areas had long made the destruction of the Amazon forest seem a tame affair. Some of the world's highest deforestation rates could be found in the region, particularly in Sichuan, where millions of people came to depend on the activity. After the great floods of the summer of 1998 – in which the tree cutting undoubtedly played a role, but was not, as is often misunderstood, their main cause – the central government issued a hasty total ban.

In short, contrary to the current Beijing leadership's mantra of maintaining stability, China's undemocratic political system is still prone to abrupt lurches from one extreme to another, bringing huge economic costs as well as disruptions to people's lives. And this phenomenon is hardly confined to domestic policies. In foreign policy, friendly overtures to the Dalai Lama are soon followed by scornful dismissals of the man as an unworthy partner in any talks. Taiwan is lured by promises of a Hong Kong-like arrangement, and then threatened with imminent military attack. Beijing's top generals are now openly talking about joining with Russia to form a counterbalance to the aggressive and never-to-be-trusted USA, yesterday's great strategic partner.

While the Chinese people have benefited from some of these shifts, like the Deng-era reforms, their frequency and impact over the last fifty years have largely served to disrupt China's economic development and destroy lives. For outsiders they carry one lesson: until China embarks on political reform, there is very little likelihood that the country's future will be a linear extension of the recent past, a matter of continuity and stability. The lessons of the past tell us to anticipate more great reversals.

Are there any good forecasts?

But examples from the world of politics and international affairs can be seen as unfairly difficult tests of forecasting success, as they deal with developments suffused with emotions and irrationality, and hence largely outside the realm of rational prediction. Stock market valuations might be seen in a similar light. Forecasts of total energy consumption and grain harvests (national or global), of global crude oil prices, of new electricity-generating capacities or emissions of greenhouse gases, should be much more successful. After all, all of these developments depend on the performance of infrastructures that are already in place, the most likely fluctuations can be judged on the basis of past experience, and long periods of planning and financial commitment are needed to effect many of these changes. All true, but not necessarily all that helpful – as forecasts of energy, food and environmental affairs offer some of the best examples of failed predictions. And it is not just that the absolute forecast values are significantly off, but that their uselessness, for forecasts looking 5–50 years ahead, often becomes obvious in just a matter of months or a few years after their publication.

Moreover, this conclusion is true for every kind of forecast – be it about technical innovations, available natural resources, gross outputs of particular commodities, their prices or their final consumption. I have gathered many such examples in a paper for *Technological Forecasting and Social Change* (Smil 2000c), whose substantially expanded version became the third chapter of *Energy at the Crossroads* (Smil 2003). An interested reader may find there astonishing dismissals of key technical inventions published just years or months before those innovations began their triumphal conquest of global markets; baseless worries about the imminent exhaustion of this or that mineral resource; and price forecasts that would have been easily beaten by entirely random guesses.

More importantly, there may be no reason for satisfaction even when some forecasts are substantially vindicated. I have no better example in this category than my own predictions of China's aggregate energy demand, which I prepared in 1975 and published in 1976. In retrospect, my median variants for the years 1985 and 1990 turned out to have errors of, respectively, a mere 2 and 10 per cent (Smil 1976a; Fridley 2001). But this record is no reason for self-congratulation, as the overall setting and countless details of the system whose performance I tried to forecast have changed beyond mine, and indeed anybody's, expectations. I had no doubts that major changes would follow Mao's death, but I could not have predicted either the speed or the extent of China's post-1979 modernization, and all of its complex implications for energy demand and economic expansion.

My forecasts assumed that between 1980 and 2000 China's economy would grow most likely by 6 per cent a year, and I derived the long-term trend of energy intensity from the regression for the 1949–1974 period. In reality, China's official statistics translate into an average exponential growth of more than 9 per cent in constant monies – but at the same time, as shown in detail in Chapter 2, the country had been dramatically reducing its relative need for energy. Consequently, my rather successful forecast of China's primary energy needs in

1985 and 1990 was the result of being doubly wrong, as my underestimate of average GDP growth rate was almost perfectly negated by my overestimate of energy intensity. And the continuing decline of the average energy intensity of China's economy means that even forecasts less than a decade old are already substantially off. Six foreign and domestic forecasts issued between 1994 and 1999 put the country's total primary energy consumption in the year 2000 at 1.491–1.562Gtce (mean of 1.53Gtce) while the actual use was 1.312Gtce, making those forecasts 12–19 per cent too high in a matter of just a few years.

But I have an even better example of a reasonable success that still misses. Better because it refers to a broad range of developments, and because it displays all the common weaknesses of long-range forecasting. I am referring to a Delphi forecast of China's future, a study I conducted with twenty experts on Chinese affairs between November 1974 and March 1975, that is nearly two years before Mao's death. The Delphi method is an extension of systematic analysis into the areas of opinion and value judgment. Its basic ideas are anonymous questioning, iteration and controlled feedback, and expression of results in terms of probability estimates. This probabilistic group response is most useful wherever there is a high degree of uncertainty and complexity, and Delphi output is a valuable heuristic tool for gaining insights into fuzzy futures. And China's future a year or two before Mao's death looked utterly fuzzy.

Our group of twenty included Richard Baum, Jürgen Domes, Leo Goodstadt (at that time at the *Far Eastern Economic Review*, later Chief Policy Adviser to Chris Patten's Hong Kong government), Michel Oksenberg, Leo Orleans and Frederick Teiwes, and, in retrospect, it did a surprisingly good job. In quantifying probabilities of important events that might take place in China between 1975 and 2000, the group assigned the highest value (median and mode of 75 per cent) to new "revisionism", that is to a major departure from the Maoist course:

> participants felt that although some aspects of the Maoist period might be retained, the evolution of a more stable society is all but inevitable due to the industrialization of the country, mechanization and modernization (e.g. fertilizers) of her agriculture, growing urbanization, greater contacts with the world, the increasing importance of scientific research, and the necessity of long-range planning and complex management.
>
> (Smil 1977b: 480)

On the other hand, we correctly saw very low probabilities (all modal values below 10 per cent) of not just Sino-Soviet and Sino-Indian war, and a new Great Leap Forward, but also of the collapse of the Communist government and reappearance of regional fragmentation.

In weighting the relative importance of China's critical problems during the last quarter of the twentieth century, we ranked population/food balance, modernization vs. ideology, youth, industrial growth and its requirements, and generational succession, as the top five items. And, interestingly enough, there was the group's difficult task of estimating dates of future developments. Its median estimates of 50 per cent probability occurrence were: 1978 for the peace treaty with Japan (it was signed that year); the first long-term credit arrangements with Western countries (China became a member of the World Bank in 1980); 1999 for Hong Kong's integration with China (its colonial status ended in 1997); and 2000 for China becoming the world's third-largest economy (true if using some higher PPP estimates).

But the group's assessment was also subject to the biasing effect of recent events, perhaps the most common weakness found in long-range forecasts. Sino-Soviet relations were ranked far ahead of Sino-American ones in terms of their impact on China's future. The second highest probability, after the new "revisionism", was another Lin Biao-type crisis (who now remembers that affair but historians of modern China?). Rumors of China's potential oil riches led the group to put a 50 per cent probability on China surpassing the USA in crude oil output by 1995. And, most importantly, the group consensus did not foresee (in spite of all the relics of Maoism in today's China) either the speed or the sweep of post-1978 reforms. We have taken these developments increasingly for granted, but they still appear astonishing when seen from the 1975 perspective.

I summarized the dismal record of long-term energy forecasting in three conjoined axioms (Smil 2003). No long-range forecast can be correct in all of its aspects; most of these forecasts will be wrong in both quantitative and qualitative terms; and while some forecasts may get a number of quantities and timings right, they will not capture the new qualities created by subtly-to-profoundly altered wholes. And so the lessons of failures in forecasting are clear: while there is no way to prevent our forecast-happy, computer-equipped civilization from issuing a ceaseless stream of outlooks and predictions and scenarios, it is imperative to understand the profoundly limited utility of this output, and to realize that even its apparent successes may not be very helpful, as it is virtually impossible to supply them in the correct, and complex, context.

A correct forecast of China's GDP growth rate for the period 1978–2000 would be one thing if it had taken place in a slowly reforming quasi-Maoist state with a high degree of autarky; and an entirely different matter when the country has been an increasingly important component of the global economy to which it is now tied by links ranging from growing foreign trade to a large population of students at foreign universities, and from membership of the WTO to an emerging dependence on imports of energy. That is why I will not offer here any new forecasts, merely some musings on possible trends.

Contending trends

A careful reading of history shows that the outcomes of complex developments are often much less circumscribed than is commonly believed. The combination of biophysical constraints, burdens of history, and peculiarities of culture and politics counts for a lot – but it does not preordain the future. Closer looks at complex situations always reveal the existence of contending trends, and hence of realistic choices. Every one of them can be handled in one of three basic ways: vigorously pursued, largely ignored or aggressively opposed – or with countless, and shifting, nuances in between. The long-term balance of these complex interplays determines the outcome.

China's dependence on coal offers a perfect example of these contending options. Recent reductions in coal extraction (leaving aside the question of their real extent) generated some exaggerated expectations – but China's high dependence on coal cannot be shed so easily. Currently some three quarters of China's electricity is generated by burning coal, and, as we have seen, the electricity intensity of China's economy, unlike its overall energy intensity, has been increasing. And although China has a very large untapped hydroenergy potential, most of the approximately 20GW of new generating capacity needed every year cannot come from hydrostations whose capital costs are far higher, and construction periods far longer, than for coal-fired plants. This kind of reasoning leads to long-range forecasts of doubled coal consumption by 2020–2025.

Yet this growing demand for electricity should also increase the efficiency with which coal is used in China. Because of the numerous advantages of electricity compared to fuels, the twentieth century saw a relentless rise of the share of coal consumption used to generate electricity. The US share rose from less than 20 per cent in 1950 to nearly 80 per cent by 2001, with residential and commercial uses accounting for the combined total of less than 0.5 per cent of the final consumption (EIA 2001). The Chinese pattern is still very different: the country converted only about 10 per cent of its coal to electricity in 1950, and about 35 per cent during the late 1990s (Smil 1976a; Fridley 2001). About 12 per cent of China's coal is still burned very inefficiently by China's urban households and commercial enterprises, and nearly 40 per cent is used directly by industries, including many small-scale operations. Shifting this fuel to large power plants, particularly those with cogeneration or combined cycles, could eventually nearly double the current output of useful energy.

Moreover, a very large share of these domestic and industrial uses can be converted relatively rapidly to natural gas: the higher cost of the gas is readily repaid by much higher conversion efficiencies of burning this inherently superior fuel, and by radically reduced air pollution. China has already embarked on this near-universal substitution, and the coming years may see anything ranging from a steady expansion to a very rapid replacement of urban coal by a combination of domestic and imported natural gas.

At the same time, China's rising affluence may lead to such a widespread adoption of air conditioning and electrical appliances that its coal-fired electricity generation will have to grow even faster than anticipated. Hence it will be a complex and dynamic interplay of rising need for electricity generated largely from coal, more efficient uses of coal in improved electricity generation, and the requirements for more efficient conversions and cleaner environment that favor natural gas that will determine the shares of these fossil fuels in the country's primary energy consumption. Realistically conceivable differences between the extreme tilts translate to very large absolute values over the course of 15–25 years.

Similar contending trends can be found in every instance of securing China's energy and food while maintaining an acceptable quality of environment. The application of nitrogen fertilizer is the best analogy to coal use in the food sector. As we have seen, China is now the world's largest user of nitrogen fertilizer – but also perhaps its most inefficient one. Field experiments have shown that nitrogen recovery rates in continuously irrigated rice in Asia are very low, averaging only about 31 per cent (Cassman *et al.* 2002), and the rates are often less than 25 per cent in some Chinese provinces.

This, obviously, leaves much room for improvement, and a seemingly unexceptional forecast of large increases of nitrogen fertilizer applications needed to produce food for an additional 200 million people from the diminishing area of farmland may be thus defeated by the concurrent aggressive pursuit of higher field fertilization efficiencies. These are harder to achieve with wet-field crops, but Japan points the way: after reaching their peak during the early 1980s, average nitrogen applications to Japanese rice began falling, and in combination with a slightly higher yield, this decline translated to an approximate 30 per cent gain in apparent uptake efficiency of the nutrient between 1980 and 1995 (Smil 2001b).

But even a significant success in reducing specific nitrogen applications may not lead to the stabilization of the nutrient's overall use if China's meat eating, and hence the need for more animal feed, should rise closer to today's Taiwanese rate. And, to make just one more switch, this need for more feed could be easily met if future genetically modified grains were to be produced with less fertilizer in a climate with higher, and better distributed, natural precipitation due to the regionally beneficial effect of global warming that may leave China better off than, for example, sub-Saharan Africa. Once again, the long-term outcome is not predetermined by today's constraints and realities, and the range of possible results remains very wide.

Finally, let us consider a key environmental example of contending trends, the one involving China's northern water supply. South/North water transfer may ease the conditions of the northern part of the North China Plain, in Shandong and in the southern Hebei (including Beijing and Tianjin), particularly when combined with higher water-use efficiency in irrigation and industrial production. The effectiveness of these steps can be clearly seen in the USA, where the absolute water withdrawal dropped by nearly 10 per cent between 1980 and 1995 (USGS 1995), even as the country's population increased by 16 per cent, and its inflation-adjusted GDP rose by about 54 per cent (EIA 2001). On the other hand, China's average per capita water use is only a fraction of the US mean and, as I stressed before, it can never come even close to the US rate. Yet increased grain imports could considerably lower the water use in farming, as one kilogram of grain typically needs at least 1,500kg of water: large-scale imports of feed grain could thus save China both fertilizer and water (Smil 2000a).

However – to switch to a counter-trend that is well documented in other countries – greater affluence means the spread of suburban housing (with its vastly higher water demand for yards and pools), and of recreational water uses (from ubiquitous golf courses to water parks). Most importantly, it will be the long-term effects of the unfolding climatic change that will either ease or intensify North China's water shortages. But I hasten to add an important caveat: even significantly higher northern precipitation may be of limited use if most of it comes down, as some climatologists fear, in a few extreme summer events when the main effect of high and rapid runoff could be more crop and property damage and accelerated soil erosion. And so, once again, the future of northern China's water is not foreclosed by today's realities, but remains much more open than those observers who resort to simplistic comparisons of the existing supply–demand imbalance would believe.

Perhaps I should have dispensed with these three examples and just cited a passage from Mencius, whose keen insights I have found always more interesting than the didactic moralizings of Confucius. He opens the second book of his sayings and conversations by the following parable (taken from D.C. Lau's translation):

> Suppose you laid siege to a city...and you failed to take it. Now in the course of the siege, there must have been, at one time or another, favourable weather, and in spite of that you failed to take the city. This shows that favourable weather is less important than advantageous terrain. Sometimes a city has to be abandoned in spite of the height of its walls and depth of its moat, the quality of arms and abundance of food supplies. This shows that advantageous terrain is less important than human unity. Hence it is said, It is not by boundaries that the people are confined, it is not by difficult terrain that a state is rendered secure, and it is not by superiority of arms that the Empire is kept in awe.
>
> (Mencius 1970)

The message is clear: while in complex matters no factor is unimportant, none is necessarily defining, and our choices, our inventiveness and our perseverance can make the greatest difference, even in situations that may seem entirely discouraging. True, in China's case the confining variables may be more acutely felt than in the case of countries that have, literally and figuratively, more room to maneuver – but the country's fate, so fundamentally dependent on its supply of energy and food and on the maintenance of a healthy environment, will be determined more by the future choices and actions of its people than by either its ancient cultural heritage or its natural endowments and challenging environment.

Appendix

Units of measurement and quantitative abbreviations

Table A.1 Units of measurement

Variable	Unit	Symbol	Equal to
Mass	gram	g	
	kilogram	kg	10^3g
	tonne	t	10^3kg
Length	meter	m	100cm
	kilometer	km	1,000m
Area	square meter	m^2	
	are	a	$100m^2$
	hectare	ha	$10,000m^2$
	square kilometer	km^2	100ha
Time	second	s	
Energy	Joule	J	1W/s
	Watthour	Wh	3,600J
Power	Watt	W	1J/s

Table A.2 Quantitative abbreviations

Name	Symbol	Value
centi	c	10^{-2}
hecto	h	10^2
kilo	k	10^3
mega	M	10^6
giga	G	10^9
tera	T	10^{12}
peta	P	10^{15}

The most commonly used large units in this book are EJ (exajoules, 10^{18}J), Gm^3 (billion cubic meters), Gt (billion tonnes) and GW (billion watts), Mha (million hectares), Mt (million tonnes) and MW (million watts), and TWh (trillion watthours). The terms kgce and Mtce stand, respectively, for kilograms and millions of tonnes of coal equivalent, the fuel containing 29MJ/kg, compared to 42MJ/kg for crude oil, $35MJ/m^3$ for natural gas, and between 15 and 18GJ/t for biomass fuels.

Bibliography

Aird, J. (1982) "Population studies and population policy in China", *Population and Development Review* 8: 85–97.

Alexandratos, N. (1996) "China's projected cereals deficits in a world context", *Agricultural Economics* 15: 1–16.

——(1997) "China's consumption of cereals and the capacity of the rest of the world to increase exports", *Food Policy* 22: 253–267.

Alroy, J. (2001) "A multispecies overkill simulation of the end-Pleistocene megafauna", *Science* 292: 1893–1896.

Ashton, B., Hill, K., Piazza, A. and Zeitz, R. (1984) "Famine in China, 1958–61", *Population and Development Review* 10: 613–645.

Banister, J. (1987) *China's Changing Population*, Stanford: Stanford University Press.

BBC News (2002) "Rare species campaign targets chefs", London: BBC News, 1 February 2002. http://news.bbc.co.uk/1/hi/world/asia-pacific/1795388.stm.

Becker, J. (2000) "Drought paralyses big hydro scheme", *South China Morning Post*, 23 June 2000. http://www.scmp.com.

Berezina, Y.I. (1959) *Toplivno-energeticheskaya baza Kitaiskoi Narodnoi Respubliki (Fuel and Energy Foundations of the People's Republic of China)*, Moscow: Izdatelstvo vostochnoi literatury.

Biswas, A.K., Zuo Dakang, Nickum, James E. and Liu Changming (eds) (1983) *Long-Distance Water Transfer: A Chinese Case Study and International Experiences*, Dublin: Tycooly International.

Blakney, R.B. (1955) *Tao Te Ching: A New Translation*, New York: New American Library.

Bolton, W. (1989) *Engineering Materials*, Boca Raton FL: CRC Press.

Boss, L.P., Toole, M.J. and Ray, Y. (1994) "Assessments of mortality, morbidity, and nutritional status in Somalia during the 1991–1992 famine", *Journal of the American Medical Association* 272: 371–376.

BP (British Petroleum) (2001) *BP Statistical Review of World Energy 2001*, London: BP. http://www.bp.com/worldenergy.

——(2002) *Statistical Review of World Energy, 2002*, London: BP.

Braudel, F. (1972) "History and the social sciences: the *longue durée*", in P. Burke (ed.) *Economy and Society in Early Modern Europe*, London: Routledge & Kegan Paul, 11–42.

Bray, F. (1984) *Science and Civilisation in China. Volume 6, Part II: Agriculture*, Cambridge: Cambridge University Press.

Brody, S. (1964) *Bioenergetics and Growth*, New York: Hafner.

Brown, L. (1994) "Who will feed China?", *WorldWatch* September/October 1994: 10–19.

——(1995) *Who Will Feed China?: Wake-up Call for a Small Planet*, New York: Norton.

Broyelle, C. and Broyelle, J. (1978) "Comment vivant ces Chinois", *L'Express* 1385(23–29 January): 67.

Buck, J.L. (1930) *Chinese Farm Economy*, Nanking: Nanking University Press.

——(1937) *Land Utilization in China*, Nanking: Nanking University Press.

——(1966) "Food grain production", in J.L. Buck, O.L. Dawson and Y. Wu, *Food and Agriculture in Communist China*, New York: Praeger, 72.

Carin, R. (1969) *Power Industry in Communist China*, Hong Kong: Union Research Institute.

CASP (Cambridge Arctic Shelf Programme) (1999) *China Basins Project 1999*, Cambridge: CASP. http://www.casp.co.uk/china2.htm.

Cassman, K.G., Dobermann, A. and Walters, D.T. (2002) "Agroecosystems, nitrogen-use efficiency, and nitrogen management", *Ambio* 31: 132–140.

CDWR (California Department of Water Resources) (2002) *State Water Project*, Sacramento: CDWR. http://www.dwr.water.ca.gov.

Central Committee of the CCP (1979) "Chung-fa (1979) no. 4", *Issues and Studies* 15(7): 105–106.

Ch'en, T. (1978) "Planned marketing by the state: economic fetters in mainland China", *Issues and Studies* 14: 28–39.

Chang, C. (1977) "Chemical fertilizer output on the Chinese mainland", *Issues and Studies* 13: 38–53.

Chang, G. (1987) "Tungtinghu is number one no more", *Sinorama* 1987(11): 8–13.

Chang, G.H. and Wen, G.J. (1997) "Communal dining and the Chinese famine of 1958–1961", *Economic Development and Cultural Change* 46: 1–34.

——(1998) "Food availability versus consumption efficiency: causes of the Chinese famine", *China Economic Review* 9: 157–166.

Chang, K. (ed.) (1977) *Food in Chinese Culture*, New Haven: Yale University Press.

Chen, C. (1991) "Dietary guidelines for food and agricultural planning in China", *Proceedings of International Symposium on Food, Nutrition and Social Economic Development*, Beijing: Chinese Academy of Preventive Medicine, 40–48.

Chen, J., Campbell, T.C., Li, J. and Peto, R. (1990) *Diet, Lifestyle and Mortality in China*, Oxford/Ithaca NY/Beijing: Oxford University Press, Cornell University Press and People's Publishing House.

Cheng, C. (1961) *Famine and its Repercussions on the Chinese Mainland*, Taipei: Asian People's Anti-communist League.

Cheng, X. (1989) "Design criteria for flood discharge at China's hydro schemes", *Water Power and Dam Construction* 41(4): 14–17.

China Daily (2002) "Water deficit haunts nation", 7 June. http://www1.chinadaily.com.cn/hk/2002-06-07/72861.html.

Chinafamine.org (2002) *China Famine 1959–61*. http://www.chinafamine.org/famine.

CIA (Central Intelligence Agency) (1975) *People's Republic of China: Chemical Fertilizer Supplies, 1949–74*, Washington DC: CIA.

——(1977) *China: Economic Indicators*, Washington DC: CIA.

——(1979) *China: Demand for Foreign Grain*, Washington DC: CIA.

CIPM Yangtze Joint Venture (1988) *Three Gorges Water Control Project Feasibility Study*, Montreal: CIPM.

Coale, A.J. (1981) "Population trends, population policy, and population studies in China", *Population and Development Review* 7: 267–297.

Comité Information Sahel (1975) *Qui se nourrit de la famine en Afrique?*, Paris: F. Maspero.

Crook, F.W. (1988) *Agricultural Statistics of the People's Republic of China, 1949–86*, Washington DC: USDA, 20.

——(1994) *Could China Starve the World?*, Washington DC: USDA.

——(1996) "China's grain stocks: background and analytical issues", in USDA, *China Situation and Outlook Series*, Washington DC: USDA, 35–39.

CS&T (Center for Science and Technology) (1985) *The State of India's Environment 1984–85*, New Delhi: CS&T.

CTSU (Clinical Trial Service Unit) (2002) *Ecological Study of Diet, Mortality and Lifestyle in Rural China*, Oxford: CTSU. http://www.ctsu.ox.ac.uk/projects/ecology1989.

Cui, L. (1995) "Third national nutrition survey", *Beijing Review* 38(4): 31.

Dai, Q. (ed.) (1994) *Yangtze! Yangtze!*, London: Earthscan.

Daly, H.E. and Cobb, J.B. Jr (1989) *For the Common Good*, Boston MA: Beacon Press.

Davis, M. (2001) *Late Victorian Holocausts: El Niño, Famines, and the Making of the Third World*, New York: Verso.

Deng, J. and Wu, C. (1984) *Rural Energy Utilization in China*, Ottawa: IDRC.

Deng, K. and Zhou, Q. (1981) "A discussion on the methods of solving China's rural energy crisis", in R.A. Fazzolare and C.B. Smith (eds) *Beyond Energy Crisis*, New York: Pergamon Press, 85–91.

Deng, X. (1977) quoted in "Wir liegen jetz 50 Jahre zurück", *Der Spiegel* 31(48): 189.

——(1985) "Current policies will continue", *Beijing Review* 28(4): 15.

Domrös, M. and Peng, G. (1988) *The Climate of China*, Berlin: Springer-Verlag.

Dong, S. (1990) "Water crisis in North China and counter-measures", *Beijing Review* 33(14): 31–33.

Economic Construction Group of the CPPCC (1987) "Sanxia gogcheng jinqi bunengshang" ("The Three Gorges Project should not go ahead in the short term"), *Diqu fazhan zhanle yanjiu (Research on Regional Development Strategies)* 9(3): 89–92.

EDMC (Energy Data and Modelling Center) (2000) *Handbook of Energy and Economic Statistics in Japan*, Tokyo: The Energy Conservation Center.

EIA (Energy Information Administration) (2000) *International Energy Outlook 2000*, Washington DC: EIA. http://www.iea.doe.gov/oiaf/ieo.

——(2001) *International Energy Outlook 2001*, Washington DC: EIA. http://www.iea.doe.gov/oiaf/ieo.

——(2002) *China*, Washington DC: US Department of Energy. http://www.eia.doe.gov/cabs/china.html.

Encyclopedia Britannica (1997) *The New Encyclopedia Britannica Micropedia*, Chicago: Encyclopedia Britannica, 4: 674–675.

Erisman, A.L. (1975) "China: agriculture in the 1970s", in *China: A Reassessment of the Economy*, Washington DC.

Fan, S. and Pardy, P.G. (1992) *Agricultural Research in China*, The Hague: International Service for National Agricultural Research.

FAO (Food and Agriculture Organization) (1971) *Food Balance Sheets 1964–77 Average*, Rome: FAO.

——(1975) *Yearbook of Forest Products*, Rome: FAO.

——(1985) *1984 FAO Production Yearbook*, Rome: FAO.

——(1996) *The Sixth World Food Survey*, Rome: FAO.

——(1997) *The State of World Fisheries and Aquaculture*, Rome: FAO.

——(1999) *State of the World's Forests*, Rome: FAO.

——(2002) *The State of Food Insecurity in the World 2002*, Rome: FAO. http://www.fao.org/DOCREP/005/Y7352e/Y7352e00.HTM.

——(2002) *Agricultural statistics*, Rome: FAO. http://www.apps.fao.org.

FAO/WHO/UNU (1985) *Energy and Protein Requirements*, Geneva: WHO.

Fisher-Vanden, K., Jefferson, G., Liu, H. and Tao, Q. (2002) *What is Driving China's Decline in Energy Intensity?* http:///www.dartmouth.edu/~kfv/files/kgv.pdf.

Fragoso, M.A. (ed.) (1993) *Optimization of Plant Nutrition*, Amsterdam: Kluwer.

Franke, R.W. and Chasin, B.H. (1980) *Seeds of Famine: Ecological Destruction and the Development Dilemma in the West African Sahel*, Montclair NJ: Allanheld, Osmun.

Fridley, D. (ed.) (2001) *China Energy Databook*, Berkeley: Lawrence Berkeley Laboratory.

Friedman, E., Pickowicz, P.G. and Selden, M. (1991) *Chinese Village, Socialist State*, New Haven: Yale University Press.

Fry, L.J. (1974) *Practical Building of Methane Power Plants for Rural Energy Independence*, Santa Barbara: Standard Printing.

Galbraith, J.K. (1973) *A China Passage*, Boston MA: Houghton Mifflin.

Gale, F. *et al.* (2001) "China's grain policy at a crossroads", in *Agricultural Outlook/September 2001*, Washington DC: USDA, 14–17.

Gangrade, K.D. (1973) *Challenge and Response: A Study of Famines in India*, Delhi: Rachana Publications.

Garbaccio, R.F., Ho, M.S. and Jorgenson, D.W. (1999) "Why has the energy-output ratio fallen in China?", *Energy Journal* 20: 63–91.

Ge, K. *et al.* (1996) *The Dietary and Nutrition Status of Chinese Population*, Beijing: People's Medical Publishing House.

Ge, K., Chen, C. and Shen, T. (1991) "Food consumption and nutritional status in China", *Food, Nutrition and Agriculture* 1(1): 54–61.

Gelt, J. (1997) "Sharing Colorado River water: history, public policy and the Colorado River Compact", *Arroyo* 10(1). http://ag.arizona.edu/AZWATER/arroyo/101comm.html.

Goodkind, D. and West, L. (2001) "The North Korean famine and its demographic impact", *Population and Development Review* 27: 219–238.

Greer, C. (1979) *Water Management in the Yellow River Basin of China*, Austin: University of Texas Press.

Guizhou Provincial Service (1976) Broadcast of 18 May 1976, *Summary of World Broadcasts*, FE/W929/A/5.

Gustafsson, B. and Shi, L. (2001) "The anatomy of rising earnings inequality in urban China", *Journal of Comparative Economics* 29: 118–135.

Hanstad, T. and Li, P. (1997) "Land reform in the People's Republic of China: auctioning rights to wasteland", *International and Comparative Law Journal* 19: 545–583.

Hao, Z. (1974) "China's views on solving world food problem", *Peking Review* no. 46 (15 November 1974): 12.

den Hartog, A.P. (1972) "Unequal distribution of food within the household", *Nutrition Newsletter* no. 4 (October–December 1972): 8–17.

Hebei Provincial Service (1986) Broadcast of 3 August 1986, *Joint Publications Research Service*, CAR 88–054.

Heilig, G.K. (1997) "Anthropogenic factors in land-use change in China", *Population and Development Review* 23: 139–168.

Houghton, J.T., Ding, Y., Griggs, D.J., Noguer, M., van der Linden, P.J. and Xiaosu, D. (eds) (2001) *Climate Change 2001: The Scientific Basis*, New York: Cambridge University Press.

Hsu, H., Chern, W.S. and Gale, F. (2002) "How will rising income affect the structure of food demand?", in *China's Food and Agriculture: Issues for the 21st Century*, Washington DC: USDA, 10–13.

Hsu, H. and Gale, F. (2001) "USDA revision of China grain stock estimates", in *China: Agriculture in Transition*, Washington DC: USDA, 53–56. http://www.ers.usda.gov/publications/wrs012/wrs012k.pdf.

Hu, Y. (2001) "Waste less, spend less", *Shanghai Star*, 10 May 2001. http://www.chinadaily. com.cn/star/2001/0510/fo6-1.html.

Huang, H. (1982) "The present situation and prospects for developing our nation's firewood energy", *Neng Yuan (Journal of Energy)* 2: 40–43.

Huang, J. and Rozelle, S. (1995) "Environmental stress and grain yields in China", *American Journal of Agricultural Economics* 77: 853–864.

——(1996) "Technological change: rediscovering the engine of productivity growth in China's agricultural economy", *Journal of Development Economics* 49: 337–369.

Huang, J., Rozelle, S. and Rosegrant, M. (1999) "China's food economy to the 21st century: supply, demand and trade", *Economic Development and Cultural Change* 47: 737–766.

Huang, Z. and Zhang, Z. (1980) "Development of methane is an important task in solving the rural energy problem", *Hongqi (Red Flag)* 21: 39–41.

ICOLD (International Committee on Large Dams) (2000) *Sanmenxia Dam and Reservoir Project*, Paris: ICOLD. http://www/icold-cigb.org.cn/icold2000/st-c6-01.htm.

India Famine Inquiry Commission (1945) *The Famine Inquiry Commission: Final Report*, Madras: Government Press.

IEA (International Energy Agency) (1999) *Coal in the Energy Supply of China*, Paris: IEA.

——(2000) *China's Worldwide Quest for Energy Security*, Paris: IEA.

——(2001) *Key World Energy Statistics*, Paris: IEA.

INSHP (International Network on Small Hydro Power) (2002) *Overview of Small Hydro Power*. http://www.inshp.org/small_hydro_power.htm.

ITESA (Institute for Techno-economic and Energy System Analysis) (1987) *Rural Energy Technology Assessment and Innovation*, Ottawa: IDRC.

Johnson, D.G. (1998) "China's great famine: introductory remarks", *China Economic Review* 9: 103–109.

Kammen, D.M. (1995) "Cookstoves for the developing world", *Scientific American* 273(1): 72–75.

Kashkari, C. (1975) *Energy Resources, Demand and Conservation*, New Delhi: Tata.

Ke, B. (1996) *Grain Production in China*, Beijing: China Agricultural University.

Khan, A.R. and Riskin, C. (2000) *Inequality and Poverty in China in the Age of Globalization*, New York: Oxford University Press.

Klatt, W. (1961a) "Communist China's agricultural calamities", *The China Quarterly* 6: 64–75.

——(1961b) "The state of nutrition in Communist China", *The China Quarterly* 7: 121–127.

Korn, M. (1996) "The dike-pond concept: sustainable agriculture and nutrient recycling in China", *Ambio* 25: 6–13.

Kung, J.S. and Putterman, L. (1997) "China's collectivization puzzle: a new resolution", *The Journal of Development Studies* 33: 741–763.

Kyodo, Dispatch in English (1975) *Summary of World Broadcasts*, FE/W850/A/19, 29 October 1975.

——(1976) *Summary of World Broadcasts*, FE/W868/A/11, 10 March 1976.

Lampton, D.M. (1986) "Water politics and economic change in China", in *China's Economy Looks Toward the Year 2000*, Washington DC: USGPO, 387–496.

L'Hirondel, J. and l'Hirondel, J-L. (2001) *Nitrate and Man: Toxic, Harmless or Beneficial?*, Wallingford: CABI Publishing.

Li, Z. (1994) *The Private Life of Chairman Mao: The Memoirs of Mao's Personal Physician*, New York: Random House.

Liang, L. *et al.* (1993) "China's post-harvest grain losses and the means of their reduction and elimination", *Jingji dili* (*Economic Geography*) 1(March 1993): 92–96.

Liaowang (*Outlook*) (1987) News item of 21 December 1987, *Summary of World Broadcasts*, FE/W0010/A/4.

Liebig, J. von (1840) *Chemistry in Its Application to Agriculture and Physiology*, London: Taylor & Walton.

Lin, J.Y. (1990) "Collectivization and China's agricultural crisis in 1959–1961", *Journal of Political Economy* 98: 1228–1252.

——(1992) "Rural reforms and agricultural growth in China", *American Economic Review* 82: 34–51.

Lin, J.Y. and Yang, D.T. (1998) "On the causes of China's agricultural crisis and the Great Leap famine", *China Economic Review* 9: 125–140.

Lin, X. and Polenske, K.R. (1995) "Input–output anatomy of China's energy use changes in the 1980s", *Economic Systems Research* 7: 67–84.

Liu, B. (1984) "Speaking of the good situation in rural areas", *Liaowang* (*Outlook*) 5: 6.

Liu, C. (1998) "Environmental issues and the South–North water transfer scheme", *The China Quarterly* 156: 899–910.

Liu, H. (1992) "A review of Danjiangkou reservoir resettlement", *Hubei wenshi ziliao* (*Cultural and Historical Documents of Hubei*) 4(41): 208–214.

Liu, T. and Yeh, K. (1965) *The Economy of the Chinese Mainland: National and Economic Development, 1933–1959*, Princeton: Princeton University Press.

LNG Express (2002) *China Surprises Industry: Guangdong LNG Contract Goes to Australia*, Houston: LNG Express. http://www.lngexpress.com/.

Long, X. (1989) "Firewood burned, thrown away", *Jingji cankao* (*Economic reference*) 15 March 1989: 2.

Lu, F. (1998) *Output Data on Animal Products in China: How much Are They Overstated?*, Beijing: Beijing University. http://ccer.pku.edu.cn/faculty/lufeng/fooddata.doc.

Luo, Z. (1998) "Biomass energy consumption in China", *Wood Energy News* 13(3): 3–4.

Ma, H. and Popkin, B.M. (1995) "Income and food-consumption behavior in China: structural analysis", *Food and Nutrition Bulletin* 16: 155–165.

Ma, M. (2001) "Northern cities sinking as water table falls", *South China Morning Post*, 11 August 2001. http://www.scmp.com.

MacLaine, S. (1975) *You Can Get There from Here*, New York: Norton.

Maddison, A. (1997) *Measuring Chinese Economc Growth and Levels of Performance*, Paris: OECD.

Malthus, T.R. (1803) *An Essay on the Principle of Population: Or a View of Its Past and Present Effects on Human Happiness*, London: J. Johnson.

Manibog, F.R. (1984) "Improved cooking stoves in developing countries: problems and opportunities", *Annual Review of Energy* 9: 199–227.

Mao, Z. (1969) *Miscellany of Mao Zedong Thought*, Washington DC: JPRS.

Mattera, P. (1985) *Off the Books: The Rise of the Underground Economy*, London: Pluto Press.

McEvedy, C. and Jones, R. (1978) *Atlas of World Population History*, London: Allen Lane, 167.

MEDEA (1997) *China Agriculture: Cultivated Land Area, Grain Projections, and Implications*, Washington DC: National Intelligence Council.

Mei, C. and Dregne, H.E. (2001) "Silt and the future development of China's Yellow River", *The Geographical Journal* 167: 7–22.

Mencius (1970) *Mencius*, trans. D.C. Lau, London: Penguin Books, 85.

Ministry of Energy (1989) *Energy in China 1989*, Beijing: Ministry of Energy.

MSHA (Mine Safety and Health Administration) (2000) *Injury Trends in Mining*, Washington DC: MSHA. http://www.msha.gov.

NBS (2000) (National Bureau of Statistics) *Urban Household Survey*, Beijing: China Statistics Press.

——(2001) *China Statistical Yearbook*, Beijing: China Statistics Press.

NCNA (New China News Agency) Dispatch in English (1975) *Summary of World Broadcasts*, FE/W845/A/20-21.

NCNA Dispatch in Chinese (1975a) *Summary of World Broadcasts*, FE/W834/A/14.

——(1975b) *Summary of World Broadcasts*, FE/W812/A/6.

Nickum, J.E. (1990) *Irrigation in the People's Republic of China*, Washington DC: International Food Policy Research Institute.

——(1998) "Is China living on the water margin?", *The China Quarterly* 156: 880–898.

Odum, H.T. (1971) *Environment, Power and Society*, New York: Wiley.

OECD (2001) *Main Economic Indicators*, Paris: OECD. http://www1.oecd.org/std/meiinv.pdf.

O'Mara, G.T. (ed.) (1988) *Efficiency in Irrigation*, Washington DC: World Bank.

Orleans, L.A. (1975) "China's population: can the contradictions be resolved?", in *China: A Reassessment of the Economy*, Washington DC: USGPO, 69–80.

Paik, K. (1997) "Tarim Basin energy development: implications for Russian and Central Asian oil and gas exports to China", *CACP Briefing* 14: 1–5.

Pedersen, W. (2000) "US had early knowledge of China's famine", *Business Week Online*, 7 February 2000. http://www.businessweek.com/2000/00_06/c3667081.htm.

People's Daily (2000a) "China's rural energy shortage alleviated", 15 March 2000. http://english.peopledaily.com.cn/200003/15/print20000315T134.html.

——(2000b) "China steps up biogas research and application", 26 October 2000. http://english.peopledaily.com.cn/english/20001026.

——(2000c) "No dried-up areas on Yellow River", 18 July 2000. http://english. peopledaily.com.cn/200007/18/eng20000718_45745.html.

——(2001) "China keeps Yellow River flowing despite droughts", 20 December 2001. http://english.peopledaily.com.cn/200112/20/eng20011220_87099.shtml.

——(2002) "Tougher fists upon small coal mines", 10 April 2002. http://english. peopledaily.com.cn/200204/10.

Piazza, A. (1983) *Trends in Food and Nutrient Availability in China, 1950–81*, Washington DC: World Bank.

Pieters, A.J. (1927) *Green Manuring*, New York: John Wiley.

Policy Research Office of the Ministry of Forestry (1980) "Run forestry work according to law", *Hongqi* (*Red Flag*), 1 March 1980: 27–31.

Power Technology (2002) "Xiaolangdi hydroelectric power plant, China". http://www.power-technology.com/projects/xiaolangdi/.

Prasad, R. and Power, J.F. (1997) *Soil Fertility Management for Sustainable Agriculture*, Boca Raton FL: Lewis Publishing.

Rabalais, N. (2002) "Nitrogen in aquatic ecosystems", *Ambio* 31: 102–112.

Railway Technology (2002) *Industry Projects*, London: Railway Technology. http://www.railway-technology.com/projects.

Rhodes, R. (1988) "Man-made death: a neglected mortality", *Journal of American Medical Association* 260: 686–687.

Richardson, S.D. (1966) *Forestry in Communist China*, Baltimore: Johns Hopkins University Press.

Riskin, C. (1990) "Food, poverty, and development strategy in the People's Republic of China", in L.F. Newman (ed.) *Hunger in History*, London: Blackwell, 331–352.

——(1998) "Seven questions about the Chinese famine of 1959–61", *China Economic Review* 9: 111–124.

Rozelle, S., Huang, J. and Rosegrant, M. (1996) "Why China will not starve the world", *Choices* 1996(1): 18–25.

Ruddle, K. and Zhong, G. (1988) *Integrated Agriculture-Aquaculture in South China: The Dike-Pond System of the Zhujiang Delta*, Cambridge: Cambridge University Press.

RWEDP (Regional Wood Energy Development Programme) (2000) "China". http://www.rwedp.org/c_cpr.html.

Ryder, G. (ed.) (1990) *Damming the Three Gorges*, Toronto. Probe International.

SB (Statistics Bureau) (2002) *Statistical Handbook of Japan 2001*, Tokyo: Statistics Bureau.

Schulte, W. *et al.* (1973) "Food balance sheets and world food supplies", *Nutrition Newsletter* 2(1973): 16.

Schumacher, E.F. (1973) *Small is Beautiful: A Study of Economics as if People Mattered*, New York: Vintage.

Shangguan, C. (1980) "Way must be found to solve energy problems in rural areas", *Nongye jingji wenti (Agricultural Economic Issues)* 4: 1056–1058.

Shen, T.H. (1951) *Agricultural Resources of China*, Ithaca NY: Cornell University Press.

Simon, J. (1996) "Population growth is our greatest triumph". http://www.juliansimon.com/writings/Articles/POPUNENV.txt.

Simoons, F.J. (1991) *Food in China: A Cultural and Historical Inquiry*, Boca Raton FL: CRC Press.

Simpson, J.R., Cheng, Xu and Miyazaki, Akira (1994) *China's Livestock and Related Agriculture: Projections to 2025*, Wallingford: CAB International.

Sinton, J.E. and Fridley, D.G. (2000) "What goes up: recent trends in China's energy consumption", *Energy Policy* 26: 671–687.

Sinton, J.E. and Levine, M.D. (1994) "Changing energy intensity in Chinese industry", *Energy Policy* 17: 239–255.

Smil, V. (1975) "Communist China's oil exports: a critical evaluation", *Issues and Studies* 11(3): 71–78.

——(1976a) *China's Energy: Achievements, Problems, Prospects*, New York: Praeger.

——(1976b) "Intermediate energy technology in China", *World Development* 4(10–11): 929–937.

——(1976c) "Communist China's oil exports revisited", *Issues and Studies* 12(9): 68–73.

——(1977a) "Food availability in Communist China", *Issues and Studies* 13(5): 13–57.

——(1977b) "China's future: A Delphi forecast", *Futures* 9: 474–489.

——(1978) "Food in China", *Current History* 75(439): 69–72, 82–84.

——(1979a) "Energy flows in rural China", *Human Ecology* 7(2): 119–133.

——(1979b) "Controlling the Yellow River", *The Geographical Review* 69: 253–272.

——(1979c) "San-men-hsia reservoir: a space view", *Issues and Studies* 15(3): 77–86.

——(1979d) "China's water resources", *Current History* 77(449): 57–61, 86.

——(1981) "China's food", *Food Policy* 6(2): 67–77.

——(1984) *The Bad Earth: Environmental Degradation in China*, Armonk: M.E. Sharpe.

——(1985) "Eating better: farming reforms and food in China", *Current History* 84(503): 248–251, 273–274.

——(1986) "Food production and quality of diet in China", *Population and Development Review* 12: 25–45.

——(1987) *Energy, Food, Environment: Realities, Myths, Options*, Oxford: Clarendon Press.

——(1988) *Energy in China's Modernization: Advances and Limitations*, Armonk: M.E. Sharpe.

——(1989) "Why Sanxia should not be built", in Tian Fang and Lin Fatang (eds) *More on the General Decision Concerning the Three Gorges Project*, Changsha: Hunan Provincial Science and Technology Publishing House, 492–493 (in Chinese).

——(1990) "Missing energy perspectives", in G. Ryder (ed.) *Damming the Three Gorges*, Toronto: Probe International, 101–106.

——(1992a) *Potential Environmental Conflicts Involving Countries of the North Pacific*, Toronto: North Pacific Cooperative Security Dialogue, York University, 18 pp.

——(1992b) "Environmental change as a source of conflict and economic losses in China", occasional paper series of the project on *Environmental Change and Acute Conflict* 2: 5–39, Cambridge MA: American Academy of Arts and Sciences.

——(1993) *China's Environmental Crisis: An Inquiry into the Limits of National Development*, Armonk: M.E. Sharpe.

——(1994) *Energy in World History*, Boulder: Westview.

——(1995a) "Feeding China", *Current History* 94(593): 280–284.

——(1995b) "China's environmental refugees: causes, dimensions and risks of an emerging problem", in K.R. Spillmann and G. Bächler (eds) *Environmental Crisis: Regional Conflicts and Ways of Cooperation*, Bern: Swiss Peace Foundation, 75–91.

——(1996a) "Is there enough Chinese food?", *New York Review of Books* 43(2): 32–34.

——(1996b) "Who will feed China?", fourth annual Hopper Lecture, 22 October 1996, Center for International Programs, University of Guelph, Ontario, 18 pp.

——(1996c) *Environmental Problems in China: Estimates of Economic Costs*, Honolulu: East–West Center.

——(1997a) *Cycles of Life: Civilization and the Biosphere*, New York: Scientific American Library.

——(1997b) "China's environment and security: simple myths and complex realities", *SAIS Review* 17: 107–126.

——(1997c) "China shoulders the cost of environmental change", *Environment* 39(6): 6–9, 33–37.

——(1998) "China's energy and resource uses: continuity and change", *The China Quarterly* 156: 935–951.

——(1999a) "Crop residues: agriculture's largest harvest", *BioScience* 49: 299–308.

——(1999b) "China's great famine: 40 years later", *British Medical Journal* 7225: 1619–1621.

——(1999c) "China's agricultural land", *The China Quarterly* 158: 414–429.

——(1999d) "China's megaprojects for the new millennium", *Asian Wall Street Journal*, 22 April 1999, 8.

——(1999e) "China's unstable past and future", *Asian Wall Street Journal*, 30 September 1999, 8.

——(2000a) *Feeding the World: A Challenge for the Twenty-first Century*, Cambridge MA: MIT Press.

——(2000b) " 'Water, water everywhere…' ", *Asian Wall Street Journal*, 22 August 2000, 12.

——(2000c) "Perils of long-range energy forecasting: reflections of looking far ahead", *Technological Forecasting and Social Change* 65: 251–264.

——(2001a) "The shadow of droughts' deaths", *Science* 292: 644–645.

——(2001b) *Enriching the Earth: Haber–Bosch Synthesis of Ammonia and Its Consequences*, Cambridge MA: MIT Press.

——(2002a) "Nitrogen and food production: proteins for human diets", *Ambio* 31: 126–131.

——(2002b) *The Earth's Biosphere: Evolution, Dynamics, and Change*, Cambridge MA: MIT Press.

——(2002c) "Three Gorges Project", in J. Barry and E.G. Frankland (eds) *International Encyclopedia of Environmental Politics*, London: Routledge, 449–451.

——(2003) *Energy at the Crossroads: Global Perspectives and Uncertainties*, Cambridge MA: MIT Press.

Smit, B. and Cai, Y. (1996) "Climate change and agriculture in China", *Global Environmental Change* 6: 205–214.

Soligo, R. and Jaffe, A. (1999) *China and Long-Range Asia Energy Security: An Analysis of the Political, Economic and Technological Factors Shaping Asian Energy Markets*, Houston: Rice University. http://riceinfo.rice.edu/projects/baker/publications/claes/cpis/cpis.html.

SSB (State Statistical Bureau) (1978–1999) *China Statistical Yearbook*, Beijing: SSB.

Streets, D.G., Kejun Jiang, Xiulian Hu, Sinton, Jonathan E., Xiao Quan Zhang, Deying Xu, Jacobson, Mark Z. and Hansen, James E. (2001) "Recent reductions in China's greenhouse gas emissions", *Science* 294: 1835–1937.

Sun, Y. (1989) "Why I am against the project", *Beijing Review* 32(27): 31–35.

Sze, M. (1959) *The Way of Chinese Painting*, New York: Random House.

Tanaka, A. (1973) "Methods of handling the rice straw in various countries", *International Rice Commission Newsletter* 22(2): 1–20.

Teng, T. (1955) "Report on the multi-purpose plan for permanently controlling the Yellow River and exploiting its water resources", *People's China* 9: 7–15.

TGP (Three Gorges Probe) (2001) "Two more Yangtze dams planned", *Three Gorges Probe News Service*, 5 March 2001. http://www.threegorgesprobe.org/tgp.

——(2002) "Radioactive debris, diseased rats, anthrax and *E. coli*: the reservoir-cleanup concerns pile up", *Three Gorges Probe News Service*, 8 February 2002. http://www.threegorgesprobe.org/tgp.

Thomas, J. (1999) "Quantifying the black economy: 'measurement without theory' yet again", *The Economic Journal* 109: 381–389.

Thomson, E. (2003) *The Chinese Coal Industry: An Economic History*, London: RoutledgeCurzon.

Tian Fang and Lin Fatang (eds) (1989) *More on the General Decision Concerning the Three Gorges Project*, Changsha: Hunan Provincial Science and Technology Publishing House (in Chinese).

Timmer, C.P. (1976) "Food policy in China", *Food Research Institute Studies* 15(1): 53–67.

Tong, D. and Tong, B. (1978) "On the policy for the construction of the northwest plateau", *Renmin ribao*, 26 November 1978, 2.

Troush, S. (1999) *China's Changing Oil Strategy and Its Foreign Policy Implications*, Washington DC: Brookings Institution. http://www.brook.edu/neasia/papers/1999_troush.htm.

UNDP (United Nations Development Program) (2001) *Human Development Report 2001*, New York: UNDP. http://www.undp.org/hdr2001/.

UNO (United Nations Organization) (1956) "World energy requirements in 1975 and 2000", in *Proceedings of the International Conference on the Peaceful Uses of Atomic Energy*, vol. 1, New York: UNO, 3–33.

——(2001) *Yearbook of World Energy Statistics*, New York: UNO.

——(2002) *World Population Prospects: The 2000 Revision*, New York: UN. http://esa.un.org/unpp.

Uppal, J.N. (1984) *Bengal Famine of 1943: A Man-Made Tragedy*, Delhi: Atma Ram.

USDA (US Department of Agriculture) (1997) "The Continuing Survey of Food Intakes by Individuals (CSFII) and the Diet and Health Knowledge Survey (DHKS), 1994–96". http://sun.ars-grin.gov/ars/Beltsville.

USGS (United States Geological Survey) (1995) *Estimated Use of Water in the United States in 1995*, Washington DC: USGS. http://water.usgs.gov/watuse/pdf1995/pdf/abstract.pdf.

Wang, D. (1985) "Water lack calls for action", *Beijing Review* 28(26): 4.

Wang, H. and Zhou, H. (1981) "Why are drought and flooding on the increase in Yunnan?", *Huanjing (Environment)* 1982(1): 20–21.

Wang, M. and Ding, Y. (1998) "Fuel-saving stoves in China", *Wood Energy News* 13(3): 9–10.

Wang, M. *et al.* (eds) (1993) *Chinese Fuel Saving Stoves: A Compendium*, Bangkok: FAO.

Watson, R. and Pauly, D. (2001) "Systematic distortions in world fisheries catch trends", *Nature* 414: 534–536.

Watts, I.E.M. (1969) "Climates of China and Korea", in H. Arakawa (ed.) *Climates of Northern and Eastern Asia*, Amsterdam: Elsevier, 1–116.

Wei, Y. D. and Kim, S. (2002) "Widening inter-county inequality in Jiangsu Province, China, 1950–95", *Journal of Development Studies* 38: 142–164.

Whitton, C.L. (1984) "Livestock", in *China: Outlook and Situation Report*, Washington DC: USDA, 11.

WHO (World Health Organization) (1973) *Energy and Protein Requirements*, Geneva: WHO.

Wittfogel, K. (1957) *Oriental Despotism*, New Haven: Yale University Press.

World Bank (1996) *Poverty in China: What Do the Numbers Say?*, Washington DC: World Bank.

——(1997) *Sharing Rising Incomes*, Washington DC: World Bank.

——(2001) *World Development Report 2001*, Washington DC: World Bank.

WRI (World Resources Institute) (1988) *World Resources 1988–89*, New York: Basic Books.

Wu, G. and Guo, H. (eds) (1994) *Land Use in China*, Beijing: Beijing Science Press.

Wu, H.X. (1996) "Wining and dining at public expense in post-Mao China from the perspective of sayings", *East Asia Forum* fall 1996: 1–37.

Wu, W. and Chen, E. (1982) *Our Views on the Resolution of China's Rural Energy Requirements*, Guangzhou: Guangzhou Institute of Energy Conversion.

Wu, Y. and Ling, H.C. (1963) *Economic Development and the Use of Energy Resources in Communist China*, New York: Praeger.

Xinhua (New China News Agency) (1980) News release of 5 March 1980, *Summary of World Broadcasts*, FE/W1972/A/2.

——(1981) News release of 6 May 1981, *Summary of World Broadcasts*, FE/W1132/A/3–4.

——(1983) News release of 23 November 1983, *Summary of World Broadcasts*, FE/W1263A/1–2.

——(1987) News release of 10 October 1987, *Summary of World Broadcasts*, FE/W1463/A/4.

——(1988) News release of 9 January 1988, *Summary of World Broadcasts*, FE/W0009/A/2.

——(1989) News release of 5 December 1989, *Summary of World Broadcasts*, FE W0109/A/4.

——(2002) News release of 31 July 2002. China.org.cn http://www.china.com.cn/english/government/38310.htm.

Yang, D. (1996) *Calamity and Reform in China*, Stanford: Stanford University Press.

Yang, D. and Su, F. (1998) "The politics of famine and reform in rural China", *China Economic Review* 9: 141–156.

Yates, R.S. (1990) "War, food shortages, and relief measures in early China", in L.F. Newman (ed.) *Hunger in History*, Oxford: Blackwell, 147–177.

Yu, K. (1983) "Some opinions on accelerating development of small-scale hydropower in China", *Shuili shuidian jishu (Water Resources and Hydropower)* 6: 59–61.

Yuan, Z. (2001) "Research and development on biomass energy in China", paper presented at the Regional Seminar on Commercialization of Biomass Technology,

Guangzhou, 4–8 June 2001. http://www.unescap.org/enrd/energy/China/ China-aBiomass.pdf.

Zhang, J. and Lin, Z. (1985) *Zhongguo zhihou* (*Climate of China*), Shanghai: Science and Technology Press.

Zhang, N. (1982) "Divert Huanghe river water to Tianjin", *Beijing Review* 25(34): 19–21.

Zhang, X. (1988) "The analysis of the index of dryness in the last 500 years in eastern China", paper presented at the Conference on Climatic Change, Beijing.

Zhang, Z. (2001) *Why Has the Energy Intensity Fallen in China's Industrial Sector in the 1990s?*, Groningen: Rijksuniversiteit Groningen. http.//www.eco.rug.nl/cds/zhang.pdf.

Zhang, Z. *et al.* (1998) "Fuelwood forest development strategy", *Wood Energy News* 13(3): 6–8. http://www.rwedp.org/acrobat/wen13-3.pdf.

Zheng, L. (1998) "Biomass energy consumption in China", *Wood Energy News* 13: 3–4. http://www.rwedp.org/wen13-3.html.

ZXS (Zhongguo xinwen she; China News Service) (1988a) News release of 24 November 1988, *Summary of World Broadcasts*, FE/W0055/A/3.

——(1988b) News release of 20 January 1988, *Summary of World Broadcasts*, FE/W0011/A/11.

Index